Klaus Daniels

Low-Tech Light-Tech High-Tech

**Building
in the
Information Age**

English translation by
Elizabeth Schwaiger

Birkhäuser Publishers
Basel · Boston · Berlin

Low-Tech Light-Tech High-Tech

for Cornelia

Foreword

A year and a half ago, the chairman of our supervisory board, Dr. Ernst Pechtl, asked me: What will HL-Technik be doing in 15 years? A straightforward yet surprisingly complex question. To answer this question and answer it well required a close look at several topics, including:
- the changes in work and activities as a result of changing markets (globalization of the world economy)
- the influence of information systems and applications on our future actions and architectural design
- influences arising from the necessity for sustainable management of resources and energies and for direct and indirect environmental protection on several levels

There are a number of interesting books on each of these topics, highlighting specific concerns in some detail. As for architecture, these topics can be narrowed down to three terms that summarize how we will approach planning and design in the future: Low-Tech Light-Tech High-Tech. 'Low-Tech' means simple building design and maximum use of the natural resources available in the respective environment. 'Light-Tech' suggests that we need to go beyond sim-ply using recyclable building materials and develop buildings that are designed for maximum resource efficiency. 'High-Tech' symbolizes the impact that future information and communication systems will have on architecture. They will change how we work, create new demands and, ultimately, call for buildings designed for change and readily adaptable to the latest technical standards. This book endeavours to present these topics in their full significance and to document the resulting measures with examples of specific building objects. It may also be understood as a response to Ernst Ulrich von Weizsäcker's book *Faktor 4* in that it translates some of those theories into concrete measures for architecture.

Many people have played an important role in the development of this book by sharing their ideas, contributions and convictions – and their buildings. I would like to give special credit to Ute Dumitrescu, whose suggestions as former editor-in-chief were invaluable; to Dr. Schmidt of Birkhäuser Verlag, who helped considerably in his role as reader and consultant to structure the book; to Dr. Jörg Schlaich, renowned not only as a gifted structural planner in 'Light-Tech' but also for his dedicated research on and contributions to resource conservation. I should also like to mention Professor Richard Horden, whose resource-efficient building projects are important models for how natural resources can be sensibly utilized; Alessandro Vasella, for his contribution on the subject of low-tech buildings in India; Professor Peter Steiger and Roland Stulz, for their contribution on ecologically correct building (Chapter 10); Dr. L. Oberascher, for his ideas on using colours; and Professor Stefan Behling for his tips on solar architecture and the use of solar energy. Furthermore, my thanks are offered to all the architects whose project contributions have made this book possible and to all the clients whose far-sighted demands have led to such projects.

To my wife, Cornelia, and our children my deepest gratitude for once again tolerating with great understanding and patience, the creation of this book. Last but not least, my thanks to Dr. Andreas Colli, whose dedication and hard work have been invaluable and who took on a major role in creating and compiling the illustrations.

Munich / Zurich January 1998
Klaus Daniels

Point of departure

What will be the future demands on architecture, landscape architecture, structural engineering, industrial design, technical building services and urban planning? What role will professionals in these fields play? What building tasks still exist for architecture in a society based on information? These questions are of vital interest both to those working in fields related to architectural planning and to anyone with an interest in ensuring good building performance in the future.

This book tries to answer how the growth of an information-driven society will impact the architecture of the future. The main issues – environmental protection, resource efficiency and related recycling methods – are as important as the shift of work from the industrialized countries to the so-called threshold countries and the diminishing role of labour in general. If the goal of reducing CO_2 emissions to 20 % of today's average levels in the industrial nations is to be realistic, the cities and buildings of the future will have to be conceived very differently, and the professions of architecture and urban planning will take on new importance.

The lifespan of buildings will have to be specifically planned for, with an absolute minimum of material expenditure, a minimal consumption of "grey energy" and a maximum of recycling. Several usage cycles must be differentiated within the lifespan of a building; they must be defined and not left to chance. Virtual reality cannot replace real life because social contact and interaction, as well as innovation, would be lost. It is therefore all the more important to plan with greater specificity the scale of building that will still be required even in the information age.

Concepts of sustainable building lead to the analysis of all currently available options for building optimization. Intelligently designed and operated buildings, sometimes erroneously called "intelligent buildings", are distinguished not by the presence of a high degree of linked information, communication and building automation systems, but rather by the fact that they can serve user needs directly from the environment and avoid the use of technical installations. Natural lighting, natural ventilation, variable thermal transmittance, changeable total solar energy transmission values, adapted daylight lighting etc., decrease the energy requirements in the operation of such buildings by approximately 30 % to 40 % by comparison with today's buildings.

The traditional buildings of the past did not profit from the great number of technical options available today, and yet they point us in the right direction, just as do contemporary buildings in which natural resources are optimally utilized and activated. Tomorrow's buildings must meet high ecological standards in construction and in technology and at the same time deliver the necessary framework for information and communication processing, as well as automation and process optimization.

Buildings deemed to be sustainable in the information age, due to their dedication to all the aspects mentioned above, are now referred to as "flexible" real estate objects: they can be assigned to new uses and modified, a characteristic that ensures a long lifespan. Typically they will be equipped technically with a minimal expense of material and only to the degree that meets the actual, current requirements and yet can be easily upgraded when necessary. They will be located in dense, planted urban environments, where living and working are once again side by side, increasing the quality of life and preventing urban sprawl.

Taking Stock

The approach of the new millennium finds us at the beginning of a post-industrial revolution, sparked by shifting variables in the areas of work, communication, high-tech development and the environment. These variables initiate a worldwide competition for work and remuneration, radically altering our life habits and requirements. The following factors determine these global trends:
– World population growth
– Globalization of the economy
– Worldwide information networks
– Increasing gap between rich and poor
– Emerging markets
– Environmental pollution
– Resource exploitation

According to research by the Resources Institute in Washington, D.C., world population may develop in two vastly different ways over the coming two hundred years. There may be a dramatic increase *(Figure 1):* with a high birth rate (2.5 children per couple) world population will reach 28 billion by 2150. If the birth rate stabilizes at 1.7 children as the lowest value, then world population will rise to over 7.8 billion until 2050 and then fall to 4.3 billion by 2150. The most likely scenario is that world population will roughly double by 2050, from 5.7 billion in 1994 to approximately 10 billion in 2050 *(Figure 2).*

This could still be manageable if the population were distributed across the entire world. Today, there are great disparities from continent to continent and country to country, with nearly 840 million people suffering from lack of food. *Figure 3* shows the population density in the western zones of the world. Central Europe and Asia already have the highest population density and will continue to do so in the future. Countries such as Canada, sections of South America and Eastern Europe, as well as some areas of Asia remain relatively sparsely populated. The same applies to Australia and areas in Africa. The table next to *Figure 3* lists the population development forecast by the United Nations, differentiated according to continent and divided into industrialized and developing nations. As is evident also in *Figure 2,* population growth is very moderate in highly industrialized countries, settling in the medium range.

The prevailing trend will bring about a flight from the countryside in many nations. (In Central Europe only approximately 2–3 % of the population still work in agriculture.) The prediction is that there will be large conurbations (highly urbanized regions) located in the threshold or newly industrialized countries (NIC) as well as in the industrialized nations. *Figure 4* provides an overview of these future megacities. The growth of such megacities is already evident, especially in Asia. Rapid urbanization in the threshold countries, and to some degree in the developing

1

United Nations population projections
Birth rate is the key statistic on which these projections are based. With an average birth rate of 2.5 children per couple, the population is projected to reach nearly 28 billion by 2150; with a lower average of 1.7 children per couple, the maximum population projected for 2050 is 7.8 billion, falling to 4.3 billion by 2150. The current average birth rate per couple is 3.3, following an average of 4.5 in the early seventies.

—— High
—— Medium high
—— Medium
—— Medium low
—— Low

2

World population growth
The world population is projected to double by 2050, from 5.7 billion (1996) to 10 billion people. This increase will be almost entirely a result of growth in the developing countries.

| | Developing countries
|||| Industrialized countries

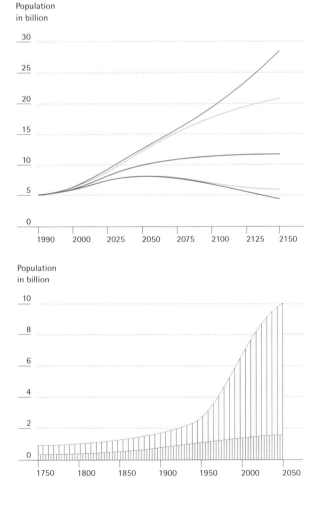

Population in billion

Population in billion

countries, leads to considerable strain in these regions. Access to consumer goods, environmental protection issues, as well as housing and infrastructure, are areas that are especially affected.

The population explosion in Asia will also boost the level of knowledge and education in that region. The International Monetary Fund (IMF) predicts that by 2004 the developing and threshold countries will outpace the production of all industrialized nations combined. According to this prognosis, by the year 2020 Germany, for instance, will rank sixth among the economic powers (between Indonesia and South Korea, far below China's number-one position).

This prognosis is qualified by barriers that are now evident in the threshold countries (for example, Korea, Indonesia, Thailand, Malaysia) and even in the developed nation of Japan. Rising wages in combination with higher living standards, increasing pollution in some instances, largely inadequate infrastructure and other factors are discouraging global capital from committing to large investments. In the "tiger states" rigid political systems and, hence, a failure to react to these changes, as well as an overvaluation of real estate and credit financing for economic growth, have led to the collapse of exchange and capital markets. At the same time, strike actions cause further insecurity among investors. While some mega-corporations have emerged in the "tiger states", an industrial middle class is virtually non-existent. Furthermore, these countries have relied for years on cheap exports; quality parts and consumer goods must still be imported. Finally, productivity is not keeping pace with wage increases. As a result, Korean companies, for example, are already outsourcing production to Vietnam. Only those countries able to create a new class of educated workers will achieve lasting wealth and prosperity; in the medium and long term these countries are, however, subject to the same laws as the industrialized nations (the only difference being that the speed of development is currently even faster.)

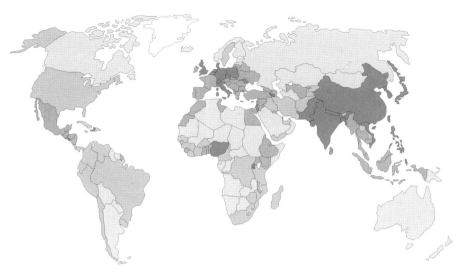

3
World population density
Population density is an important indicator for the future of humankind. The regions with highest population densities are Europe and Asia. Africa, despite its high population growth rate, is not densely populated.

People per 1,000 hectares
- 2–175 people
- 176–475 people
- 476–1,200 people
- 1,201 or more people
- missing

Table to figure 3
World Population Trends and Projections 1990–2005 (in millions)

	1990	1995	2000	2005
Europe	722	727	731	730
Africa	633	728	832	945
North America	278	293	306	319
Latin America	440	482	525	564
Asia	3186	3458	3737	4003
Australia and Oceania	26	28	31	33
Total	**5285**	**5716**	**6162**	**6594**
Industrialized countries	1143	1166	1185	1200
Developing countries	4142	4550	4977	5364

4
Megacities
Megacities will continue to expand rapidly until the new millennium. Most of the largest cities (with more than 10 million inhabitants) will be located in Asia. The value in the first column indicates population in 1991; the second column is the projection for the year 2000.

1 Mexico City	17.3 / 25.8 million	10 Rio de Janeiro 10.4 / 13.0 million		19 Los Angeles	10.1 / 11.0 million
2 São Paulo	15.9 / 24.0 million	11 Jakarta	7.9 / 13.0 million	20 Bangkok	6.0 / 10.7 million
3 Tokyo	18.8 / 20.2 million	12 Delhi	7.4 / 13.0 million	21 London	10.4 / 10.5 million
4 Calcutta	11.0 / 16.5 million	13 Buenos Aires	10.9 / 13.0 million	22 Osaka	9.5 / 10.5 million
5 Bombay	10.1 / 16.0 million	14 Karachi	6.7 / 12.0 million	23 Moscow	9.0 / 10.4 million
6 New York	15.6 / 15.8 million	15 Beijing	9.3 / 11.2 million	24 Tianjin	7.9 / 9.7 million
7 Shanghai	12.0 / 14.3 million	16 Dacca	4.9 / 11.2 million	25 Lima	5.7 / 9.1 million
8 Seoul	10.3 / 13.8 million	17 Cairo	7.7 / 11.1 million		
9 Teheran	7.5 / 13.0 million	18 Manila	7.0 / 11.1 million		

Multinationals have been developing the global market for years and, in doing so, take advantage of all available options to reach a minimal (pre-tax) return on equity of 15 %. Thus more and more production sites have been created in the new urban centres: on the one hand, everyone wants to be part of the market, and on the other hand, everyone wants to profit from the extraordinarily advantageous wage differential by comparison with the developed countries. As a result of this trend, Bangalore in India is currently growing into the second-largest software centre in the world after Silicon Valley.

Japanese companies are considered leaders in the "global market" in terms of worldwide networked production. Global labour distribution has enabled multinationals to avoid rising wages, social security costs and taxation by the simple expedient of shifting production sites. Already close to 20 % of all industrial workplaces (approximately 400,000) have been transferred out of Europe during the past years. The new form of capitalism ("killer capitalism") has resulted in a decrease in real wages, an inability to maintain social systems and an increase in unemployment despite increased productivity. At the same time there is a very real threat that poverty and unemployment will create enormous tensions between rich and poor, leading to more crime, violence and terrorism; the proliferation of ghettos may well become a reality.

In the end only a small class of employed – highly qualified concept developers, co-ordinators, systems experts and marketing specialists – will emerge as the winners next to investors. Knowledge will be internationally accessible at any time, anywhere, through the worldwide network and will become an important production factor. Expertise that relies on brain work will set the tone and will no longer be limited to specific locations. Micro-electronics, biotechnology, the raw materials industry, telecommunications, aircraft construction and the computer industry can locate almost anywhere, especially since these industries do not rely on natural resources.

In 1995, the largest multinationals had already reached a billion-dollar turnover, which is larger than the gross national product of Austria, for example. Among the twenty largest worldwide enterprises, eleven were from Japan, seven from the United States, one from England and one from Germany.

The giants among the Global Five Hundred *(Fortune magazine)* increased their turnover by 11 % in 1995, thereby growing at a rate four times that of the world economy. *Figure 5* illustrates the dramatic rise in world trade over the past twenty years; *Figure 6*, the flow of trade between continents in 1994.

Over the past ten years the flow of capital and goods has increased tenfold. In this process the market and its tools, chiefly modern communication systems, have forced governments to dismantle customs fees, weaken employment protection laws, drop currency controls, abolish state monopolies to a large extent, privatize public services and, increasingly, lower social security benefits.

5
Development of world trade
volume in billions (US dollars)

Billions of $

5000
4940
4000
3000
2000
1000
769
0

1974 1980 1985 1990 1995

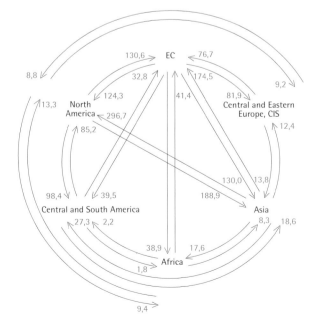

6
Global flow of trade
Import and export in 1994
in billions (US dollars)

According to the United Nations Conference on Trade and Development (UNCTAD), of 373 amendments to basic economic legislation in the past years, 368 were targeted at dismantling the states and their monopolies. A limited number of multinational enterprises (banks, insurance companies, investment firms and funds, industrial enterprises) control the global economy (the 20 largest multinationals generate more revenue than all 86 of the poorest countries). For instance, the American investment firm Fidelity Investment currently manages $ 548 billion in capital – a sum that holds the attention of central bankers from Washington to Tokyo.

The per capita gross national product in 1991 for industrialized, threshold and developing countries reflects the enormous differences that can be traced back to differing per capita production *(Figure 7)*. It is already evident that these conditions are changing, however. Countries like China and India will catch up in great strides over the coming years.

Opposition to the power of the multinationals can come from charitable organizations and activist organizations such as Amnesty International and Greenpeace that act locally while thinking globally. This was demonstrated by their success at the environmental conference in Rio de Janeiro, despite opposition from governments and international enterprises. These organizations may provide an escape route from the "end of the employment world". Another alternative is the "third sector", the independent or volunteer sector of non-profit endeavours (health and welfare, education, the legal system, the sciences and the arts.)

The problem areas of environmental pollution and resource exploitation persist, problems that affect humanity as a whole and that are allowed to slip into the background from time to time, unless extraordinary events and natural phenomena converge, resulting in "ecological catastrophes" (e.g., forest fires in Southeast Asia that last for months and are disastrous for the environment). Especially in the threshold countries, these two topics have received too little attention until now, although these countries also depend on ample energy supplies and outside resources and require a healthy environment. Providing solutions may therefore become a major cornerstone in a new ecological industrial strategy. As part of the third industrial revolution, this new strategy may help to define the future high-tech economy. If the industrialized nations want to continue to be "players", they must form sufficient groups of qualified individuals.

How do these topics impact on architecture not only in the information-based societies, but also in the developing countries? What are the characteristics of an architecture that meets these challenges and can thus be sustainable? Before these questions are answered in Part 2, the trends outlined above will be presented in more depth.

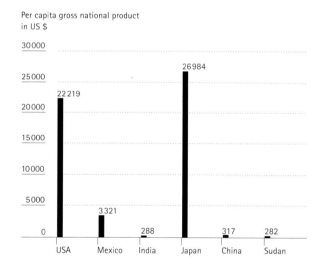

Per capita gross national product in US $

7
Per capita GDP (gross domestic product)
There are huge differences between the GDPs of industrialized and developing countries.

Part 1   The Path to an
Information Society

Basic Principles

1   At the End of the Century: Trends and Demands of the present

1.1   Destruction or Conservation of the Environment?

New demands have emerged and become more defined in all of the industrialized countries over the past 15 years, impacting building strategies for the information age. (Can the same be said of Japan and will it not also affect the "tiger states" a few years from now, or are there distinct cultural differences?) Demands, too, grow in part out of historic conditions and occur in bursts, which can be recognized as trends. A primary and essential demand in European society is a high degree of individualization, where the "I" replaces "we" as the central focus.

Individualization in turn is based on one essential condition, which is part of the economic environment; that is, the strong "I"-focus must be financially viable and is usually a privilege reserved for the few. General prosperity and the creation of a broad middle class allow the individual to exercise sufficient freedom of choice. Individuality goes hand in hand with a high degree of technical mobility, manifested in portable computers, Walkmen, cell phones, cars etc. Individuality does not harmonize, however, with true commitment to and responsibility for others – because individuality develops along the evolutionary principle by which each individual expands his or her area of control as much as possible, avoiding displeasure whenever possible and seeking pleasure. One consequence of these demands is the gradual collapse of traditional family structures in the western industrialized nations. Urbanization and women's education also contribute to the marked decrease in birth rates in these countries.

To what degree can individualization continue to grow in the western industrialized countries? There is no doubt that the world is rapidly shrinking: international problems are growing, poverty is once again present even in prosperous countries and the fear of unemployment is increasingly real.

Individuality means mobility, space, resource consumption – and this is where we encounter limitations. Never-ending luxury, consumption and pleasure no longer deliver the satisfaction they once promised. There are indications that the singles trend has peaked, and that many no longer regard themselves exclusively as independent individuals but as part of a larger whole. It is therefore only apparently a paradox that ecological demands can succeed in the long term only in a society where the life and health of the individual are a central value. One can reasonably assume that the coming years will bring about a shift in national and international industrial policies towards a worldwide ecological policy, less for moral reasons than because of the growing realization that evolutionary adjustment is necessary. This shift will be spearheaded by activist organizations, who act locally and think globally.

Despite global problems, we cannot and must not leave the preservation of our environment to chance, nor can we live by the motto "It'll take care of itself." On the contrary, we must join in a worldwide, intensive effort to ensure that our world continues to be worth living in.

We can begin by looking at different countries and take as an example their respective use of energy to generate one US dollar in GNP (see *Figure 8*). In 1993, while Japanese industry required only five megajoules to generate US$ 1, industry in the United States consumed 12 megajoules. Poor energy efficiency in China until 1989 was primarily the result of the use of coal-burning to generate energy. For some years now, this situation has been improving through a shift to other fuels and newer technologies.

Energy
in megajoules per US$ GDP

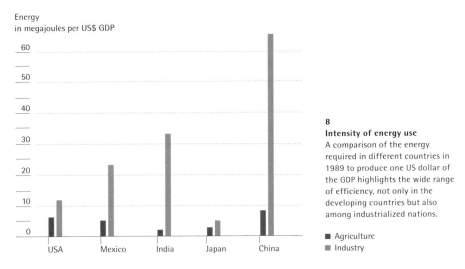

8
Intensity of energy use
A comparison of the energy
required in different countries in
1989 to produce one US dollar of
the GDP highlights the wide range
of efficiency, not only in the
developing countries but also
among industrialized nations.

■ Agriculture
■ Industry

This consumption, divided into individual areas, results in different energy requirements for the previously listed countries. As *Figure 9* illustrates, energy is consumed to varying degrees for different purposes; naturally, the geographic location and the industrial infrastructure of the relevant countries play a considerable role as well.

The combustion of fossil fuels between 1950 and 1989 led to a build-up in CO_2. *Figure 10* shows the countries with the highest levels of CO_2 emissions: the United States is the "leader" by comparison with other industrialized countries, primarily because, at least prior to the first energy crisis, the Americans did not pursue energy-saving measures. Even today, 32 % of worldwide energy is consumed in the United States, although it houses only 5 % of the world population.

9
Energy use
Distribution of energy use across
different economic sectors varies
greatly from country to country.

■ Industry
■ Transportation
■ Agriculture

■ Trade
■ Housing
■ Other

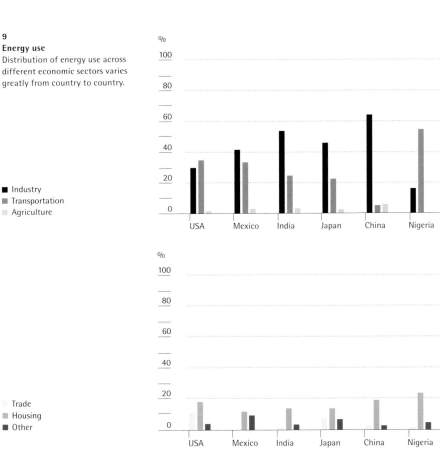

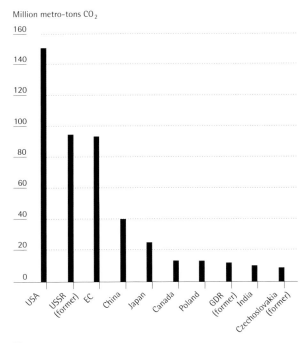

Million metro-tons CO_2

10
Top CO_2 emitters
The countries with the largest
cumulative CO_2 emissions from
fossil fuels (1950-1989).

As shown in *Figure 11,* the United States is once again top among the ten largest emitters. The greenhouse effect varies widely among this group, since the calculations take into consideration how much fossil fuel was burned, how many cement factories were in operation and how much clear-cutting of forests took place. Other considerations include the amount of methane gas and fluorocarbons released into the atmosphere.

Based on extensive simulations carried out by the Intergovernmental Panel on Climate Change (IPCC), the potential for global warming was established according to documented emissions and in consideration of other factors. One of the essential variables was the emission of carbon dioxide as a parameter. *Figure 12* shows the steady increase in CO_2 levels over the past 130 years from 289 ppm to 350 ppm. As a result of these emissions of carbon dioxide and other gases, as well as air-polluting elements, the global temperature has changed considerably *(Figures 13.1 and 13.2)*: next to the combustion of fossil fuels, the combustion of vegetation for land clearing and other agrarian processes is responsible for a rise in global temperature by a total of 0.3 K.

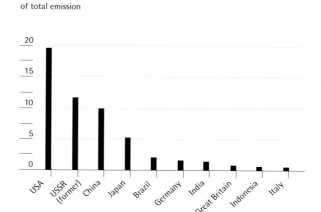

11
Greenhouse gas emitters
The "Top Ten" in 1991

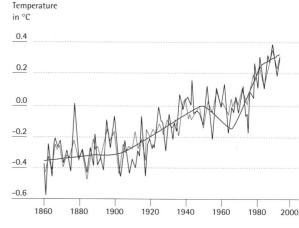

12
Development of atmospheric CO_2 concentrations since 1860

13.1
Temperature changes and atmospheric CO_2 concentrations over the last 160,000 years

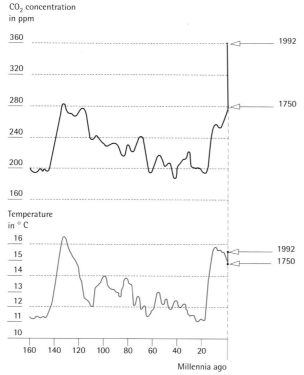

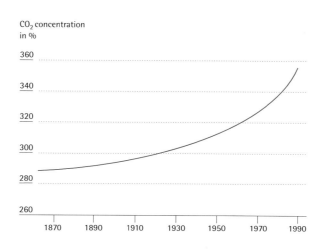

13.2
Simulation calculations take into consideration the various human and natural factors which influence climate; they are used to analyze climate development and to determine temperature increase due to human factors.

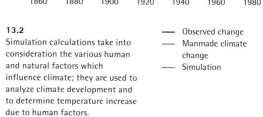

Observed change
Manmade climate change
Simulation

Many international climate experts assume that should the pollution rate remain unchanged, global temperatures will rise 1 K by the year 2025 unless decisive countermeasures are taken. Even the seemingly negligible temperature increase has already contributed to a 250 % increase in natural catastrophes in the past years. Survival alone, for all nations, will therefore dictate that ecology be given precedence over economy in our systems. Still, economy has a special role to play: industry must become the vanguard of ecological change, installing energy-preserving systems across the board and employing renewable energies.

However, there is a lack of consensus among climate experts. Some are of the opinion that the causes for climate change lie in solar activity.

Over a period of approximately 10 to 11 years solar winds shield the earth from cosmic radiation (flows of atomic particles).

The particles of cosmic radiation serve as condensation nuclei in the formation of clouds, so that the solar activity leads to a reduced cloud formation and thus to higher temperatures on earth. The climate changes are thus not traced to man-made causes and the greenhouse effect is ranked as less significant.

One of the fundamental trends is expressed in the buzzword "sustainability". This word describes economic cycles that do not harm the environment and do not consume more energy, raw materials, etc., than are re-created in the natural cycle. A call for sustainability is imperative if we wish to pass on a living environment to our descendants. To stabilize the climate, for example, it is necessary to reduce greenhouse gas emissions worldwide by 60 %. For Germany alone, this translates into a reduction of emissions by at least 80 %. The measures that have already been taken are far from sufficient because profit still rules over preservation. And yet anyone with an interest in these topics clearly understands that we have at best half a century to re-create a balance in the world.

It is also evident that five years after the environmental summit in Rio de Janeiro, the environmental balance sheet is still rather poor. Agreements on climate change and the convention on the conservation of species have not been widely implemented – the American Senate has still not ratified the species variety convention, for example (three-quarters of all bird species in the world are endangered; one-quarter of all mammals are close to extinction). Stress on the atmosphere continues due to toxic elements, deforestation and the destruction of ecosystems – not least of all because we continue to claim more space for agriculture and real estate development.

China, India, the United States, Indonesia, Brazil, Russia, Japan and Germany house 56 % of the world population and generate 58 % of CO_2 emissions. Some 53 % of the world's forests are located in these countries. They must initiate action if environmental damage is to be stopped. Growth at all costs leads to a dangerous destabilization of ecosystems and the natural resource base.

Since we cannot assume that the industrial nations will be willing to lower the standard of living in order to protect the environment, we must instead aim for a considerable increase and improvement in the efficiency of energy-consuming appliances, buildings, means of transport and industrial processes in use on a daily basis.

1.2 Resource Consumption or Conservation

The main issue in the discussion of sustainability is the challenge to limit resource consumption and prevent compromising the needs of future generations. This applies equally to renewable and non-renewable resources. Despite this, there continues to be a dramatic increase in resource consumption, not least of all due to the rapidly growing Asian economies, where the assumption is that resources are inexhaustible and the rate of consumption is therefore unimportant.

The same can be applied to the total inhabited land mass. *Figure 14* shows the use of land in various regions. Human disturbance, however, must be differentiated as follows:

- First category: Low human disturbance means that fewer than 10 people inhabit each square kilometre (barren, partially barren or tundra regions).
- Second category: Medium human disturbance describes land used for agriculture and then allowed to regenerate naturally.
- Third category: High human disturbance defines land that is continuously farmed and that does not regenerate naturally. This includes all types of developed and urban areas as well.

As is evident in the comparison given in *Figure 14*, Europe's position is very poor compared with all other world regions because of its high population density. At the same time, a glance at planned building developments gives the impression that land is in plentiful supply in parts of Europe, especially in Germany.

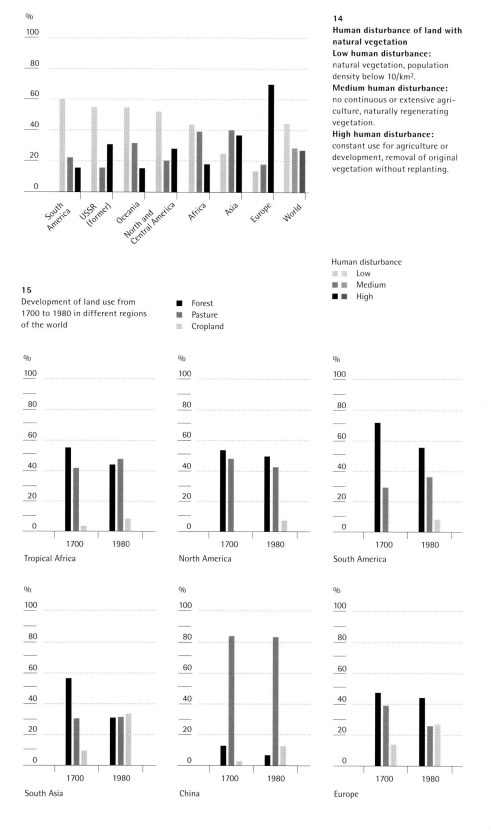

14
Human disturbance of land with natural vegetation
Low human disturbance: natural vegetation, population density below 10/km². **Medium human disturbance:** no continuous or extensive agriculture, naturally regenerating vegetation. **High human disturbance:** constant use for agriculture or development, removal of original vegetation without replanting.

Human disturbance
Low
Medium
High

15
Development of land use from 1700 to 1980 in different regions of the world

Forest
Pasture
Cropland

Tropical Africa

North America

South America

South Asia

China

Europe

Species extinction
in %

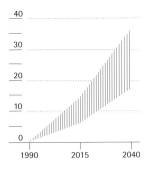

16
Species extinction in rainforests
If 15 million hectares of tropical
rainforest continue to be clear-
cut on an annual basis, between
6% and 14% of local species will
be extinct by 2015 and between
17% and 35% by 2040.

The steady growth in world population has brought about a dramatic change in that new areas of land have been created for agriculture hand in hand with a massive reduction in forest areas *(Figure 15)*. From 1700 to 1980 approximately 20% of the world's forests were destroyed and agrarian areas were enlarged by 460%. Taken together with the necessary reduction of air pollutants, this can only be described as a dramatic change.

The destruction of forests, at the rate of approximately 15 billion hectares a year, will lead to the permanent extinction of roughly 6% to 14% of all animal species by the year 2015 and 17% to 35% by the year 2040; *Figure 16* illustrates this trend, which could still be averted. Biologists speak of the destruction of the rich variety of species as the crime that future generations will find the least forgivable. A wealth of different species can be seen as insurance against unpre-

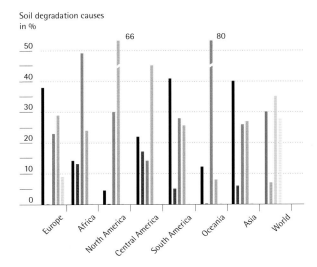

17
Causes of soil erosion
Overgrazing, agriculture and
deforestation contribute more or
less equally to soil erosion,
although wide variations are evident in different regions. Industrialization and its consequences,
such as waste and excessive use
of pesticides, factor in only 1% of
soil erosion worldwide.

■ ■ Deforestation
■ ■ Overexploitation for fuel wood
■ ■ Overgrazing
■ ■ Agriculture
░ Industrialization

dictable biospheric, climatic or other changes, and it is hence foolhardy to sacrifice the conservation of species for the sake of short-term economic gain.

The reasons for environmental destruction differ in various regions, as is shown in *Figure 17* for the period up to 1990. Clear-cutting, gathering firewood, the creation of pastures, an extensive agrarian economy and industrialization all play a role. The figure further illustrates that by comparison with all other regions, soil reduction and destruction respectively are especially rampant in Europe for the sake of development.

The issue of resource consumption is further illustrated with several examples shown in *Figures 18–21*.

Figure 18 shows the consumption of sawlogs from 1961 to 1990 in the industrialized, threshold and developing countries. The consumption of wood for wood products, paper and firewood has increased moderately; wood as a renewable resource remains the least critical issue, since it is still at least a partially renewable resource.

Figure 19 illustrates per capita aluminium consumption and proves that industrialized countries consume approximately twenty times more aluminium than developing countries. The strong tendency to increased consumption in this area poses the question whether and for how much longer we can afford it. Serious recycling must be practised to prevent an irreversible exhaustion of the world's reserves.

Figure 20 illustrates global metal consumption from 1900 to 1983, again with a steep upward tendency. Here, too, recycling is the only answer, because the production of different metals requires displacing huge amounts of earth in order to gain the desired raw material. Here are some of the ratios for further clarification: iron ore, 1:14; bauxite, 1:5; manganese iron ore, 1:420; zinc, 1:27; lead, 1:19; silver, 1:7,500; gold, 1:350,000; platinum, 1:350,000. The ratios indicate the tonnes of material that have to be displaced to gain 1 kilogram of the respective metal.

In their book *Faktor 4,* Ernst Ulrich von Weizsäcker and Armory B. and L. Hunter Lovins made the memorable comparison that one wedding band carries with it an "ecological backpack" of approximately three tonnes. Scientists researching the causes for soil and water acidification have determined that in European latitudes the shifting and displacement of soil alone creates more sulphur dioxide than all other industrial combustion processes.

Lastly, *Figure 21* illustrates the per capita consumption of fossil fuels in industrialized, threshold and developing countries and shows that energy consumption in industrialized countries increased only moderately after the first energy crisis in 1973, in some areas even falling slightly, while in the threshold countries energy consumption is rising unchecked, although it is a known fact that fossil fuels are not inexhaustible.

Dennis H. Meadows and Jørgen Randers used computer programs for the first time in the book *Die Grenzen des Wachstums* [The Limits of Growth] to demonstrate what a growth model for the current condition of the world might look like. In *Figure 22* we see the image of a growing population with increasing industrial production and a concurrent increase in food production, but also an increase in environmental pollution up to the year 2010. At the same time, raw materials decrease steadily, settling at a low level. Due to the steady population growth, simultaneous decrease in food supplies (from circa 2010 onward) and industrial production, there is a reversal of the overall tendency (period from 2010 to 2030). What emerges is that population growth and industrial production are clearly limited by environmental pollution and the reduction in raw materials.

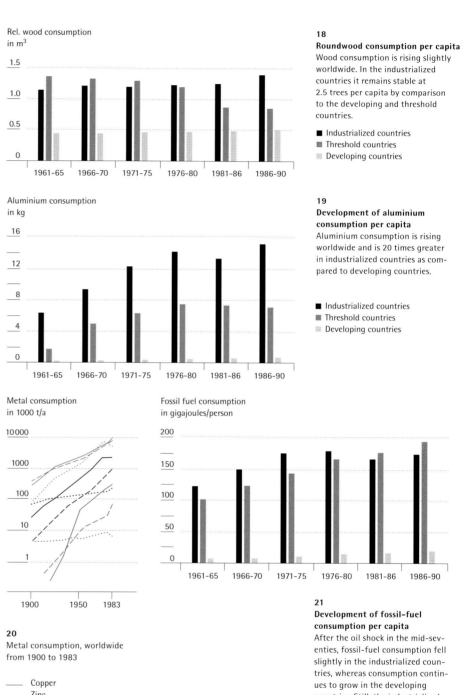

Rel. wood consumption in m³

18

Roundwood consumption per capita
Wood consumption is rising slightly worldwide. In the industrialized countries it remains stable at 2.5 trees per capita by comparison to the developing and threshold countries.

■ Industrialized countries
■ Threshold countries
▨ Developing countries

Aluminium consumption in kg

19

Development of aluminium consumption per capita
Aluminium consumption is rising worldwide and is 20 times greater in industrialized countries as compared to developing countries.

■ Industrialized countries
■ Threshold countries
▨ Developing countries

Metal consumption in 1000 t/a

Fossil fuel consumption in gigajoules/person

20

Metal consumption, worldwide from 1900 to 1983

——— Copper
— — Zinc
······ Manganese
——— Chrome
— — Nickel
······ Tin
——— Magnesium
— — Molybdenum
——— Mercury

21

Development of fossil-fuel consumption per capita
After the oil shock in the mid-seventies, fossil-fuel consumption fell slightly in the industrialized countries, whereas consumption continues to grow in the developing countries. Still, the industrialized countries consume approximately nine times more than the developing countries.

■ Industrialized countries
■ Threshold countries
▨ Developing countries

Figures 23 and *24* present the growth model based on the assumption of a yearly increase of 3 % and 5 % respectively in resource productivity, indicating that in this case the system will stabilize. The requirements set forth in *Figure 24* are the only ones that could ensure the stability of an affluent society over the long term.

22
Growth model according to Meadows
Only when environmental pollution and raw-material consumption have reached their limits, and when the lack of investments can no longer be compensated, will population growth and growth in industrial production cease.

— Raw materials
— Population
–·· Food
— Industrial production
---- Environmental pollution

23
Growth model for a rise of 3 % in resource productivity
Assuming an annual rise of 3 % in resource productivity, Harry Lehmann of the Wuppertal Institute, using the World 3/91 model, projects a system stabilization by the year 2150.

— Raw materials
— Population
–·· Food
— Industrial production
---- Environmental pollution

24
Assuming an annual efficiency increase of 5 %,
stabilization occurs much earlier and at a higher level of economic wealth.

— Raw materials
— Population
–·· Food
— Industrial production
---- Environmental pollution

Rel. units
of model parameters

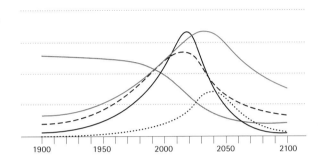

Rel. units
of model parameters

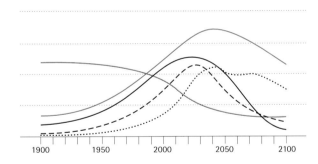

Rel. units
of model parameters

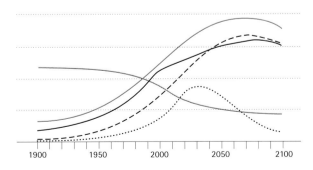

1.3 Recycling Instead of Single-Use Products

To show the percentage of building waste to total waste, here are some figures for the Federal Republic of Germany (former West Germany) from 1987.

Assuming the entire waste production to equal 100 %, one can divide it into contributing factors as follows:
– Household waste, bulk waste,
 trade waste   approx. 12 %
– Toxic waste   approx. 5 %
– Production waste   approx. 35 %
– Construction waste   approx. 48 %
Construction waste is nearly 50 % of the total waste, a primary target for the recycling economy.

A further differentiation of construction waste (100 %) for the same period leads to the following percentages:
– Excavation   approx. 78 %
– Roadwork   approx. 8 %
– Rubble   approx. 14 %
Rubble is here understood to be all hard materials that result from building demolition and that contain mineral components, depending upon the type of building and method of demolition.

For 1994 the construction industry aimed for the following recycling targets:
– Excavation   reuse 70 %
– Roadwork   reuse 90 %
– Rubble   reuse 60 %
– Other construction site waste   reuse 40 %

In building excavation, it's necessary to differentiate between uncontaminated and contaminated earth. In the case of the excavation of uncontaminated earth, the recycling factor can be 100 % – in the sense of recycling, it is not waste but rather raw material. To avoid great distances for the disposal of excavated earth, it is sensible to determine where the excavated earth can be reused when the environmental feasibility study is done. Possible balancing and substitution measures may include landscaping plans: excavated earth can be used for recultivation.

Contaminated soil, for instance at industrial sites, is processed and decontaminated and then channelled for recycling. Known soil decontamination procedures include soil vapour extraction, soil washing and microbiological cleansing processes which utilize the ability of adapted micro-organisms to consume pollutants as a source of nutrients, thereby transforming them into harmless substances. This creates a product that is useful for recycling in agriculture and horticulture.

In roadwork excavation as well, it is necessary to differentiate between uncontaminated and contaminated material. Technical progress means that recycled material has nearly the same quality as the new material, and the recycling success rate is therefore correspondingly high. Even contaminated waste resulting from roadwork is rendered usable through treatment and separating out the noxious material.

The recycling of building material is the basis for developing an intelligent and judicious material economy in the building sector. The following sequence applies:
– Waste avoidance
– Material use of waste
– Thermal use of waste
– Waste disposal

Due to high dumping fees, several competitive options for recycling have been developed for used building materials; with few exceptions, all standard materials can now be recycled to some extent. To reach the highest possible rate of building-material recycling, the following conditions must be considered in the initial planning phase:
– Material homogeneity
– Separability of different materials
– Low material diversity
– Building material identification
– Recovery when possible

Mineral Building Materials

Mineral building materials such as concrete, calcareous sandstone and bricks are easily re-used. Light building materials such as aerated plaster, drywall and foam mortar can be channelled through separate cycles into the new production of these building materials.

Wood

Wood can be processed in the form of strands or used as insulation. Older, treated woods may contain contaminants (e.g., PCBs), which make re-use more difficult. For improved recyclability in the future, wood treatments should be free of heavy metals.

Metals

Metals can usually be treated and re-used without any loss in quality. Coatings somewhat limit recycling options.

Glass

Glass recycling usually consists of a long process from plate glass through cast glass to container glass, wherein high-grade recycling depends principally upon the pollution abatement in the manufacture of the glass panes.

Bituminous Materials

Rolled building material, such as tarpaper for roofing, is recyclable; coatings with a mineral base can easily be re-used as rubble or ballast. Coatings for insulating materials can only be separated out with great effort and must usually be completely disposed of. The same applies to composite materials.

Insulating Materials

Polystyrene can be integrated into the recycling process as an insulant (granulates, insulating grist, new panels). Mineral-strand boards or panels for interior construction are not yet recyclable, since possible health hazards posed by aged strands cannot be ruled out. Multi-cellular or foamed glass, on the other hand, can be processed into sand. Light building boards are usually re-used as insulation; in-situ PUR foams (in-situ cellular plastics) are usually present only in small amounts and are therefore disposed of.

Synthetic Materials

All types of purely extracted thermoplastics such as roofing, flooring, framing materials etc., are in principle recyclable. Jointing compound, adhesives and coatings are not recycled because of the small volumes in which these materials are used.

Textiles and Wallpapers

Textiles and wallpapers are generally used for insulation, taking into consideration that they must be treated with safe paint coatings.

To ease the treatment and processing of building materials, the basic premise must be to avoid any pollutants (heavy metals, organic solvents, halogenated hydrocarbons, formaldehyde, benzoate, toluol, polycyclic aromatic hydrocarbons). Here, older building materials pose a much greater risk than do modern materials.

The building industry has come to understand that a positive corporate image cannot be maintained in the future if ecological sensibilities are ignored, and furthermore, that recycling creates new service industries and markets. One can thus reasonably assume that the necessary path will be followed in an appropriate fashion. This means that planners must contribute in advance and that the public sector must offer massive support for recycling, even in cases where it may not appeal to the individual. *Figure 25* shows a cost representation for a utilization period ranging from 30 to 60 years for one building, which clearly demonstrates the actual value of demolition: the percentage of cost and hence the volume of the material ultimately consigned to disposal is relatively small and the best form of recycling is undoubtedly ensuring the longest possible lifespan for each building. Thus environmental economical costs and ecological stress are kept at a minimum.

25

Building costs

Costs for construction and renovation, operation, demolition and recycling for a commercial highrise per square metre of usable area, calculated for the number of years the building is in use (excluding VAT and financing interest). (Energy consumption in kWh/m² of primary energy per annum.)

- ■ Total
- ■ Dump
- ■ Raw materials
- ■ Energy
- ▦ Depreciation
- ▦ Other
- ▦ Labour

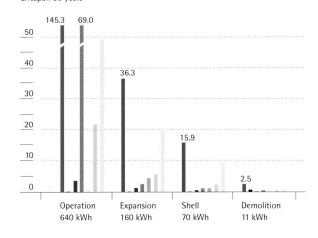

Total cost in DM/m²a
Lifespan 30 years

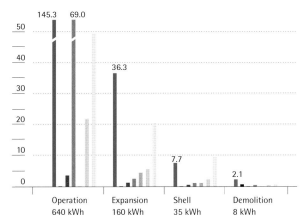

Total cost in DM/m²a
Lifespan 60 years

1.4 The Worldwide Net and the Virtual Universe

The road towards the information age has many unknown twists and turns. Depending on whether one identifies with the new technologies and what they have to offer, completely different projections can be made. At the very least, one can recognize that "artificial environments" are already affecting our lives and are being accepted to some extent. As we move beyond the era of individualism, our needs can no longer be the sole motivating factor for our actions; we have to be prepared to consider a range of alternatives.

Our knowledge, and the possibilities of increasing our knowledge, surpass our options for action. It is clear that the perception of "civilized" human beings in an industrial society is increasingly rooted in a domain of symbols, in a virtual universe of images. This, however, also engenders a collective malaise which might be paraphrased as "media irrationalism". The feeling that everything is becoming more and more fleeting, artificial, unreal, irrational and meaningless creates massive psychological reactions. What is more, the human brain is not necessarily capable of dealing with a virtual world: this statement originates from studies of individuals who have worked with virtual reality for years. The brain reacts defensively against a suspension of tactile, manifest reality; individuals ultimately complain of a growing feeling of disorientation and malaise. Psychological studies have furthermore led to the realization that the constant transformation of images (humans become robots, unicorns turn into cars etc.), which is standard fare in film and advertising today, have affected the consciousness of adolescents in that they increasingly believe that anything is possible and are disappointed when reality cannot be bent and reshaped at will.

There is no doubt that the information age and virtualization are affecting our perception of space: basically, there are no longer spatial distances. Furthermore, virtualization can lead to the loss of connection to one's body; at the same time, it can overthrow the time dimension since it, too, can be shifted. The arti-ficiality of our perception reduces our world to a universe of shadows, where we are threatened with the loss of Self.

A recent study by H. Frey and the German Federal Research Ministry points out that electronic communication systems impoverish language skills, which in turn leads to a paralysis of innovation in both individuals and even entire companies. Electronic communication carriers (e-mail, multimedia mail, video conferencing, video telephones) reduce complex information to a minimum and change living language into abbreviated image symbols. Emotions and body language, which communicate more than pure information, are no longer present between colleagues, managers and team members. Creativity and innovation suffer as a result, and responsibilities are delegated to the system, a development with unfortunate consequences. Communication technologies should be understood as they were intended, namely, as tools to improve efficiency for data transfer with higher transmission rates than previously available.

A counter-movement against virtualization can be felt in our culture. The "retro-trends" call for tactile reality and localization (the search for spatial "rootedness"), and a consciousness of the passage of time and related feelings of nostalgia. Researchers of trends have found that this counter-movement will be one of the biggest and most influential trends at least up until the turn of the millennium.

At the same time, approximately 30 million people currently use the Internet, with growth projected at an annual increase of 100 %. The system acts like a self-fulfilling prophecy: whole industries are created based on the vision of a limitless, borderless data highway.

To draw up plausible prognoses for the development of the electronic future, trend researchers look to experiences from the past. One of these experiential potentials applies to the video telephone. According to futurists in 1950, all households should already be equipped with a video telephone. This is, however, not the case. The reason for the relatively low popularity of this technology is found in the cultural domain – that is, people have not developed rituals and social codes for its use. Since a video telephone would force us to adopt behaviours that would collide with our daily habits, most people today still prefer the conventional telephone (possibly in combination with the computer network); it provides the ability to maintain a comfortable distance. The interlocutor is accessible and yet the telephone keeps him or her at a distance. People have learned to manipulate with their voices; this is easily achieved with the conventional telephone. The video telephone demands role-play as well, which would draw upon intimate reserves.

Trend researchers posit that a psychological defence may arise against computer networks. In the technology-crazed United States, almost half of 600 office employees that were surveyed admitted to an antipathy towards computer technology. Motives were fear of loss of personal contact and the feeling of not being equal to the professional requirements of the future. Information stress also came into play. The question used to be, How do I effectively gain access to information? It has become, How do I reduce the information? Another query posed by the average consumer with regard to the new technology is at the same time a question of survival: What good will this do me? Supporters of the data highway say simply, Information is valuable. Yet a further question requires an answer: What is valuable information to each individual? Numerous studies show that people handle information very differently. Each person clearly links information with meaning or sense. When information makes no sense, it is ignored and perceived as excess weight. The human brain has an ability computers still lack – it can forget. This form of reducing complexity may be a true blessing in the information age, for the actual problem of the individual in a modern society is often not how to gain access to more information but rather how to differentiate important from unimportant information and how to get rid of the latter as quickly as possible. The possibilities provided by the information age and the data networks are indeed powerful tools, but they can only realize their full potential when there is communication – in other words, when information exchange occurs, rather than a mere accumulation of information.

Tangible advantages in networking lie in the areas of medicine, interest groups, hobbies, sex and purchasing consumer goods. The computer network achieves its full potential above all when personal interests can be organized by individuals. This is the case especially in the field of medicine, more precisely in the area of diagnostic medicine.

Other noticeable advantages of the network technologies can come into play in the area of consumer goods, since a purchaser can search for and locate the product he or she is looking for with the help of worldwide search programs, no matter how unusual the product may be. For hobbies, special interest groups and sex, the data highway is also an important tool, since it brings together those of the same persuasion in an uncomplicated fashion.

To arrive at a clear image of the electronic future, one must comprehend the social aspects of the network euphoria. It is not technical or financial facts that will ultimately determine the future of data networks, but social evolution. Today, data networks are mainly operated for professional reasons. Aside from this, adolescents may use the Internet to participate in an "alternative" subculture. This international subculture functions according to the laws of a "closed minority". The source code of the network culture is communication. It expands across cyberspace through MUDS (multi-user dungeons, meeting places in the computer network where many subscribers communicate simultaneously).

At the same time, the Internet is still an amorphous and more or less self-organizing structure which anyone with some know-how – and the right computer – can access. Commercialization may soon define user privileges and exclude the "have-nots" from the data flow, which may lead to personal and professional disadvantages.

The implications of the Net may in the long term lead to a marketing revolution. The extension of computer networks may even spell the downfall of mass media; where marketing formerly addressed the public, individuals now search for the specific in the mass marketplace of the Internet. This results in atomized perception in that the structure of the network gives each consumer a choice.

Trend researchers give the following prognoses a high rating of probability based on previous experience:

– The digital, individual newspaper will be a flop.
– Atomized, individualized information is only important for the professional.
– Exchange, sale, service, classifieds thrive.
– Interactive television will be a flop.
– Actual media events will take place on site, at the theatre, opera house etc.
– Excessive stimulants will be excluded from homes.

Since the main gate to interactivity will open only for our children and grandchildren, most trend researchers are of the opinion that a period of at least three generations is necessary before relevant key technologies can be permanently established. Only after 2010 will nearly 75 % of all German households likely own a PC (30 years after the manufacture of the first home computers).

In conclusion, one can say that the information age will begin later than believed – not least of all because cost-benefit relationships determine the real future of interactive utopias.

1.5 Changing Markets, "New Work"

The construction and real estate markets are deeply influenced by the requirements and demands described above: the preservation of the environment, the conservation of resources, the necessity for recycling, the dawning of the information age and the new production and service markets, as well as company and enterprise development.

The main centres function increasingly as short-term way stations: young people move into the cities for education and training, immersing themselves in the singles culture, only to return to the suburbs when they are ready to start a family. They choose to escape the urban stress in search of more space, more security, more time at home, more air, more happiness. Cities are confronted increasingly with poverty because of the influx of cheaper work forces, slower growth and high social costs. Already they appear more miserable, more polarized and tougher than in their heyday. The urban dream is increasingly giving way to a feeling of alienation, exacerbated by the cut-backs of government "rationalization" and corporate "restructuring". This urban flight is closely linked to the new drop-out trend, which is not related to "doing nothing", but rather to becoming independent, relying on the strength of one's own professional experience.

The boundaries between national economies are dissolving in the drive towards a world economy; especially in the search for cheap labour, there has been worldwide competition for many years. European companies in particular are being forced to implement rationalization measures because of this worldwide competition and must sometimes enter new markets in order to maintain at least a part of their market share. The first wave of the "emancipation from above", which has already reached many companies, is based clearly on one single formula: more profit with fewer people. Classic leadership models do not serve this dynamic. The creativity of all employees must be exploited, resulting in new work models.

The future market in Europe will be a service and software market, not a hardware market. This development also means that the major industrial societies in the West will enter increasingly into an era dominated by an economy of ideas: a wealth of ideas and innovation will be the decisive competition factors, while the production of goods will be either delegated to other countries or reorganized. In an economy of ideas, however, the deciding cost factor is the human brain: the employee. A company that wants to hold on to good employees and has high qualification and remuneration levels is threatened by excessive redundancy costs. The habits and milieus established in Central Europe with regard to social demands, safety, etc., become a burden. An even greater burden can be the "this is not my job" factor, one of the most prevailing patterns in employee culture: many strive to keep the range (or radius) of their responsibilities as small as possible and to reject any task that they have not explicitly been ordered to perform.

In contrast, large software companies are already demonstrating the evolution of companies in the information age. At the core lies the realization that production in the future will no longer be driven by work function but by problem solution. An economy of ideas is fundamentally different from mass production. Problems must be solved by a creative process, and in a race against time. Hence, software companies no longer have regulated working hours; instead, teams gather to work on problem-solving and are then dissolved again. Team leaders may be simply team members on the next case. This new employee structure ultimately leads to a radical dissolution of hierarchies and to an employee type who performs "network tasks" in the company and need no longer be dependent upon instructions from above. Modern companies must therefore bring their employees to accept more self-responsibility and greater flexibility. In this way the new structures of the information age are diametrically opposed to the old hierarchies.

While the latter aimed for the greatest degree of con-
flict-free functioning of employees, "new work" in
the widest sense means independence, with all its
inherent advantages and disadvantages.

2 The Dissolution of Architecture or Denser Building: Scenarios for the Future

2.1 Data Highways Instead of Highways, Databanks Instead of Libraries

On the road to the information age, visions develop along the way. In *The City of Bits: Life in the City of the 21st Century,* William J. Mitchell describes the city of the information age not only as a city of computers and data highways, but also as a city which is still very much inhabited, where people may still work or pursue activities outside the home, not totally absorbed into cyberspace but still searching for the same things that interest us today. Thus the city in the information age will have a real building mass, a real exterior space, buildings that serve for meeting and congregating, houses that consume energy whose efficiency, however, should be far better than those we currently inhabit. Hence a multitude of aspects will be explored in the "forecast" of a city in the information age. These scenarios of the future naturally also discuss whether we do not already have at our disposal the basics of what we require, albeit with a need for retrofitting, concentrating and optimizing in order to meet future requirements in a sustainable fashion.

The worldwide computer network (the Internet) has a fundamentally different physical structure and is governed by different rules than public interaction in conventional cities. Mitchell extrapolates from this that the Internet will challenge how we think of community and urban life and will provide a radically new definition of these terms. As a result we discover such diametrically opposed topic pairings as:

- Spatial / antispatial
- Physical / aphysical
- Synchronous / asynchronous
- Narrow band / broad band
- Voyeurism / direct participation
- Neighbouring / interconnected
- Focused / fragmented

The computer network negates geometry and is antispatial in a fundamental and profound sense. One cannot describe its typical forms, its proportions; one can, however, find "things" within it without knowing exactly where they are. The Net is an environment into which one doesn't enter but logs in (phoneline-modem-access code-password-network). This antispatial element is already fully present: e-mail messages give no clue as to where they were sent from; people communicating exclusively via the Net do not reveal where they are.

Since network connections are often executed through neutral identifications, one cannot ascertain with certainty who and what is behind the identification code. The participants become aphysical; bit by bit an electronic identity is constructed.

Personal conversation between people is linked to a geographically contextual, physical and hence strictly synchronous event. A telephone connection, while separating the interlocutors geographically, nevertheless requires synchronicity of action. Answering machines and fax machines as well as state-of-the-art voice-mail systems are contemporary means of asynchronous communication. In the asynchronous mode we do not hear the words when they are spoken, instead they are reproduced later in time. In the case of e-mail systems, we do not hear the other person's voice. In these modes of communication, responses are usually delayed and thus the continuity of personal conversation is not only geographically but also temporally broken.

To avoid being one of the disadvantaged on the Net, it is vital to be able to absorb or release sufficient volumes of information via corresponding bandwidths. This ensures direct profit from and through the data network. While real estate value in the traditional, urban constellation is driven by location, the value of a network connection depends upon the bandwidth.

The steady improvement in information and communication technology results in a steady increase in broadband connections. Electronic interaction is becoming increasingly multi-modal; video conferencing unites image and sound, robot effectors – combined with audio and video sensors – make a telepresence possible. Intelligent exoskeleton devices (data gloves, data suits, robotic prostheses, "intelligent second skin") enable us to feel touch while serving as tactile output devices by exerting force and pressure in a controlled manner. Portable stereo sight devices or holographic television enable us to immerse ourselves in simulated environments.

Cities are not only dense fields of activity where access options are maximized and direct interaction is promoted, but also highly developed structures for the organization and control of access (subdivided as they are into municipalities, neighbourhoods, etc.). Property borders are marked by fences or walls. In the data network the situation is parallel, but the rules are different. The access and connecting structures have an entirely different architecture: one no longer enters or leaves a location through physical movement but through establishing or breaking logical connections. Locations, sites in the cyberspace of the Net, are software constructs. The software of a machine or group of machines on the Net creates interaction environments, virtual domains, into which potentially anyone can enter. Text windows, character surfaces, three-dimensional model rooms are such locations one enters. These include desktops and files in computer operating systems, mailboxes and billboards. Virtual sites can be so configured as to allow only one person to occupy them at a time. Others, however, are multistation systems that allow several users simultaneous access to common or shared activities (electronic calendar, CAD files, virtual conference rooms). The digital city, the network, is – if we believe the prognoses – the new urban location without geographic reference, resting solely upon networking and bandwidth.

Current research is geared towards developing miniaturized electronic products that can be connected to human organs through exonerves. Where these electronic organs and the sensory receptors and muscles interface, bits are constantly exchanged between the external digital world and the nervous system, which

is thus coupled to the worldwide digital net. Man and woman become modular, reconstructible, endlessly expandable cyborgs.

Imagine that all personal electronic devices – wireless headphones, cell phones, beepers, dictation machines, camcorders, personal digital assistants, electronic pens, modems, computers, satellite navigation systems, "intelligent glasses", video remote controls, data gloves, electronic jogging shoes, medical monitoring systems, pacemakers – could be connected to a continuous network so that the body could function as an integrated system and be linked to the worldwide net. We might then, with PDA programme videorecorders, be able to listen to beeper messages on a walkman, with intelligent glasses display the co-ordinates of a navigation system, transfer physiological data from an electronic training machine to the PDA and transfer camcorder output to remote locations via a wireless modem.

In the wake of size reduction and ever closer connection to the body, the electronic organs will develop from the plastic housing used now into a kind of body-fitting clothing item. Micro devices may be surgically implanted, as is already the case with pacemakers. Currently, systems for neuromuscular stimulation are being developed to compensate, for example, for spinal cord injuries or to give sight to the blind by implanting a silicon retina. Once the barrier of the skin has been broken in this described manner, barriers between surroundings and architecture will gradually dissolve as well.

In conventional buildings, space and time are continuous. A window pane separates interior and exterior, but inside and outside are at the same location, and there are no differences in time. In a world inhabited by cyborgs, video cameras create shifts and fragments as electronic retinas; rooms and buildings have new kinds of openings. Scenes viewed through glass have new dimensions and are possibly far distant. The place on the other side of the glass pane may change from one moment to the next; a sequence may repeat itself. In buildings designed for the information age, interior walls are not what they seem but rather enormous video screens that simulate a surface in repose and open electronic windows to show whatever one intends when activated.

In this time of electronics, the Net is becoming a worldwide optical nerve transcending all time zones with electronic eyes on all its extremities. Locations, demarcated by walls and horizons, defined by sunrise and sunset, no longer exist. This doesn't apply only to sight but to hearing as well. A convolvotrone is a digital device that can place electronically synthesized and reproduced sounds at specific locations. It can create illusions with sound backdrops issuing from empty space.

Actuators transmit precisely synchronized movements and thrusts, possibly with recorded images, whereby simulated movements are perceived much more intensely than they actually are. Physical and simulated movements can be uncoupled. In the future, telemanipulators will replace hands to such a degree that a surgeon will be able to manipulate a scalpel by remote control: the surgeon may be hundreds of kilometres distant, holding a back-coupled instrument while watching the output of an imaging system on a video monitor. (In March 1991, the first active surgical robot operation was performed on a living patient.)

Telemanipulators will become increasingly important in the organ repertoire of cyborgs. There are many practical reasons to expand the use of robots; dangerous tasks will require only the appropriate video eyes and electromechanical gloves for their precise execution. Already in 1988, a cockroach-sized robot was developed at M.I.T. (Massachusetts Institute of Technology). Since then R. Brooks has led a team of scientists at the same university in the research of piezoelectric, motor-driven ant robots 1 mm in diameter. If a microscope were used instead of a video camera and a micro-manipulator instead of a telemanipulator, one could penetrate to the atomic level and work within that world.

For thousands of years, architects have studied and worked with the body as it is, delimited by the skin and its immediate sensory environment. Architects provide shelter, warmth and security, illuminate surrounding surfaces, create rooms for entertainment and music, bring soft, rough and smooth materials into harmony and take care to create hygienic conditions in a house. In the expanded field created through electronics, architects will have to work with reconfigurable virtual bodies, which can feel and act from a distance and yet are still partially rooted in their immediate environment. By donning a data helmet the immediate visual environment is replaced by virtual space; only sensations of touch remind us of the solid objects surrounding us. Increasingly the architectures of physical space and of cyberspace will overlap, intersect and merge.

In architecture past and present, façades show what takes place inside the building, which activities, organizations or social groups are within a building. In like manner, the inner configuration reflects the structure of the company or institution, thus delivering a physical diagram of the pattern of activities. Today, companies are not only supported in their activities by architecture and interior design, but also by modern electronic media and software. In this process the digital, electronic and virtual side is gaining ground compared to the physical; bit storage is replacing physical artefacts such as books. The need for walled-in space is lessening.

This shift is most evident in the area of information. Books, magazines and newspapers can be mass produced at one central location; their distribution, on the other hand, requires tremendous effort. However, if we separate information from its usual carriers (paper and plastic), storage and transport become superfluous. In the future the majority of information will be stored on a central server in digital form and distributed to output sites via computer networks. Clients can select the desired information from a menu, download it on site and copy it to CDs or print it on laser printers. This electronic, digital distribution of information can reach into homes and other consumer locations.

Similarly, sound and image recordings can be transmitted to private stereo systems, televisions or home computers. By changing the manner of information distribution, the forms of consumption can be changed as well. Instead of looking through a newspaper or magazine for specific information, one uses software that selects those topics one is especially interested in; databases search information by keywords. One can imagine that book, music and video stores will in the future be replaced by small and omnipresent electronic devices. Through the Net and the data highway, where each node can be a site both of reception and of publication, concentrations of activity will be centrally replaced by millions of dispersed fragments.

This may mean, for example, that libraries as well as books and magazines will become superfluous. Computer graphic user interfaces will fulfil the same function as the corresponding buildings used to. Someone searching for information can download staggering amounts of information (comparable to several books) onto a personal workstation and print them within a few minutes. It is unimportant where the digital source material is located. Instead of filling and organizing large central book repositories or bookshelves in homes, we may in the future create a database with integrated search and retrieval functions.

Museums, new and old, mount exhibitions with carefully designed display sequences. These must be accommodated by certain types of buildings and suites of rooms or spaces. In the virtual museum digital images of paintings, videos of living organisms or three-dimensional simulations of sculptures and architecture take the place of physical objects. At the same time the virtual museum offers a far greater range for exploration than even the largest museums in the world. In fact, all individual works and exhibitions at any museum in the world may become available via server and data highway and be brought straight into the home.

In the field of entertainment (theatre, concerts, opera, dance etc.), the revolution triggered by the new media may be even greater, for entertainment is information. Entertainment is produced and consumed by the public in specific buildings. Radio and television broadcasts expand the audience from a few hundred or thousands to millions. The flow of information runs in one and the same direction. New bi-directional broadband systems change this insofar as subscribers can choose videos from a wide menu in order to view them at any time (video on demand). Interactive productions will become the norm. When television "receives" three-dimensional events, viewers can control the directional functions themselves by operating a virtual camera. If we take these futuristic visions to the extreme, the architectural relationship between the production site and the audience space falls apart. These types of buildings will no longer be needed and will be replaced by studios as production sites, on the one hand, and computer systems with monitors, on the other.

Places of education also serve to pass on information. When teachers and students no longer need to be brought together in one place, when network connections distribute information to any location, then – instead of traditional classrooms – we will require a room with a workstation and a computer-driven video projector to complement the current set-up. Students can gather bits of information directly via information systems; teachers can teach from a great distance. There is no need for the students to be at any specific physical location.

Hospitals can be partially replaced by telemedicine, which reduces the need for transporting patients to a special medical facility. The family doctor can get advice from distant specialists by video and can thus assume some of the tasks available only at major clinics today. If more and more private households come online, residential diagnosis and monitoring devices will eventually make the virtual home visit possible, turning long-term care into telecare. Microwave devices will be used to monitor the vital signs (pulse, respiration, temperature, blood pressure). Special heating and air-conditioning systems and bathroom facilities will automatically take samples and analyse them. Homes will be built with technically correct health care instruments in place. In some ways, medical care will become even more impersonal and technical than it already is. At the same time, this revolution in information and telecommunication will lead to decentralization and a more even distribution of medical services.

Buildings that house people for institutional reasons can be similarly redesigned if not abolished altogether to create, for example, prisons without cells and walls. Individuals will be monitored by transponder (ankle brace) and modem. Overstepping the default distance will automatically trigger an alarm.

Banks can be transformed completely into money machines, since money can also be understood as digital information endlessly circulating in cyberspace. We are currently experiencing the step-by-step evolution of digital banks (24-hour banks), which are accessible from an infinity of locations and able to handle all transactions electronically. Deposits and withdrawals can be integrated into laptops or electronic notebooks through personal terminals. There are already gambling casinos where visitors are given "smart" credit cards that electronically store credit and debits. Bank buildings will no longer be places where money is stored; bank robbers will have to break into computer security systems rather than safes.

The same scenario applies to stock exchanges and round-the-clock trading systems for futures and options transactions. The globalization of financial markets divides traditional markets for financial trading, while integrating them by electronic means. The new technology reduces the importance of human participation. At the same time, it considerably increases the risks, as recent events have demonstrated. Moving financial markets into cyberspace goes hand in hand with a change of what is being traded. The full palette of split-second electronic derivatives trading which has developed in the nineties – computer-generated financial tools that move financial data in seconds via networks; high performance workstations that execute complicated operations – is a creation of cyberspace.

Warehouses and department stores could develop into pure teleshopping. Futurists imagine that customers may put on a data helmet and slip into data gloves to inspect goods for sale. Traditional displays will be virtualized with computer simulation, allowing one to step into and view the display at any time. Electronic shopping centres will eliminate the trip to the market, as display windows are replaced by windows on a computer screen. Sales representative, customer and delivery agent no longer need to come together at one place since they only require electronic contact with each other. Delivery is direct from warehouses with advantageous transport connections; goods distribution systems are equipped with wireless computers to handle delivery services precisely and quickly.

Since offices are places of work with information, this type of work environment may also be replaced by a network environment. Architecturally, office buildings represent the power and prestige of information-processing organizations. They are usually grouped around central, well-connected points of transport and infrastructure, since employees move back and forth twice a day between home and workplace. The current structures arise from the need for personal contact with colleagues and clients, for direct access to expensive information-processing machines and direct access to information. Telework replaces this procedure – in part or wholly. Subordinate office tasks can be relocated from urban centres to less expensive suburban or rural areas; the employees living there can maintain close electronic contact with the headquarters (the office located in the urban core). Work sharing, which makes it possible to relocate lesser tasks not only to the suburbs but to other countries, is becoming more common. This decentralization of work opens up, among other things, the possibility of telework centres (e.g. small office complexes close to homes and apartments) with telecommunication links reaching right into the home. Project-oriented satellite offices in an environment conducive to creativity may accommodate groups for a given time period to complete a specific task. (Intellectual productivity, a trend clearly evident for the future, requires greater concentration and hence an environment that promotes creativity.)

Between 1991 and 1993, telework has increased by 20 % in the United States – a rapidly accelerating trend with lasting repercussions. The living-room becomes a site where digitally driven activities are newly configured and take root again in the physical world. It seems that we are currently experiencing a reversal of the separation of living and work place. Urban planners of the future will have to grapple with the question of how virtual and real public spaces should relate to one another. Communities and planners will need to weigh whether they wish to use their purses for development and expanding parks and communal buildings or, instead, for the installation of high-performance electronic networks.

The electronic "undercarriage" of cyberspace consists of modules that are geographically distributed and operate on a redundant level, and are hence practically indestructible. A new society or societal structure

can thus emerge. Human laws are replaced by software codes, rules formulated in accordance to which a certain action takes place when a specific condition is given. For the citizen of cyberspace, the computer code is the medium by which intent is translated into action and by which plans are realized.

But how will this historic development continue? While the pre-industrial settlements (1850 – 1930) were followed by industrial zones and "sleeping" cities (1930 – 1990), the era characterized by an emerging telepresence (1990 – 2000) begins to show signs of the binary world (2000 – ...): cyberspace has opened up and everyone can stake a claim. Are we already in the process of entering the era of the electronically expanded body? Do we already live on the interface of the physical and the virtual world?

No doubt the binary world will become a complex reality: a worldwide, electronically communicated environment with omnipresent networks, where most artefacts are equipped with intelligence and telecommunication systems. This may, however, also mean that the binary world will form a layer over and, ultimately, inherit the agricultural and industrial landscape inhabited by humans. But will it really be as described in the previous scenarios by Mitchell? Clifford Stoll, an expert and co-founder of the Internet, voices misgivings in *The Desert Internet,* which we cannot ignore for long:

Computer networks isolate people and reduce the significance of real experience. They undermine educa-

Limitations of the Internet

tion and creativity and counteract schools and libraries. Entering into a nonexistent universe cannot fail to have consequences. The modern computer world and all that is offered by and through the Net are a poor substitute for reality. Virtual reality is inherently full of disappointments – important areas of human relationships are ruthlessly devalued. The blessings of the Internet are often shamelessly exaggerated, and our expectations are consequently unrealistically high.

Stoll also poses the question whether national information infrastructures should keep available, on cable, a programme for hundreds of video channels and whether the Internet, issuing directly from universities into our homes and schools, isn't becoming more of a commercial event than a public service.

In the United States and some other countries, governments are already subsidizing the information industry. A September 1994 research report on national information infrastructure predicted that in the US alone this sector would reduce health costs by 36 billion dollars annually. Furthermore, children are being prepared by this medium for the knowledge-based economy of the twenty-first century. Between 1994 and 1996, 500,000 new workplaces were created by this industry alone, which is also expected to improve the quality of professional life and ensure social partnerships.

On the one hand, few aspects of daily life truly require computers, digital networks and massive cable links. On the other hand, many computer freaks already spend more than 10 hours a day on-line. This group may well be dismayed at the widespread belief that they lack a meaningful life. To them, the Internet is a tool and a community, a workplace and a home – and they don't even notice that many popular programmes and services are hardly worth the price of the floppy disc on which they are stored. Since anyone and everyone can feed messages into the Net, and many do, a cacophony of senseless gabble results. Furthermore, extreme views are polarized and the

medium runs the risk of turning into an impoverished environment of banalities and hobbies.

At this point, the Internet is painfully slow during business hours, dispelling the myth that any information is available from around the world at top speed. It is usually better to send a letter by fax than by e-mail because services such as on-line, audio, video and graphic application interfaces clog up the system. The Internet is still very much a domain of wishful thinking and brazen exaggeration.

Interactive television supposedly offers a choice between many different experiential variations – and yet they are all pre-programmed. The word "multimedia" is in itself a contradiction in terms: only the computer, a single medium, is being used.

In frustration, Stoll and others ultimately conclude that they spend as much time trying to establish what went wrong with their computers as they do in actually using them. And the long-awaited paperless office has failed to materialize. It is doubtful whether in the future the majority of people will work from home and offices will be vacant. Recent studies show that without meetings and personal exchange, employees become increasingly isolated and the feeling of belonging to a firm or company is weakened.

Institutions of all kinds can gather tons of data and information about each individual Net user, which is a very real threat to privacy. Each insignificant unit of data information poses no threat; it is the totality of these bits of information that seriously threatens the anonymity and privacy of our whole society.

Special programs can already search through networks and locate public information about each and every one of us. For this reason alone, many important computer systems are not linked to the network.

The very nature of data processing is in direct contradiction to the flight of the imagination. In the Darwinian sense, creative people are poorly equipped for survival in a computer environment. And yet, the medium one uses to communicate with others changes the way in which one's thoughts are formed. People program computers and vice versa.

Another argument that contradicts Mitchell's futuristic vision is that even good computers have a short lifespan. Hardware is usually an expensive investment, yet powerful computers bring few advantages for on-line use because the modem and the netlink are the bottleneck one must pass through. The short lifespan of computers is further exacerbated by the continual need for further development of the network infrastructure. It may well turn out that networks become obsolete just as quickly as computers do.

Although software cannot physically deteriorate, its value is usually rapidly diminished by the fact that more powerful computers and operating systems require compatible software, that is, software has to be upgraded constantly. This in turn means that one must always use the latest version of a software program, and these new versions are notoriously full of bugs as the software companies tend to issue them prematurely for competitive reasons. The strengths of contemporary computer technology lie in copying and modifying – in repetition, not in creation; these are images devoid of creative power.

In his critique, Stoll also addresses the issue of how the Internet can in no measure replace a visit to a real museum. Although 50 or more masterpieces can flicker across the screen via the Internet in the space of two minutes, art is cheapened in the process and loses its aura. Furthermore, computer reproduction can never replace a real painting. Look closely at the screen, and the details of the image dissolve into pixels; at any rate, the mere 236 colours available on the standard monitor cannot possibly do justice to the wealth of colours in a real painting.

In the world of trading and stocks, current experience shows that fully electronic trading systems cannot replace the marketplace of traders. After several years of operation at the product stock exchange in Chicago, the record of an average day shows that of approximately 800,000 transactions, only some 4,000 deals were actually struck by computer.

A similar weakness is becoming evident in the area of e-mail systems: large companies are beginning to lock out this system for several hours each day to ensure that work gets done. The rather humdrum reason for this is that often hundreds of messages accumulate and need to be processed, although the majority are only dead weight. Not to mention the impersonal nature of this system, which creates more distance.

Long-distance data transfer is often expensive with only limited advantages; it is difficult to create sturdy, reliable and expandable data-transfer systems. When they work, we become dependent upon them; when they do not work, we may be forced to stop our productive work. One should also question whether the Internet is truly more effective in selling products than good sales personnel. The latter represent an important group of professionals who not only offer demonstrations and information but also communicate consumer wishes to the company. Personal customer service tends to be an essential part of any enterprise and is hardly replaceable by lists of available products.

To summarize, we can state that there is a risk of the Internet turning once again into what it originally was – a technical society of sociable neighbours. Its initial friendly anarchy promised a revolution in social relationships and a breakdown of political barriers. There has been a regression in the meantime. On-line databases answer straightforward questions without difficulty and provide simplified, direct information (a black-and-white vision of the world). Since good questions are rarely answerable by a simple reply, the system quickly reaches its limits. Creative problem solving requires context, reciprocity and experience. This frame of reference may be more important than the individual data bits, and only human beings can communicate the context that links issues. Sensual experience knows no Ersatz.

It is becoming increasingly clear that Net access in schools is far from a cure-all. Teaching by computer requires hours of staring at the screen and an unquestioning acceptance of the computer's output. The world is not a passive, pre-programmed place where a mouse click provides the correct answer. School and teaching entail training in analytical thinking and the building of human relations.

It is equally uncertain whether the server and the Internet can replace libraries, as has been claimed. The Gutenberg project in the US will install a complete library for on-line access; approximately 10,000 books are to be processed over a period of six years. They will then be available for inexpensive CD-ROM publication. This endeavour is countered by an annual publication rate of 40,000 new titles. This seems to make the whole thing questionable from the very start, although a Net research study has shown that no books were digitized prior to 1980. Copyright and human nature speak against the utopia of universally available information, for without a total overhaul of copyright law, libraries cannot simply put their collections onto the Net. In-depth research on any topic is extremely time consuming on the Net. The dream of a universal fountain of information freely available to all will most likely remain a dream.

The often-praised information infrastructure bypasses most contemporary questions in the social and scientific fields, while threatening valuable components of social life. Deep scepticism is fully justified in considering whether the promises of virtual communities will be utilized by people, or whether they wouldn't after all prefer a real life in an environment worth living in. Information structures are not synonymous with a culture of knowledge, and electronic networks cannot replace social networks. People who do not feel liberated by information systems may well choose to free themselves from these systems.

2.2   Compactness Instead of Dissolution

26
The breakdown of population and settlement areas in the Federal Republic of Germany, 1950-1987

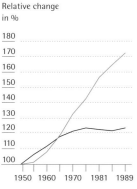

Relative change
in %

180	
170	
160	
150	
140	
130	
120	
110	
100	

1950 1960 1970 1981 1989

—— Developments and traffic areas
—— Population

Returning to the real world, we are faced with urgent problems that must be solved if we want to meet the demands of the next millennium. We must, especially in Europe but also elsewhere, put a stop to urban sprawl and environmental destruction.

We can note that population growth is not necessarily reflected in the development of housing requirements. *Figure 26* shows these relationships in the Federal Republic of Germany. From 1950 to 1987, the per capita requirement has risen from 14.3 to 35.5 m². The requirement for living space is comparatively even greater in Sweden (40 m²/capita) and in Switzerland (50 m²/capita). Obviously there is no ceiling to the demand for living space, and we must be prepared for a continued increase in living-space demands in the coming years.

Depending on business cycles, ecological problems repeatedly spark debates on what contemporary housing architecture should look like and how compact or integrated it should be. Continued expansion, above all on the peripheries of large cities, as well as increased traffic and the energy consumption linked to it, are naturally not a solution for these problems - on the contrary, the opposite approach would be the right one.

New buildings cannot replace low-cost housing space, which is disappearing as a result of decreasing social security and more stringent lease and tenancy legislation. Any easing up in the housing market must be encouraged through political measures, such as fees levied for greater-than-average living space, a special fee for excessive expansion in housing development, etc. On the other hand, greater economy in living space and housing developments could, in the future, be rewarded - the same could apply to reduced energy consumption. First and foremost, however, there has to be a growing awareness of these problems.

Residential building must be qualitatively concentrated architecture: concentration is more than merely crowding a greater building mass into the available space. It must focus above all on the preservation of green and forest zones. Even better, it should help increase such zones. Combined utilization, utilization value, attractive surroundings and, above all, high-quality architecture must compensate for the reduction in living space. Compact, integrated building can provide solutions for these problems as is evidenced by several recent examples, some of which are more or less familiar to all of us.

Urban Approach: Essen, Germany

The Passarea project for the reorganization of built space surrounding Essen's main train station (Architects Ingenhoven, Overdiek, Kahlen + Partner) will create approximately 200,000 m² in office, service, retail and living space. To the north of the train station lies the old shopping district, to the south the plan foresees further development of residential and office/retail buildings. As part of the process, the area around the train station is freed of local traffic to regain urban space and to redesign green zones. *Figures 27* and *28* show the current and the projected state of this urban area respectively. Especially *Figure 28* demonstrates how potentially attractive living and working in a dense urban structure can be.

27
Passarea project,
Essen, Germany
Original condition of site in city centre, view from south along Rellinghauser Strasse

28
Model photo
Design by architects Ingenhoven, Overdiek, Kahlen + Partner
View of trainstation from the north along Rellinghauser Strasse

Urban Consolidation: Chicago, Illinois

Bertrand Goldberg designed and built the famous Marina City Towers in Chicago between 1960 and 1964. *Figure 29* shows the dense urban core of Chicago, with the Marina City Towers clearly visible. These towers are considered prime apartment high-rises with adjoining park and service areas and count among the most striking buildings of this city. They meet a high aesthetic standard in themselves, and at the same time this is architecture that gains its liberating form within a context of expediency. The unusual form brings together various economic, functional and ecological advantages; it is this integration that makes the buildings so convincing.

The inner, circular core with elevator shafts and fire escape forms the spine of the building, demonstrating maximum utilization of the structural characteristics of reinforced concrete. Louvre-like segmental arches reach across to the outer posts of the scaffold, which has made considerable savings in materials possible by comparison to rectangular structures (approx. 10 % compared to standard building costs). Despite the attractive location, the Marina City Towers are in no way an enclave of luxury apartments, but simple, affordable apartments of different sizes. The smallest single-unit apartments are complemented by larger ones with 2 $1/2$ to 3 units *(Figure 30)*. Interior walls vary from unit to unit, creating great flexibility throughout the building. The entire front of each room is marked by large window surfaces providing sufficient daylight for the interior. The apartments occupy the upper two-thirds of the building, with the lower third reserved for parking.

Since the swampy shore of the Chicago River was poorly suited to the construction of an underground garage, Goldberg used the riverbank substructure to house expansive business and meeting spaces as well as restaurants. The deep pier construction provides mooring facilities for motor boats. Integrating the architecture with the riverbank has revived the riverside. *Figure 31* shows these linkages and indicates the

29
Dense urban centre of Chicago

various utilization areas. The entire Marina City complex – in combination with the office buildings to the rear – is the densest building complex in Chicago, without any loss of spacious airiness. The development is excellent proof that urban cores can remain dense and compact without loss of spontaneity and openness. Furthermore, Marina City is a prime example that high-rises need not be anti-urban.

31
Marina City Towers,
Chicago, 1960-1964,
architect: Bertrand Goldberg

30
Floor plan structure
of Marina City Towers

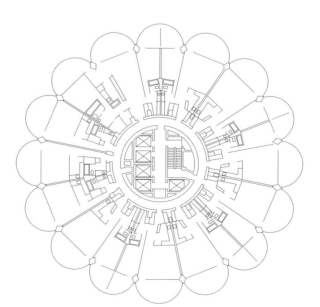

32.1
Site plan of Ried W2
housing development,
architects: Atelier 5

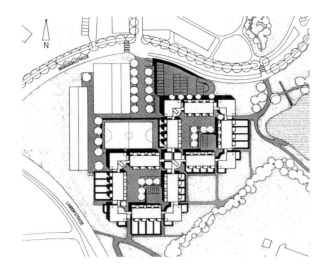

Densification on the Urban Periphery: Niederwangen, Switzerland

High-quality but compact housing is being developed on the periphery of urban cores or smaller towns, as is demonstrated in the following example of the Ried W2 complex designed by Atelier 5 in Bern. Completed in 1990, it houses condominiums and retail spaces. The individual building blocks are accessed from the courtyard as a semi-public open space, complemented by private patios and gardens. Additional access is created on the ground floor by a central stairwell. There are corner apartments with full-length interior living space, maisonette or multi-level condominiums with connecting stairs and small apartments with single-face orientation at the block corners. All apartments have a direct view of the courtyard and balconies or verandas adjacent to it, encouraging the occupants to take part in the social life of the courtyard. The private gardens of the ground floor apartments face out *(Figures 32.1 to 32.5)*.

32.2
Aerial view

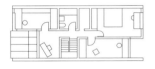

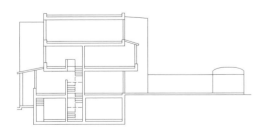

32.4
Floor plans and section

32.3
Access stairs from courtyard

32.5
Interior view

Prototype Wood Building: Sulzbach-Rosenberg, Germany

Another example of compact living is a group of homes in Sulzbach-Rosenberg designed by architects Fink + Jocher, Munich *(Figures 33.1 to 33.4)*. The project, rental apartments in wood construction, was developed as a pilot for low-cost building. The novel aspect of the design is the creation of a multi-functional stairwell that provides access space. It clearly exceeds the standard minimum measurements; its 45 m² are almost equal to the smallest apartment, made attractive by large kitchen windows opening to the outside. The ground plans follow a layering of the various utility areas, from the open kitchen facing east to the sheltered bedrooms and living areas on the west side. The stairwell takes on the function of an extended hallway. Neighbours find a common territory, where they can interact. Apartments are usually inadequate for large gatherings; here, they can spill over into the stairwell and onto the landing, weather permitting. Each floor has a combination of one-, two- or three-bedroom apartments, ensuring mixed-use and multi-generational living. The Spartan design of the buildings has been realized with prefabricated wood panels, which are stacked from floor to floor; self-supporting aluminium corrugated roof slabs stretch across the entire building to form a shed roof.

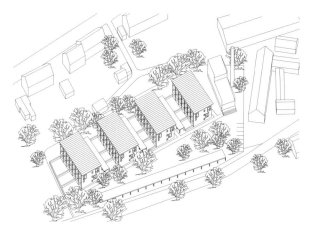

33.1

Isometric of housing group in Sulzbach-Rosenberg
Architects: Fink + Jocher
The drawing illustrates the density in the centre of the development. To the south, covered parking shields the meadow from the road and traintrack; to the right, the chimney of the old boiler is the landmark of the development.

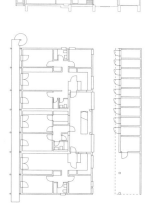

33.3
Elevation
The open meadow with old tree growth provides an individualized setting for the four identical housing blocks.

33.4
View of exposed stairwells
The stairwell is more than just an access; it is also a meeting place. Storage rooms open onto the paths between the buildings, replacing expensive basements.

33.2
Floor plan and section

3   The Knowledge of Building Masters: Solutions from the Past

Traditional building design makes use of the natural resources in the environment and responds to the specific locality. Sun and wind, rain and light have always played a special role in building. The reciprocity between these factors regulates climate and weather. Experience enabled the building masters of the past, who were responsible for "architecture without architects", to use what the local environment had to offer for heating, cooling, lighting and water supply. We know today that the world climate functions as a complex system distributing the sun's energy evenly across the earth. Before these ideas and solutions of the past are presented, here is a short outline of the climate system.

The sun, approximately 150 million kilometres distant from Earth, releases daily nearly 175 billion kilowatts onto the earth in the form of radiation. The amount of radiation energy received by the earth varies according to latitude. Near the equator the earth heats up much more intensely than in the polar regions, where direct sun incidence may fall to zero. Large masses of warm air move from the equator in the direction of the poles; together with an exchange of cold air masses flowing from the poles towards the equator, they create a balance in surface temperatures.

The radiation spectrum of the sun runs from extremely short-wave radiation (gamma, X-ray and ultraviolet radiation) to the spectrum of visible light all the way to long-wave infrared radiation. The electromagnetic radiation emanating from the sun is absorbed in the atmosphere in whole or in part depending upon the wavelength and results in substantial heat build-up *(Figure 34)*.

At a height of approximately 50 kilometres, the ultraviolet radiation is almost completely absorbed by the ozone layer. This absorption has decreased as the ozone layer is depleted, due to increases in fluorocarbon and carbon dioxide in the atmosphere. The damaged ozone allows more UV radiation to reach the earth's surface, leading to global warming. In the lower level of the atmosphere (troposphere), large amounts of incident solar energy are absorbed, owing to the high air density, and then dispersed.

Sun rays within the wavelength area of visible light pass through the atmosphere almost unfiltered, while infrared radiation is absorbed to a large extent. The radiation that actually reaches the earth (incident radiation) is, however, full of energy and warms the earth's surface sufficiently, heating land masses more than oceans because the latter absorb energy without warming to a large degree. The equalizing action of the oceans also contributes to the fact that certain climate zones benefit from comfortable temperatures all year round.

The sunlight that reaches the earth is partially absorbed by it and partially reflected and dispersed in the atmosphere. Nearly 70 % is reflected again through cloud formations. Carbon dioxide and hydrogen in the troposphere also serve to diffuse radiation in the long-wave range, thus affecting total energy supply and radiation balance. Solar energy is the vital force for human life.

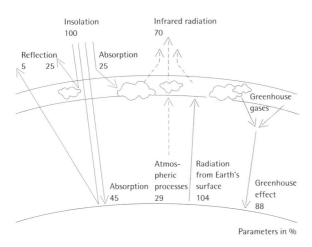

34
Radiation spectrum
The earth's atmosphere consists of several layers that filter the sunlight and reflect or absorb parts of the sun's radiation.

The space in which humans exist is the biosphere, the area reaching from the depths of the seas to a height of approximately 15 kilometres above sea level. In the biosphere several ecosystems work in tandem; together, they constitute life: the absorption of water, carbon, nitrogen and oxygen, and the release of oxygen through plants, etc. The added solar energy and the resulting warming of land surfaces induce wind movements, which in their totality make up the planetary wind system *(Figure 35)*. The earth's rotation also contributes to the creation of a similar climate worldwide. The rotation diverts air streams westward, to the equator, and eastward, to the poles (Coriolis effect), resulting in the familiar eddies manifested in the high and low pressure areas that pass over the earth's surface. High pressure zones – regions with predominantly dry, warm air – are created by heat radiation from the earth as it warms the air in certain regions. The warm air rises, depleting the air masses at the earth's surface and creating a low pressure zone. At the border to the troposphere the air cools to such a degree that the vapour in the air condenses; clouds form, and in some regions, tropical rain falls. Consequently, the air expands sideways, cooling as it grows more distant from the equator. Near the 25th latitude the air stream begins to sink as a result of the cooling: we then experience a high pressure zone.

When low pressure zones form above the oceans near the equator, extremely humid air rises, having stored the latent evaporative energy. The condensation of the absorbed vapour releases energy in layers of colder air, which often lead to tornadoes in tropical regions and to thunderstorms in other regions. The vapour transported across continents in the air masses has an important function for maintaining life. Next to the air movement between equator and pole, there are similar movements between land and water due to significant temperature differences. This creates a complex system of wind and vapour transport, distributing the sun's energy evenly across the earth.

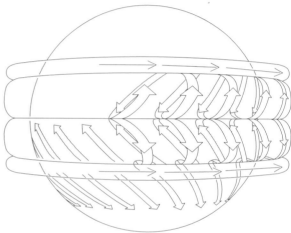

35
Planetary wind system
Air movements on a large scale compensate in part for the temperature differences created in the atmosphere as a result of uneven solar incidence.

3.1 Building According to Climate Zones

Beginning in Africa, Homo sapiens began his journey around the world some 100,000 years ago. To survive, he developed techniques and technologies over time and began to settle in different climate zones. The history of building in different regions is closely linked to these climate conditions. *Figures 36.1 and 36.2* show the main climate zones and their global temperature zones and precipitation volumes respectively.

The four main climate zones – tropical, arid, moderate and cold – are spread across the earth and are the basis for traditional building approaches in these

solar heating, air streams, relative humidity and rain volume are the influencing factors at each locality. In hot and arid zones, water is a question of life and death. When annual precipitation volumes fall to below 100 millimetres, a naturally adapted life is no longer possible, and technical intervention is necessary to create living space for human habitation.

In all climate zones, human adaptability and appropriate shelter were the prerequisites for survival. Based on local conditions, the following requirements have emerged for each zone:

Deserts
Extreme heat and severe water shortage led to:
– Mobile, light-weight shelters.

Steppes
Heat and poor water supply led to:
– Light-weight shelters to protect against heat and sand using evaporative cooling, earth cooling, air movement and geothermal energy.

Savannahs
Ideal climate conditions with favourable external temperatures all year led to:
– Light building structures without insulation for protection against sun and heavy rainfall.

Rainforests
Hot, moist regions led to:
– Building structures with good ventilation for evaporative cooling and protection against sun and rain. Building materials must dry quickly.

Subtropical regions
Warm, humid summer and mild winter led to:
– Light building structures with good ventilation characteristics, some insulation for winter.

36.1
Climate zones

▨ Hot and humid
▨ Hot and arid
▨ Temperate
▢ Cold

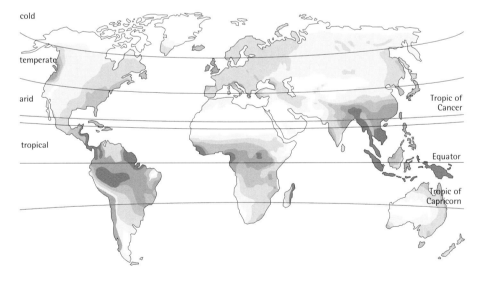

cold

temperate

arid — Tropic of Cancer

tropical — Equator

Tropic of Capricorn

cold

temperate

arid — Tropic of Cancer

tropical — Equator

Tropic of Capricorn

36.2
Precipitation zones

Annual precipitation
▰ 200 cm and over
▨ 150 – 200 cm
▨ 100 – 150 cm
▨ 50 – 100 cm
▨ 25 – 50 cm
▢ less than 25 cm

Mediterranean region

Ideal climate with summers neither too hot nor too humid, as well as mild winters, led to:

– Building structures that provide good shade with advantageous ventilation characteristics. In winter, some heating is required.

Moderate zones

Warm to cool summer season, cold winter season with low humidity led to:

– Building structures that compensate for heat as well as for very low outside temperatures, i.e., wall structures with good insulating effect, partial heat absorption.

Alpine regions

Moderate summer and very cold winter seasons with high wind velocities led to:

– Building structures that are solid and well insulated.

Tundra and taiga

Moderate summer and very cold winter seasons led to:

– Mobile structures with optimal insulation and wind protection.

Arctic regions

More or less constant cold to very cold outside temperatures with high wind velocities led to:

– Building structures (ice) with good insulating characteristics and wind protection in combination with extremely warm and thick clothing.

3.2   Environment and Town Structures

Deserts

In desert areas, humans could survive only as nomads and therefore developed a preference for tents, which created their own micro-climate. Black tents of material woven with goat hair were used as shelter from the sun during the day and closed at night to retain the heat and offer protection on cold nights. Clay structures were also built and partially sunk into the ground to fend off heat. Massive walls and roofs allowed the highest possible absorption of thermal energy. Due to low precipitation, humidity and water-proofing were lesser concerns; consequently, following heavy rainfalls, buildings were sometimes damaged and had to be reconstructed. *(Figures 37.1 and 37.2)* illustrate the predominant building type. Another important element is shown in *Figure 37.3:* covered, shaded outdoor living space. Narrow paths and lanes between tall buildings created not only comfortable external spaces but also offered shelter from sandstorms.

37.1
Desert building type
Elevation, Kasbah, Morocco

37.2
The narrow lanes and overhead screens protect the bazaar from sunlight.

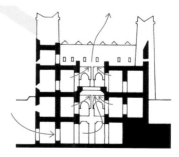

37.3
The principle of natural ventilation of buildings in desert areas

Steppes

In the hot, arid climate of the steppes, houses were built with local materials to absorb heat through the thick exterior walls. Wind towers were erected to ventilate the buildings; these towers drew fresh air flow into the building so that the warm outside air was first cooled by the building mass and then flowed out again. Houses in Hyderabad *(Figures 38.1* and *38.2)* illustrate the principle: the wind towers in the buildings face the predominant wind direction for optimal ventilation. Building masses with high storage capac-

ities are essential in this approach, since wind pressure and thermal currents together contribute to cooling and ventilation in these buildings. These traditional systems and techniques for using natural resources in the operation of a building are currently experiencing a revival. In the steppes, as in deserts, urban areas are dense, again for reasons of protection against wind and sun.

Savannahs

Savannah areas are warm and humid regions, offering almost ideal conditions for human survival. Owing to a favourable climate and moderate air flow, buildings can be light and permeable. There is no requirement for protection against extreme sun radiation and prevention of heat loss. The predominant building material in these zones is wood; floor and ceiling structures tend to be light. *Figure 39* shows this type of light construction with a straw-covered roof and walls made of matting. The extremely light construction means that these structures are literally transportable: one can, if necessary, move with the house. Houses in savannah areas offer protection from direct sun and rain. The favourable climate conditions have led to predominantly open settlement structures; outdoor areas heavily protected against sun or storms are not necessary.

Rainforests

Tropical rainforests are ideal environments for plant life, but not necessarily ideal for human habitation. Here, houses must above all be well ventilated to promote evaporative cooling. The old buildings in these zones were fitted with large gable roofs to draw wind into and around the building and to ensure sufficient air circulation. *Figures 40.1* and *40.2* show the main characteristics resulting from this requirement. The wide roof overhang creates well-shaded areas and simultaneously promotes wind intake. Insulation is not a requirement in this zone; rather, it is much more important that building materials dry quickly after

38.1
Steppe building type
The wind towers in Hyderabad

38.2
The air from cool breezes is conducted into the lower areas of the building and exits again through the courtyard.

39
Savannah building type
Thin permeable walls provide optimal ventilation of the buildings.

heavy rainfall, hence wood is the primary material. The hardwood structures sit on piles, and are thus naturally ventilated from below and benefit from a faster drying process after rain. Settlement structures in these areas can be both open or closed.

Subtropical regions

In subtropical areas the predominant climate is warm and humid; however, temperatures can fall below 0°C in winter. The classic example of building in subtropical zones is the light Japanese home, which grew out of the requirements and conditions of the environment. These buildings provide comfortable room temperatures in summer with wide roof overhangs and good ventilation facilitated by moveable wall panels. In winter, poor insulation makes these buildings unsatisfactory; this is especially true in traditional homes, where inhabitants warm themselves around a single firepit. To improve heat insulation, natural building materials such as wood and rice straw were used; sometimes mud walls were reinforced with bamboo grids.

Many traditional Japanese buildings are erected 40 cm above ground level to protect the wooden structures from the moist ground and to create a dry interstitial space for ventilation from below. In addition, the reciprocal radiation exchange between the floor of the house and the cool ground below helps to cool the building in summer (Δt approx. 0.5 K). These traditional one-storey houses use post and lintel construction, which is especially stable in an earthquake. *Figures 41.1* and *41.2* show the main characteristics of a traditional Japanese house and the classic building style. Japanese cities have always been densely populated – probably also a result of the predominantly one-storey buildings, as there were no urgent requirements for density of buildings to protect against sun or strong winds.

40.1/2
Rainforest building type
The houses are elevated on posts and open on all sides for optimal ventilation. The roof overhang provides shade.

41.1/2
Subtropic building type
The moveable walls allow for a flexible arrangement of the rooms in response to seasonal conditions.

Mediterranean areas

The Mediterranean zones (the Mediterranean region, southern Africa, southern Australia) provide the ideal climate for living. In these zones, all that is required is protection against too much sun in summer and the creation of some shaded outside areas. To achieve comfortable room temperatures, the standard approach is to build with stone masses, which are capable of absorbing the heat energy radiated in daytime, allowing it to penetrate into the building only partially. Cooling being the principal objective, minimal light through small windows is generally accepted; light is further minimized by dense building masses in urban areas.

Aside from the use of building masses with high storage capacity, great effort was expended to create shaded outdoor areas. A densely built environment with extremely narrow streets *(Figure 42.1)* fulfilled this requirement, as did the equally classic building type of atrium houses with inner courtyards and arcades with living areas behind them. Due to the comfortable climate, daily life in these zones occurs equally inside and outside of the building. *Figure 42.2* shows how closely buildings are grouped around a

corner and also the characteristic light-coloured surfaces, which serve to reflect the sun.

Urban development in these areas was heavily influenced by the need to erect houses that would shade each other and also the street areas. Heating during the winter months was neglected in the past but has become necessary today because of higher comfort requirements. On cold days, electric heat is used, although these zones would be ideal for collector installations.

Continental areas

In the moderate zones we encounter a continental climate with temperatures in winter to -15°C and in summer to 32° C. Hence these areas require houses able to meet both temperature extremes. Buildings in the continental areas must therefore be well insulated. Wood was the natural choice of building material since it has a high resistance to thermal transmittance combined with a low heat capacity *(Figure 43.1)*. The more frequently seen buildings in city cores were and still are the well-known frame houses, with a primary structure made of wood. The primary structure was filled with brickwork, in earlier times often clay-based brick elements with windows *(Figure 43.2)*. To protect exterior walls from severe weather conditions, upper storeys were stepped back or terraced in some cases.

Settlement patterns reflected the external conditions, leading to dense urban development, not to the same degree, however, as in the Mediterranean areas. Here, the main objective was protection from strong winds and heavy rains.

42.1
Mediterranean building type
Narrow lanes create a cool micro-climate in the street areas.

43.1/2
Continental building type
Well-insulated houses keep the cold out in winter. Protection from rain and snow defines the building form.

42.2
Building with mass creates cool interiors.

Alpine areas

Alpine and mountainous zones are subject to hostile weather conditions with an abundance of snow, rain and strong winds. Traditional buildings were constructed to deal with this: ecologically well-adapted buildings in these areas are located on southern slopes or with a southern exposure, low to the ground, thus utilizing passive solar heat gain and keeping heat loss to a minimum. The difficult transportation routes necessitated the use of local building materials (wood, stone). To protect against rain, which falls mainly from a westerly direction, roof structures were sometimes extended towards the ground, creating a natural protective shield.

Tundra and taiga areas

Tundra and taiga areas are located in cold zones (Siberia, Alaska), where short, warm summers are followed by long, very cold winters. In these regions the main objective is to achieve good insulation and to protect against strong winds. Tundra and taiga areas have traditionally been inhabited by nomadic peoples who carry their shelters with them. *Figure 44.1* shows the light tents of these nomads: a circular ground plan enclosed by an exterior wall, which is formed either with wood poles or woven grids. To protect against the wind, these structures are then covered in furs and skins.

Permanent dwellings were sensibly dug into the ground, as *Figure 44.2* shows, to minimize heat loss to the outside. To prevent wind from penetrating into the building, the entrance areas are protected with long barriers facing the main wind direction, thus creating a porch. Open fireplaces heat these earth homes, necessitating good smoke exhaust openings. All buildings in cold zones must limit heat loss to the tures for the inner surfaces (zero-energy house). Not only convective heat loss but heat loss as a result of ventilation must be considered as well. The overall low population density in these regions has more or less made it unnecessary for specific settlement forms to develop.

All these examples show that in the past people have reacted appropriately to their environment: they utilized wind, solar and thermal energy to achieve comfort, and built well-insulated structures in cold climates. The book *Sol Power: The Evolution of Solar Architecture* by Sophia and Stefan Behling is an excellent presentation of further examples for the correct use of solar energy and wind in the development of building types from their origin up to the present day.

44.1
Tundra and taiga building type
The sparse landscape enforces a nomadic lifestyle.

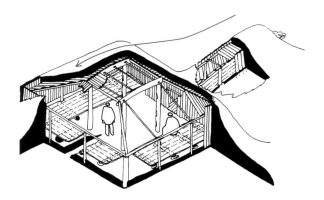

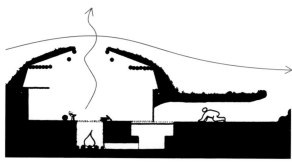

44.2
Permanent buildings are partially sunk into the ground to minimize exposure to wind.

3.3 Building in Extreme Climate Conditions: Low-Tech Architecture

Conforming to local conditions and being restricted to local resources are not impediments to good architecture. Simplicity and restriction may well be the source of diversity and true variety. Consider the following examples, compiled by Alessandro Vasella of Berlin.

Jaisalmer, Jewel of the Indian Desert

Jaisalmer, the caravan city in the Thar Desert *(Figure 45)*, was founded in the twelfth century. Although the city lost its economic base after the railroad spread across the Indian subcontinent, it is still so well preserved in its original yellow sandstone – the only locally available building material – that visitors today can easily imagine its former splendour and unity. The most noticeable characteristic of the buildings at Jaisalmer *(Figures 46.1 to 46.7)* is the high level of workmanship involved in their construction; the fine-grain sandstone was used as a substitute for almost all unavailable building materials. Posts and girders as well as the ashlar masonry were fashioned from sandstone and in some instances even joined without the use of mortar, made possible by

the precise handling of the material. Instead of the usual plank floors, the ceilings and floors of these buildings are also constructed of sandstone: as perforated slabs they replace the wood panels used elsewhere in the Orient for walls, and in this treatment also serve as ventilation grids for natural ventilation, maintaining privacy while offering a view of the outside and softening the harsh sunlight. Used as thin cantilever plates, they function as sun protection. Sandstone units, shaped into half bowls, double as water reservoirs for rare, but sometimes intense, rainfall.

The entire city is based on the module of the sandstone girder with its limited span width, whereby the basic grid of two to seven axes is the same for all houses *(Figure 46.3)*. Each house has a raised frontal zone above the narrow street, which provides additional shade. From the entrance a diagonal path leads to the inner courtyard, which operates as an "integrated air-conditioning system"; in other words, incoming wind and thermal currents cool the houses from the direction of the courtyards. Slender shafts inside the homes create the necessary thermal up-currents, and the recirculating flow of air is facilitated by air-permeable stone grids. Thus the air can circulate, ensuring relatively comfortable conditions for living in this desert area. The storage capacity in the sandstone building masses compensates for low night-time temperatures by thermal transmittance.

45
Map showing the low-tech sites in north-west India described in this section.

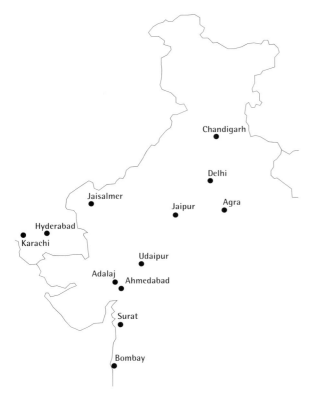

46.1
View over the rooftops of Jaisalmer

The rooms facing into the home are naturally lit from the courtyard. Kitchens are located on the ground floor and always lined up with the courtyard in such a way that the yard is simultaneously a ventilation shaft for this area. On cold nights a fire can be lit in the courtyards, which also ventilate the smoke fumes. The closeness of the row-houses creates narrow, shaded street areas; the whole is based on an extraordinarily compact urban plan with high building density. This jewel of urban planning and architecture demonstrates that extreme paucity of resources and restriction to a single available building material can still result in a high quality of living and astonishing variety, despite the hostile environment. It is a teaching model for climate-oriented, ecological architecture: this is low-tech of the highest stature.

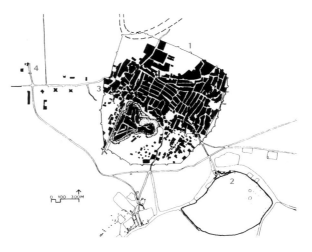

46.2
Site plan
Protected from sandstorms in summer, the early settlement lies to the north of the battlement with subsequent additions arranged in an almost right-angled grid.
1 City wall (18th century)
2 Gharsi Sagar Lake
3 Badal Nivās, the Rajah's palace
4 Jawahār Nivās, the Rajah's palace

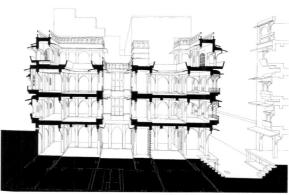

46.4
Section of typical home

46.3
Typical floor plans of a house

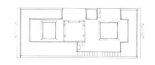
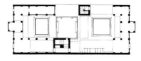
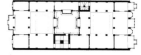
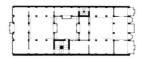
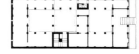

46.6
View into courtyards

46.7
Typical courtyard

46.5
Street area

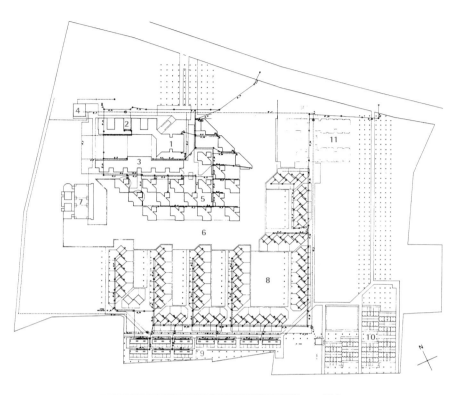

47.1
Indian Institute of Management,
Ahmedabad University

Master plan: Louis I. Kahn

1 Library
2 Faculty administration
3 Lecture rooms
4 Service tower
5 Dormitory
6 Lake
7 Kitchen and dining hall
8 Faculty apartments
9 Employees' apartments
10 Apartments for married
   students
11 Management development
   centre

47.2
Model photograph,
north elevation

Indian Institute of Management, Ahmedabad

In Ahmedabad, a university city with two million inhabitants, the urban and architectural concept developed by Louis I. Kahn offers a modern response to the extreme climate conditions in this part of the country.

When compared with Le Corbusier's buildings in Ahmedabad, created for identical climate conditions, Kahn's design is clearly more appropriate. Kahn's architecture is an ecological, low-tech building, reaching back to local predecessors, resources and techniques. Oriented to the sun and wind, the severe geometry of the whole complex, including teaching facilities and buildings and housing for students and teachers, is enlivened by a great variation in the repetition of the basic elements. *Figures 47.1* and *47.2* beautifully illustrate the play between inside and outside, and between built volume and open space.

The climate is amenable to windowless openings. Ventilation, so important for the inhabitants in this area, is made possible through narrow, room-height slits with simple, hand-operated louvers to activate or reduce air circulation in combination with large, circular openings.

The paths between the individual buildings form a sequence of open and covered areas, brought to life by a rhythm of light and shadow. Kahn used as his basic building material a locally manufactured solid brick for the massive walls and heavy support posts. The openings were constructed with segmented and round arches according to traditional brick building practices. Reinforced concrete was used sparingly in the floor zones. In contrast to Le Corbusier's design, concrete is used only in the areas where tensile forces are present. The concrete is visible on the exterior as a functional and ornamental tensile element and merges with the brick into a logical unit. The solid bricks were cut at the site into the forms required for

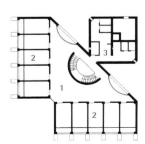

47.5
Inner courtyard

47.4
Elevation

47.3
Floor plan of dormitory
(third floor)

1 Lounge
2 Bedroom
3 Tearoom and wet cells
  (sanitary area / bathroom)

the arch constructions. In other words, even in this aspect the construction served a local need for employment of unskilled labourers. The typical floor plans and views *(Figures 47.3 to 47.5)* confirm Kahn's design as a good example of climate-appropriate, ecologically correct low-tech architecture on the highest level of building art.

Step-Well at Adalaj

Immediately to the north of Ahmedabad is the step-well of Adalaj. In this region the rainy season is limited to the monsoon in summer, coming from the south late in the season after a long hot season with daily temperatures of up to 45° C and extremely low relative humidity. The monsoon rains are short and heavy, and create a hot, moist, almost unbearably humid climate. These extreme conditions led to a unique architectural response to the commonplace problem of water supply from a traditional draw well. The original well was expanded in the late fifteenth century into an underground building with access via generously proportioned steps, sometimes with as many as six levels and galleries with seating on each level *(Figures 48.1 to 48.2)*. The communal space in this interior climate was created with the help of water evaporation and cooled by the earth. The well provided access to water regardless of the water level. The design is a strikingly simple response to the hardship created by the climate. Building step-wells also ensured that the smallest possible surface of water would be exposed to the sun, preserving as much water as possible far into the dry season.

Step-wells in villages and settlements were often much more than simple sources of water; at crossroads and way stations along caravan routes they were inviting rest areas deep in the earth. Each level within the well is sufficiently lit by daylight through a skylight, the sky being reflected on the surface of

the water. These buildings are witness to masterful work in architecture, design and structure, surpassing modern concrete cisterns for collecting rainwater.

48.2
Step-well, Adalaj
The galleries are decorated with carved columns, plinths and beams.

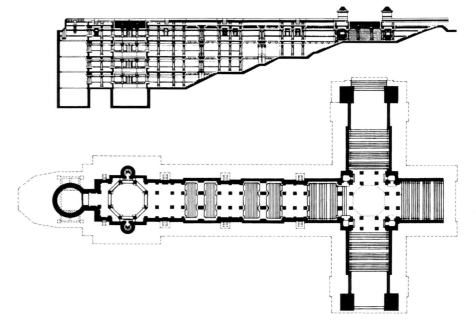

48.1
Step-well
Floor plan and section

4 Resources in Nature: The Potentials in our Environment

49.1
Average annual sunshine hours in Central and Northern Europe

- ☐ up to 1500 h/a
- ▨ 1500 – 1700 h/a
- ▨ 1700 – 1900 h/a
- ▨ 1900 – 2100 h/a
- ☐ 2100 – 2300 h/a
- ☐ 2300 – 2500 h/a
- ▨ above 2500 h/a

49.2
Average annual insulation rating in Germany in kWh/m²a (German Weather Service)

- ▨ 900 – 950
- ▨ 950 – 1000
- ▨ 1000 – 1050
- ☐ 1050 – 1100
- ☐ 1100 – 1150
- ▨ 1150 – 1200

As members of a well-informed society in the information age, we have access to excellent historical examples of building in harmony with nature. These traditional solutions provide a rich store of ideas to draw on as we tackle the challenge of designing buildings that harness natural resources in an appropriate manner. The basic requirements for building design in harmony with nature are preservation of the environment, resource protection and recyclability. All three examples described in the previous chapter fully meet these requirements. We, too, must struggle with these issues not in theory but in practice, in the interest of a future worth living. Before moving on to Part 2 of this book, where detailed solutions for information age architecture are presented, we would do well to take a closer look at the great diversity of what nature has to offer.

Utilizing environmental resources is inextricably linked to local meteorological conditions. These are discussed on the following pages, taking Europe and more specifically Germany as an example. For other regions the relevant weather data should be collected case by case. These include:

- Outside temperatures in summer and winter, for establishing exterior dimensions of the building
- Average annual incident radiation as well as maximum radiation values for individual façades and horizontal structures
- Precipitation frequency and annual average precipitation
- Annual percentages of distribution of oncoming wind direction, including wind velocities

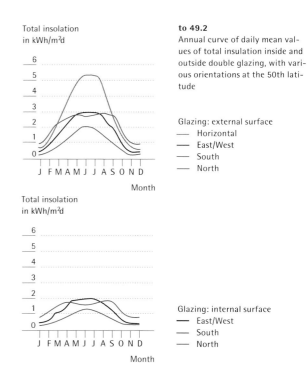

Total insolation in kWh/m²d

to 49.2
Annual curve of daily mean values of total insulation inside and outside double glazing, with various orientations at the 50th latitude

Glazing: external surface
— Horizontal
— East/West
— South
— North

Total insolation in kWh/m²d

Glazing: internal surface
— East/West
— South
— North

4.1 Solar Energy

The annual averages for total sunshine hours in the Mediterranean and in Northern Europe are listed in *Figure 49.1*. The map clearly shows the differences between Mediterranean regions, countries with continental climates and areas with high mountains. The range of sunshine hours even in this narrow scope is approximately 50 %, which gives some indication of how solar energy may be harnessed with the help of technology. *Figure 49.2* details the average global annual radiation for Germany and average daily values over the course of a year, in front of and behind glazed walls with different orientations. Illumination strengths are indicated for direct and diffuse sun radiation; all calculations conform to pertinent norms and guidelines and are based on readings taken on overcast days *(Figure 49.3)*. Figures *50.1* and *50.2* shows the radiation values for direct and diffuse radiation for individual months on southern façades and on roof surfaces respectively.

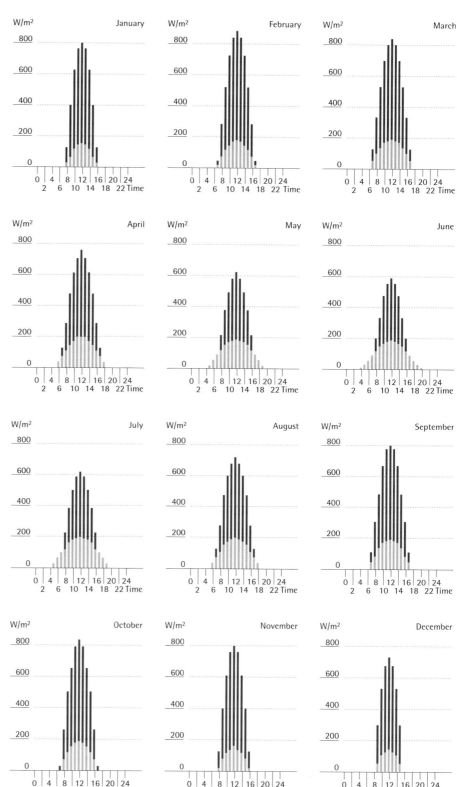

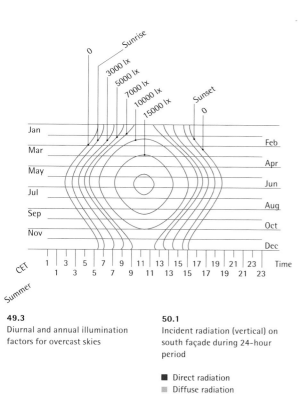

49.3
Diurnal and annual illumination factors for overcast skies

50.1
Incident radiation (vertical) on south façade during 24-hour period

■ Direct radiation
▪ Diffuse radiation

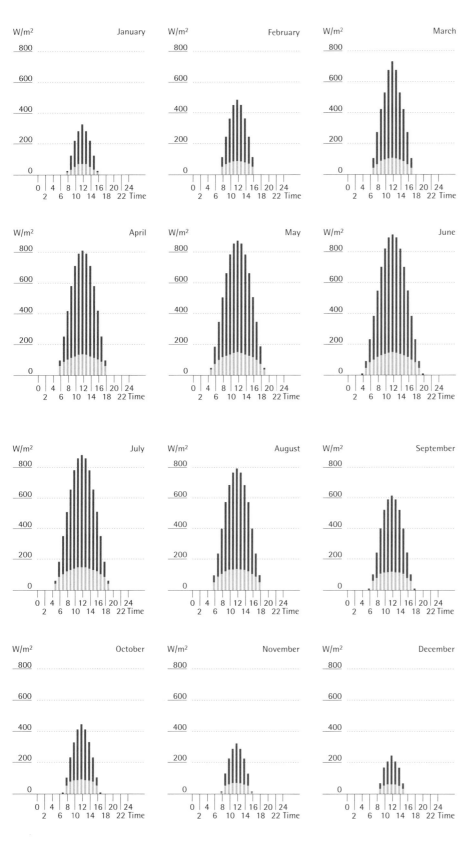

Direct radiation is the sunlight that falls onto the earth's surface without diffraction and is the principal design parameter for solar technology. Either black surfaces absorb the sunlight and generate heat energy (thermal energy), or incident sunlight falls onto photovoltaic elements to generate electricity. Incident radiation can be directly harnessed for thermal use when radiation transformers absorb the energy. These transformers may be blinds, heat-absorbing Venetian blinds, heat-absorbing surfaces and similar installations.

Systems for transforming sun energy into heat:
– Window collector panels
– Air collector panels (wall or roof installation)
– Transparent insulating materials in front of absorbing walls
– Solar absorber (simple absorber mats)
– Flat plate collectors
– Evacuated flat collectors
– Evacuated tube collectors
– High-efficiency collector systems

To create electrical energy there are different types of photovoltaic elements:
– Monocrystalline silicon cells
– Polycrystalline silicon cells
– Amorphous solar cells (opaque module)
– Amorphous solar cells (semi-transparent)

Ample reference material is available regarding installation, operation and energy efficiency of photovoltaic elements, not to mention the manufacturer's information. In each case, the components for harnessing solar energy should be an integral part of the architecture itself and not simply added on. The models listed above for solar energy use in buildings are widely known; however, the thermal air tower generator, an innovative prototype developed by Jörg Schlaich in Stuttgart, deserves separate mention. This system is used as a large technical installation to cre-

50.2
Incident radiation on roof surface
during 24-hour period

■ Direct radiation
▨ Diffuse radiation

ate electricity. *Figure 51.1* is an overview of the regions with radiation energy greater than 1950 kWh/m²a and greater than 2200 kWh/m²a respectively. The thermal air tower generator is potentially applicable in both regions, because sufficient radiation is available. The total area that would be needed in theory to meet the global primary energy requirement with thermal air tower generators in neighbouring deserts with high solar radiation is shown in *Figure 51.2*.

In thermal air tower generator, heat energy is absorbed by simple flat plate collectors placed in a ring around the air-current chimney. Thus the air entering below the glass roof collectors is heated from ring to ring, flowing to the chimney duct, through which it rises and enters the surrounding area. At the lower end of the chimney there are wind turbines, which can agitate the air flowing through the chimney and which ultimately produce electrical energy via generators *(Figure 52.1)*. All building components of the thermal air tower generator are known and tested. Therefore, to generate a large amount of energy from the environment in this manner, the only remaining problem is the availability of appropriate locations.

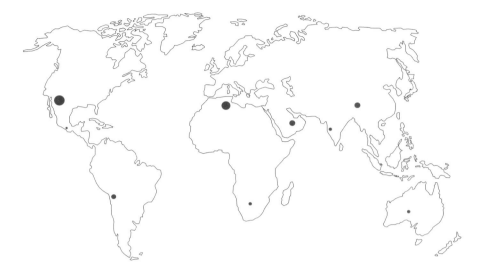

51.2
Area required to meet total world primary energy requirements with thermal air tower generator located in the nearest desert area with excellent solar radiation

The areas indicated below symbolise the areas required for using in each case one thermal air tower generator to meet the total energy demands of the world, Europe and Germany, respectively.

Area requirement for global total primary energy requirement:

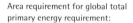 World   ø = 2000 km

 Europe   ø = 950 km

Germany   ø = 440 km

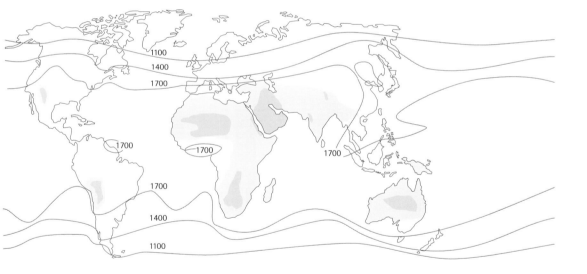

51.1
Distribution of global solar radiation
Regions with more than 1950 kWh/m²a are suited for solar production of electricity.

▓ >2200 kWh/m² excellent suitability
░ >1950 kWh/m² good suitability

52.1

Principle of thermal air tower generator:
glass roof collector, chimney pipes, wind turbine

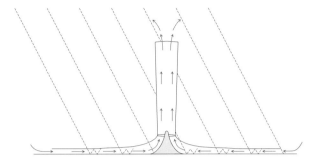

Relative global radiation and energy production curve

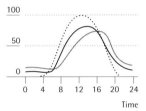

52.2

Diurnal curve of solar radiation with maximum value at noon and in relation to energy production curve, reaching into the night hours owing to thermal storage in the ground below the glass-roof collector.

Energy production for:

.....   Global radiation

——   Low (thermal) storage ground (sand, gravel, volcanic ash)

——   High (thermal) storage ground (clay, loess)

Annual energy production in GW/a

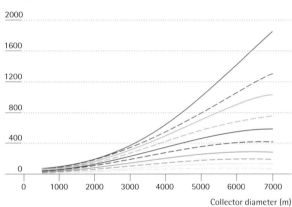

Collector diameter (m)

52.3

Annual energy production in thermal power stations (for 2300 kWh/m²a global radiation), dependent on collector diameter and chimney height

——   Single glazing
– –   Double glazing
Chimney height
——   1500 m
——   1000 m
——   800 m
——   600 m
——   445 m

Figure 52.2 shows the daily course of solar radiation and the energy produced by electricity dependent upon different types of soil; *Figure 52.3* indicates the annual energy produced in relation to collector diameter, glazing type and chimney stack height. Professor Schlaich and his team of trained structural engineers studied all types of chimney stacks *(Figure 53.1)* before using very light, braced steel plate tubes in the thermal air tower generator in Manzanares, Spain. This choice was not for financial reasons alone, but also to keep the material used for the installation to a minimum. The thermal air tower generator in Manzanares *(Figure 53.2)* has unfortunately remained a prototype to the present day – a lack of progress difficult to understand in view of the worldwide discussion on energy and the urgent need for environmental protection. Oil-exporting countries in particular could benefit from this technology and make the switch to being electricity-exporting countries, since they above all "possess" not only natural oil but also ample solar energy.

53.2
Thermal air tower generator in Manzanares
(Prof. Jörg Schlaich)

53.1
Different tower structures

4.2 Wind Energy

The annual averages for the distribution of wind direction at different sites in Germany are illustrated in *Figure 54,* while *Figure 55.1* shows wind statistics for different locations, including average wind velocity and wind direction distribution. These data form the basis for the study, analysis and planning of buildings with partial or full natural ventilation, which are at the same time expected to meet room-temperature standards. Wind has only recently been directly utilized to reduce the long-term need for ventilation, heating and air-conditioning installations or to replace them altogether. For the utilization of wind, predominant wind directions and velocities at the site are of primary importance, as is the consideration of the degree to which planted and built areas or urban centres lessen the relative wind velocity at the specific location where a building is to be naturally ventilated. *Figure 55.2* shows the interdependence of the area exposed to wind (height above ground) and relative wind velocity. As will be shown, the use of wind for natural ventilation in buildings is not merely a question of building depth or height, but primarily a question of whether sufficient, average wind velocities are present at the site. We have already mentioned the important practical use of

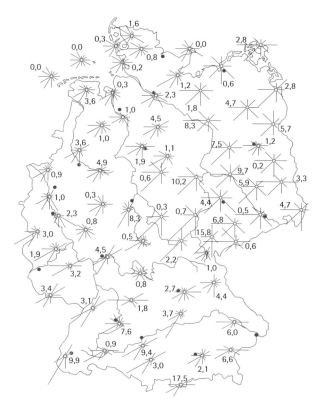

54
Average annual percentage distributions of wind direction at selected locations in Germany (German Weather Service, Report 147)
100% = 30 mm
numbers = % of still days

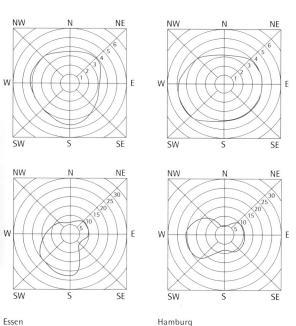

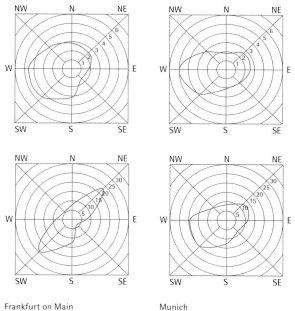

Essen   Hamburg   Frankfurt on Main   Munich

55.1
Wind statistics for Essen, Hamburg, Frankfurt am Main, Munich

Mean wind velocity in m/sec

% of distribution of wind direction

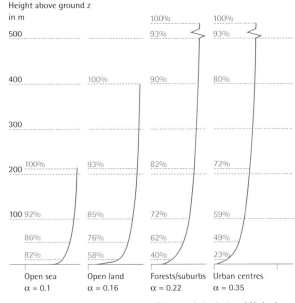

Height above ground z
in m

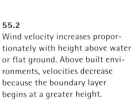

55.2
Wind velocity increases proportionately with height above water or flat ground. Above built environments, velocities decrease because the boundary layer begins at a greater height.

$w(z) = w(z_{ref}) \, (z/z_{ref})^{\alpha}$

$w(z)$ wind velocity
$w(z_{ref})$ gradient velocity
       = 100 %
z_{ref} reference height
α profile exponent

Relative wind velocity $w(z)/w(z_{ref})$

The performance contained in wind flow is described in the following formula:

$$P = \frac{\rho}{2} v^3 A.$$

The performance of wind flow is raised with the third power of wind velocity v and increases in a linear fashion with the cross-sectional surface A of the energy transformer through which the wind flows (e.g. the area covered by a rotor in a full rotation). The influence of different air densities is negligible. According to the elementary impulse theory, the efficiency quotient is approximately 60 % under ideal flow conditions – that is, when transformation is nearly loss free.

With regard to the economic viability of the installation, the most influential parameter is the average annual wind velocity v̄. The prerequisite should be a minimal average wind velocity of 4.5 m/sec with the rotor mid-point positioned at a minimal height of 10 metres. The size of the whole installation is mostly determined by rotor dimensions.

wind in past architecture. This use, however, was followed by a long period during which it was ignored in the planning of buildings, probably because the conceptual approach in architecture had grown stagnant and not enough related information was generally available.

Aside from a direct utilization of wind energy for ventilating buildings, there are well-known indirect uses of wind energy. Indirect use and transformation of wind energy into electricity respectively are connected with terms such as wind mill, wind wheel, wind turbine etc. Probably the most appropriate term in the context of contemporary technology is wind-energy conversion system. The installation and operation of wind-energy conversion systems are, as with all other systems, subject to strong economic constraints, whereby wind-energy performance is largely transformed into electricity.

56
Areas in Germany where wind velocities can be utilized to produce energy

- ▪ v̄ > 5m/s
- ▫ 4 < v̄ < 5m/s

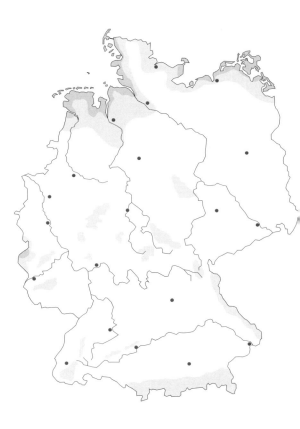

Wind-energy conversion systems are currently classified as follows:
- Large wind-energy conversion systems (megawatt performance range, rotor diameter > 50 m)
- Medium wind-energy conversion systems (performance range up to 1,000 kW, rotor diameter approx. 20 – 40 m)
- Small wind-energy conversion systems (performance range up to 100 kW, rotor diameter < 20 m).

The construction forms of wind-energy conversion systems are primarily characterized by the rotational axis. One distinguishes between systems with a vertical rotational axis and those with a horizontal rotational axis. Although wind systems with a vertical rotational axis are the most traditional form of construction, systems with horizontal rotational axes are the most important models in this field. How viable these systems are remains to be seen.

Any discussion of wind energy use ultimately leads to questions regarding manufacturer prices for electricity, amortization periods and adequate sites. The construction costs are approximately 600 DM/m² rotor surface, yielding electricity production costs in the range of 0.16 to 0.12 DM/kWh. These costs, however, are only achieved when high technical availability is given (95 %) and with an average wind velocity of 6 m/sec. In areas where winds are less strong, electricity production costs quickly climb to 0.3 to 0.4 DM/kWh. *Figure 56* identifies the areas in Germany where wind velocities are appropriate for technical utilization; the images in *Figure 57* show different types of wind generator construction. In recent years different wind farms and wind parks have been set up in coastal areas. There is currently a discussion on the usefulness of erecting large wind-energy conversion stations in the sea in order to take advantage

version stations in the sea in order to take advantage of the higher wind potential available there. Their use in urban areas is generally not sensible, due to higher noise levels and also because wind velocities tend to be slower near the ground. The only solution in urban environments would be to erect wind towers that would stand high above the surrounding buildings.

57
Wind generator types

– Horizontal axis installation, wind park in North Friesland

– Horizontal axis installation, Saal wind park

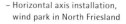

– H-rotor installation, Kaiser-Wilhelm-Koog wind park
– Darrieus wind power station

4.3 Rainfall and Surface Water

Fresh water is our most valuable resource; there is no adequate replacement for it. Water supply enterprises produce it at considerable expense and market it to consumers under stringent hygienic quality controls. It seems senseless that much of this valuable resource is being literally flushed down the toilet in residential housing (approx. 33%), and further large amounts are used for watering gardens and plants, washing cars and general cleaning. A map of average annual precipitation at different locations, like the one shown in *Figure 58* for the example Germany, can therefore help in planning and provide a basic outline when the use of rainwater for toilet flushing or for cooling is at issue.

Figure 58 also indicates several areas in Germany with low annual precipitation averages. Among others, the area Berlin-Brandenburg with an average annual precipitation of approximately 530 to 600 millimetres. In addition, potable water in this region is a mix of ground water and the shore filtrate of surface waters without chlorination. The total water price (water and waste-water price) is 8.30 DM/m³ (1997 prices). This seems to indicate that rainwater should be used for property seepage and for other secondary uses.

Figure 59 shows the water requirements in private households: 56% of potable water could be replaced directly with rainwater as utility or grey water.

A school complex in Berlin, developed by the architectural team of Grossmann & Vasella, Berlin, is an outstanding example in this context. *Figure 60.1* illustrates the main elements of how rainwater is used in this project. It is collected on the roof and stored in a simple cistern constructed of concrete rings. An overflow links the cistern to a gravel ring. The collected water is transported in a pressurized pipe system to the sanitary installations in the building, from where it is diverted to the main drains as waste water after usage. In this school project, not only is rainwater utilized as grey water, but all additional rainwater is allowed to seep into the property, the schoolyard is

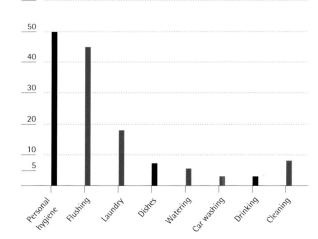

58
Rain chart of average annual precipitation (DIN 4108 part 3)

☐ Annual precipitation below 600 mm
Annual precipitation 600 to 800 mm
▨ Annual precipitation above 800 mm
In northern coastal region of Germany (strong winds) above 700 mm.

Daily water consumption in litres

59
Water requirements in private households
56% of potable water consumed in private households could be replaced with grey water.

unsealed and newly landscaped areas are covered in surfaces that allow seepage, draining the gravel trench *(Figures 60.2 and 60.3)*.

There is no doubt that collecting rainwater and direct seepage make ecological sense. It's not only a question of reducing the consumption of highly processed potable water; rainwater drainage must be controlled after intensive rainfall, which can flood the system, especially in mixed sewage systems and overload sewage treatment plants. The amortization of such systems (rainwater collection, rainwater storage, service water distribution in integrated networks) tends to come up with a negative balance, given today's extremely low potable water prices; nevertheless, the balance will shift in the future.

Principal arguments against rainwater utilization are:
– Potential contamination of the rainwater cistern
– The resulting risk of contaminating potable water in case of links between rainwater and potable water
– Possible links as a result of improper installation
– Low savings potential and high costs, especially for private households
– Water shortage is almost unknown in some countries (e.g., Germany)

Water prices and operating costs are rising steadily, though moderately, and we can reasonably expect a final breakthrough in rainwater utilization in a few years. Although it is certainly true that water shortages are rare in Germany and in other Middle European countries, the cost of maintaining the quality of water is already remarkably high.

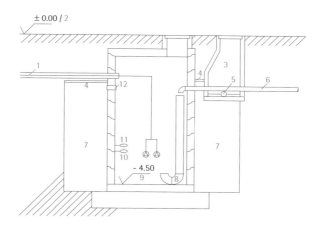

60.1
Section of rainwater reservoir and seepage
School building in Berlin, Prenzlauer Berg
Diagram: SanitärSystemTechnik, Berlin.
Architect: A. L. B. Vasella

1 Sheath, pressurized pipe system and control for operating water
2 Schoolyard level
3 SW-control shaft
4 Drainage
5 Overflow trench
6 Rainwater intake
7 Gravel trench
8 Sedimentation zone
9 (Sill) floor
10 Dry-run safeguard
11 TW-emergency intake
12 Overflow

60.2
Cistern (12 m³ content) constructed of concrete rings (Ø 250 cm) in the excavation of schoolyard area

60.3
Cistern (6 m³ content) with ring-form gravel trench (drainage pit) prior to back-filling of courtyard

Rainwater can serve not only as grey water for toilets; it can be used for cooling purposes. This is basically the cooling of glass roof surfaces or glazed slanted roofs, or direct cooling of building components and evaporative cooling near buildings respectively. Here, too, exemplary pilot projects exist and new ones will soon appear on the market. An especially interesting topic in this context is temperature reduction created by water surfaces near buildings, but not much data is available. To determine how temperature is reduced by this process, a model calculation is used based on the design of a building's skin, the average wind velocity and the distance of water surface across which the air flows before it reaches the building.

When air passes over a water surface in the direction of a building, the resulting evaporation humidifies the air in the boundary layer and creates adiabatic cooling of approximately 1–2 K, depending upon the distance the air travels. Furthermore, the air flowing across the water surface blends with air layers that lie above it; the cooling effect, therefore, decreases proportionate to the height of the wall towards which it flows *(Figure 61)*. The cooling effect can be considerably improved by guiding the air flow towards the building through a double-skin façade. *Figures 61 and 62* illustrate the basic interactions and can serve as models for approximate calculations.

A reduction of cooling energy requirements is not only a matter of designing the buildings themselves, it applies also to the open space surrounding them. In other words, if the micro-climate is sufficiently improved, technical measures for cooling can be considerably reduced. Another way to use rainwater for cooling purposes is through fountains, which hasten the evaporation water collected in large water basins; this produces cooling effects of approximately 2-3 K and creates intake temperatures of 18°C or less, which can then be directly used to cool building components.

61
Temperature decrease through humid air: single-layer façade
Adding moisture to the air by locating a horizontal water surface in front of a single-layer façade
Outside air:
Temperature 32°C
Relative humidity 40%
Wind 3 m/s

— 5 m
– – 10 m
— 15 m
····· 20 m

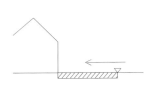

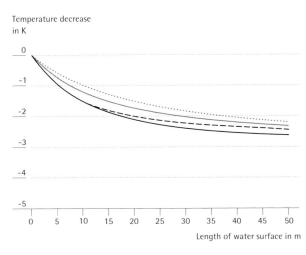

62
Temperature decrease through humid air: double-layer façade
Adding moisture to the air by locating a horizontal water surface in front of a double-layer façade
Outside air:
Temperature 32°C
Relative humidity 40%

— 2 m/s
– – 3 m/s
— 5 m/s

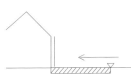

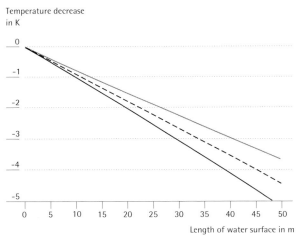

In areas with proven water shortages, one can envision a "zero-waste water house" *(Figure 63)*. Here, all water is collected in a three-chamber sewage pit, where it is biologically pre-cleaned. The treated waste water is either allowed to seep into the ground in a plant sewage system, after UV disinfection, or collected in a cistern. When there is a surplus of water, an additional reservoir basin or evaporation pool can be used to accommodate these volumes. From the cistern, used water is returned to the building as service water; the same could apply to treated rainwater, and all the building would then require would be a hook-up for potable water.

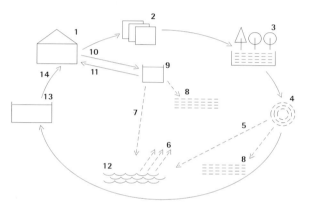

63
The zero-waste water house
Short water cycles help save and recycle water. The techniques used in these cycles are based mainly on purifying the water in nature.

1 Residential home 1-4 families Waste water approx. 1.6 m³ per day (for 100 l per person)
2 Buffer, e.g. three-cavity pit
3 Biological post-treatment, e.g. biological treatment plant, waste water pond
4 UV disinfection
5 Open run-off possible
6 Evaporation
7 Open overflow
8 Seepage
9 Rainwater reservoir
10 Rainwater
11 Utility water for washing machines etc.
12 Reservoir-/evaporation pond
13 Cistern
14 Utility water, for toilet flushing etc.

4.4 Planted Areas

This topic is often limited to a discussion of landscaping, forgetting its potentials for energy savings. Following are two statements from publications, the first by Professor Klaus-D. Neumann of Munich and the second by Ina Bimberg of Iserlohn, which broaden the perspective and inspire further thought or serve as models for action.

Building in Planted, Interior and Exterior Spaces
(Professor Klaus-D. Neumann)
Everything that is usually said with regard to building in a specific landscape also applies when one focuses on a specific building: the built object influences the space surrounding it as much as the open space acts on the object. Modern landscape architecture operates, therefore, on the basis of design in a global sense. It is an all-encompassing architecture, and interprets the building process as a co-operative effort between diverse disciplines, resulting in a conscious handling of the exterior space.

Aesthetic Dimension
Based on a dialectic relationship between building and exterior space, issues of opposition, constancy and change become important. The construction of buildings generally aims for longevity and solidity. A desirable condition is defined for the time period during which a building is put to use; change and movement are minimized through choice of material and construction. The exterior space, usually a green area with some plants already in place, is characterized

64.1
Flowering aspect

64.2
Autumn foliage

precisely by changeability over time as the plants grow. Our fascination with planted surfaces may well be tied to this natural growth and change independent of human design, and thus the impossibility of total manipulation. Deliberate work with the inherent characteristics of plants, with their ability to change, is therefore one of the foundations of design in landscape architecture *(Figures 64.1 to 64.4)*.

64.3
Old tree in front yard

64.4
Green outdoor space

Ecological Dimension

In any discussion of the ecological dimension, the functional aspect of plants is of central importance: plants can be used to protect against extreme environmental conditions, against wetness, cold or heat. Wall planting as weather protection, wind shields created with hedges, shading through climbing plants in summer – these are all familiar uses. Planted roof surfaces can help absorb peak precipitation, passing on the moisture in a time-release process. Surface water can be cleansed by passing it through or letting it seep into planted ground layers before it flows into the groundwater. Specific grasses bind toxins in biological treatment plants, toxins that could only be separated out with great effort in a chemical process. *Figure 65* shows a biological treatment plant. Aside from the familiar, more passive examples of applying the characteristics of plants, the active characteristics are especially interesting in the context of low-tech architecture. Plants can be used intelligently for correct building operation. The leaves of large trees filter toxins from the surrounding air, increase the humidity in the immediate surroundings and reduce temperature by virtue of an interaction between evaporative cooling, reflection of solar radiation and absorption of energy from solar radiation.

Open Spaces and Green Systems in Cities
(Ina Bimberg, Landscape architect)
City centres and areas near urban cores are characterized by dead materials such as concrete, asphalt, stone and metal, and by a more or less complete displacement of nature. The environment of urban dwellers is almost completely devoid of nature – and this has demonstrably negative consequences for the basic physical and psychological needs of humans, but also for the energy household and the ecological cycles in the urban systems. The scope and character of urban planted areas, open spaces and green systems have a long-term influence on the living conditions in a city and thus on the well-being of its

65
Biological treatment plant

inhabitants. The social significance of useable open spaces for recreation and sports is indisputable, as they provide physical and emotional relaxation, enabling city dwellers to take a break from work and recuperate in the open air. For people of all ages and social backgrounds, open spaces are areas for communication. Above all, inner-city parks and the plant and animal world in them are places where seasonal changes and a multitude of colours, smells and sounds stimulate sensual perception. There, nature can be experienced in a wider context, and natural cycles are made visible.

Streets and squares are traditional spaces where urbanism and urban life are tangible, where people meet and pursue diverse activities. Planted zones and squares help organize the built environment, creating areas of quiet in the sea of houses, articulating traffic arteries and facilitating orientation and identification *(Figure 66)*. Planted courtyards and gardens are private oases, as *Figure 67* illustrates. They clearly separate private buildings from the public domain by providing play areas for children close to home and opportunities to pursue gardening and other hobbies. The city climate differs from the rural climate in temperature, humidity and air quality; it is noticeably warmer, dryer and more polluted. The concentration of building mass and the large surfaces mean that energy is absorbed in times of strong solar radiation and the air above the city warms up considerably. Building materials such as asphalt and concrete store heat, releasing it in the evenings and overnight. At the same time, the constellation of built forms often prevents the intake of fresh air from the open countryside near the city and thus hinders air exchange within the city. Overnight cooling is reduced and delayed, and a temperature increase of 2-6 K in comparison with the surrounding countryside is the average norm, and that is often surpassed.

Stretches of diverse planted and open spaces – parklands, natural riverbanks and creeks, forested areas, gardens and cemeteries – all contribute considerably to a balanced urban climate, especially when these green areas connect within the city and with the open areas on the periphery. In a planted area of 50 to 100 metres in width, for example, the temperature may be approximately 3.5 K lower than in the adjacent built environment. For sustainable urban planning, the plotting of built and planted areas to create and maintain a free flow of cold air streams is of vital importance. Planted courtyards and core areas around which blocks are built, treed streets and squares, planted empty lots and fallow land, as well as planted façades *(Figure 68)* and roofs all help balance and improve the micro-climate in city neighbourhoods.

The shade provided by trees and dense bushes lessens the heat increase in sealed surfaces and built masses. A forest can evaporate more water, owing to its large leaf surface, than a comparable water surface. The photosynthetic process in plants produces oxygen and reduces the CO_2 concentration in the air. The leaf mass enables plants to bind air pollutants such as SO_2 or CO and to counteract their toxic effects; dust particles are filtered out. At the same time, planted façades and roofs provide protection for the built mass itself

66
Street with planted borders

67
Front yards

68
Foliage on façades

with regard to preventing overheating. On exposed asphalt roofs, temperature variations of up to 100 K are quite normal over the course of a year, whereas planted roof surfaces exhibit balanced temperature curves with a variation of only 30 K. The average change in climate parameters in densely built zones is shown in *Table 1*.

Open spaces in the city provide habitats and shelter for many animal and plant species. This is especially true of barren land, railway lands, overgrown gardens and clusters of trees. Forests are important areas of refuge for local species that have been driven out of other places. Natural riverbeds and permeable surfaces stabilize and ultimately safeguard the water table; they allow precipitation to seep into the ground and contribute to the creation of new groundwater while protecting against flooding.

Building with Environmental Resources
(Professor Klaus-D. Neumann)

Building with natural resources is as old as humankind. Human beings have always erected structures in the open by changing their environment to secure their own existence, making use of the materials available in nature to do so. Cutting down branches and trees for wood, terracing land on slopes, stacking rocks and stones to create enclosures and walls – all these are traditional practices.

Our inherited cultural landscape – here understood as the land surface of our segment of the globe – is changed in terms of architecture and landscape architecture by the types of manipulation arising from forestry and agriculture. Deciduous and coniferous forests, wheat fields, rice paddies, orchards and vineyards are examples of the anonymously created designs of green space illustrated in *Figures 69* to *71*. It is interesting that the disciplines with the greatest influence on the recognizable image of our environment – the landscape – namely forestry and agriculture, have also been the least communicative with regard to the visual consequences of their actions.

The changes most commonly associated with intervention by construction in the landscape are in fact secondary: engineered structures such as roads and power lines, or dams that regulate rivers and other bodies of water. At this level of interference in the

Parameters	Variables	Comparison to surroundings	
Air pollution	Condensation nucleus	10	times more
	Gaseous impurity	5 – 25	times more
Radiation	Global radiation	15 – 20 %	less
	UV (winter)	30 %	less
	UV (summer)	5 %	less
	Hours of sunshine	5 – 15 %	less
Temperature	Annual average	0,5 – 1,5 °C	higher
	on sunny days	2 – 10 °C	higher
Wind velocity	Annual average	10 – 20 %	less
	No wind	5 – 20 %	more
Relative humidity	Winter	2 %	less
	Summer	8 – 10 %	less
Precipitation	Total precipitation	5 – 10 %	less
	Snow	5 %	less

Table 1
Average change of climate parameters in dense urban areas

natural landscape, planning – that is to say studying the landscape conditions prior to plotting the project – is indispensible. Although designers, both architects and landscape architects, tend to rate their own activities highly, the most striking changes in the landscape effected by them through erecting tall buildings, and entire neighbourhoods with gardens, squares and parks figure last in this list of structural changes to the environment. *Figures 72* and *73* illustrate two examples.

69
Aerial view of Morocco

70 (far left)
Cinque Terre: vineyards

71
Agricultural landscape

72
Skyline, New York

73
Baroque garden

4.5   The Energy Potential of the Soil

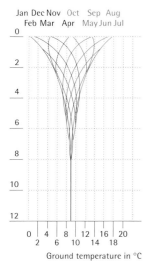

Temperature in °C

74.1
**Temperature profile
of lithosphere**
In Central Europe thermal temperatures increase by 3K per 100 m
of depth. In regions with so-called
"geothermal anomalies", thermal
temperatures increase more
rapidly.

Ground depth in m

74.2
**Average monthly ground tem-
peratures at the earth's surface**
To a depth of 4.5 m, ground temperatures are influenced by seasonal fluctuations. The influence
of weather is barely noticeable at
greater depths; ground temperatures are constant throughout the
year, ranging from 8° C to 10° C,
depending on the soil.

Earth or soil heat offers a safe alternative for heating
and cooling buildings: this approach harnesses the
natural heat, which rises from the centre of the Earth
and heats the surface. A comparison of the energy
available in the earth's surface, $43 \cdot 10^{24}$ joule, with
the world energy consumption (1987 = $0.3 \cdot 10^{21}$
joule/a) gives insight into the potentials of this energy source. Assuming that all geothermal energy is
usable, one can estimate supply timeframes of
approximately 140,000 years. The source of this heat
is, on the one hand, the hot core of the earth (approx.
5,000° C), whose temperature results from the residual
heat from the original creation of the earth, and, on
the other hand, to a large degree the natural radioac-
tivity of the earth's crust (mainly from thorium and
uranium). This heat rises to the surface because of the
temperature difference between the centre of the
earth and space. The average amount of heat transported to the earth's surface is approximately
$0,08$ W/m² and the temperature quotient in the outer
layer is approximately 3 K per 100 metres in depth
(Figure 74.1). Near the surface of the earth, temperature is determined by the radiated solar energy and by
weather *(Figure 74.2)*. Only in deeper layers does the
heat flowing from the centre of the earth totally
define the temperature in the soil. There are several
methods for utilizing this heat; which is suitable
depends upon local geological conditions. These
methods are:

Hydrothermal Geothermics
In this process warm deep waters from a depth
between 1,000 and 3,000 metres are brought to the
surface, where they are heated and then pressurized
back into the soil through a second bore hole. In this

technology, a distinction is made between high and
low enthalpy (heat content). Systems with high
enthalpy usually display local geothermal anomalies,
i.e., there are very hot areas near the earth's surface
of approximately 150 to 500° C, often present in hot
sources and similar phenomena near the earth's surface (geysers in Iceland and in the United States;
boracic water thermal sources in Larderello, Italy).
When steam escapes at the surface, it can be utilized
directly to produce electricity.
Systems with low enthalpy utilize groundwater with
temperatures ranging from 20° C to 150° C. This is
used to supply district heat networks, which are
linked to a heat exchanger or through a heat pump to
the transported groundwater.

Petrophysical Geothermics
In the Hot-Dry-Rock (HDR) process, hot rock formations preserve steam for creating electricity. Water is
pressed into the rock formation through a bore hole
with a depth of approximately 2,000 to 3,000 metres;
there it creates fissures in the rock where the water
heats up (hydraulic fracturing). Through a second
baracicwater in the area of the resulting fissure system the hot water, approximately 150° C to 200° C, is
then transported to the surface and used.

Shallow Bore Holes, Earth Coils
Shallow bore holes reach to a depth of approximately
100 metres. Earth coils deliver water with a constant
temperature of approximately 10° C to 15° C, which
can be used as a heat source for heat pumps or as a
cold water source. *Figure 75* illustrates the schematic
structure of this type of installation.

Thermal Tunnel, Thermal Labyrinth
Aside from the technologies mentioned above, earth
heat and coolness, respectively, can also be utilized
by guiding fresh air flow through the soil before it
enters a building. In a thermal tunnel, smaller air volumes for the ventilation of residential buildings are

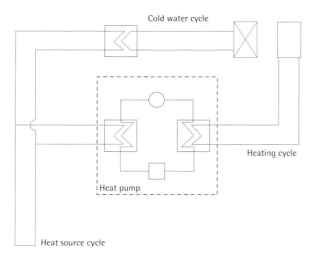

Cold water cycle

Heating cycle

Heat pump

Heat source cycle

75
Diagram of geothermal bore-hole
installation with four closed circuits: heat-source circuit, heat-
pump circuit, heating circuit and
cold water circuit

guided through clay, concrete or plastic pipes and installed in the ground, where the air naturally warms or cools to approximate the soil or ground temperature after some time. This process gains at least some of the energy required for heating or cooling.

In thermal labyrinths, larger air volumes are generally guided through uninsulated basement areas. Here, too, the result is cooling in summer and warming in winter respectively, with an average temperature reduction in summer by approximately 3 – 4 K and temperature increase in winter by approximately 2 – 3 K. Investment costs are still quite high and these system solutions receive therefore only moderate attention; however, they can at least contribute to a reduction of energy consumption.

4.6   Daylight

Humans, like all living organisms on Earth, depend on light and sun for their survival. In ancient times, people adjusted their life rhythm to daylight. They lived according to daily and annual changes in light. The advent first of fire and then of candles made it possible to light up the night hours, so people could change the rhythm prescribed by nature.

The spectral composition of daylight is never constant. The intensity of the total spectrum, as well as the individual colours, change over the course of a day and a year *(Figure 76)*. This spectrum determines the activity of human beings in approximately constant cycles from which many analogies can be formed, such as :

– Spring	Blossoming
	Morning
	Awakening
– Summer	Growing
	Noon
	Becoming active
– Fall	Harvesting
	Evening
	Enjoyment
– Winter	Renewal
	Night
	Sleeping

Colour temperature
in K

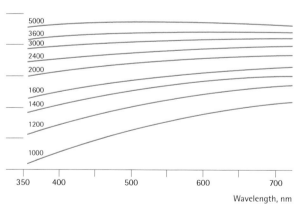

76
Spectrum of daylight
The daylight spectrum changes in analogy to the spectrum of a full radiator, shown in this figure, to the spectral distribution and to the intensity, symbolised by the colour temperature.

Today, working hours no longer coincide with natural cycles and we have become used to being active even in winter and at night.

In our buildings, artificial light replaces the daylight necessary for these activities. Modern fluorescent and discharge lamps with high light efficiency do not have a light spectrum that changes over the course of a day as daylight does. Their spectrum is composed of selected colours in various intensities. Light imitated by these means has the quality of daylight, and yet it has a different impact on the person whose immediate surroundings it illuminates.

Daylight and Daylit Rooms

Light has always played an important role in architecture: the building masters of the past often incorporated the sun as a source of light when plotting the designs of buildings. We have already described how differently buildings and openings were designed in Northern Europe by comparison with Mediterranean areas and even more markedly in Africa. The path of the sun and its intensity in summer and winter had to be considered for the building concept, if inhabitants were to feel comfortable.

After years of building design, especially during the sixties and seventies, in which the interior space was totally sealed off from the exterior space, ignoring the human need for daylight, the latest trend is a return to a conscious integration of daylight in building concepts.

Glare problems associated with visual-display surfaces such as computer monitors and undesired room temperature increases in summer make sun and glare protection necessary. Office buildings in Mediterranean regions often keep windows covered with blinds, and artificial light is used even when there is sunshine or when sky luminosity is high. To reduce energy consumption, this type of situation should be avoided altogether.

Ultimately, the following conditions for light technology have been established as universally desirable:
- Sufficient daylight, adjustable to each person's needs
- Good mix of diffuse and direct light
- Good visual contact with the outside to experience weather and time of day

Hence we need sun and glare protection that is responsive to different daylight conditions and window glass that does not change the spectrum of the daylight.

Part 2   Sustainable Building:

Examples and Ideas

Information technologies promise to expand communication horizons; radical visions in architecture and urban design dissolve into cyberspace and virtual cities. At the same time, ecological responsibility imposes new limits on individualism. How can architecture do equal justice to both of these developments? How can architecture move towards the information age without losing sight of the fact that this era, too, will achieve architectural longevity only through sustainability?

Trend researchers conclude that we are currently in the last of three phases:
- Phase 1   Era of economic growth
- Phase 2   Era of the ego
- Phase 3   Era of soft individualism

Soft individualism is characterized by engagement, composure, friendship, honesty, responsibility, experience and spirituality. Three of these attributes – engagement, honesty and responsibility – are particularly applicable to living environments and, to some degree, to working environments as well. Honesty has become the driving principle behind the promotion of consumer goods. This will lead to a broader commercial concept of "new basic goods", which are sensible, solid, necessary, simple, classic, durable and yet fashionable, and economical (but not cheap). These attributes apply not only to objects for everyday use but also to interior design and furniture.

In Part 1, we mentioned that the industrialized nations will re-group, using state-of-the-art technologies, especially electronic media, to produce knowledge instead of goods. This type of work requires surroundings that foster creativity, rooms that permit a higher level of concentration and intellectual productivity. These issues relate to both office buildings and to home offices.

The oil crisis of 1973 initiated a concerted effort in the United States to study the profitability of home-based telework. The findings prompted strong support for this approach from futurists, their main argument being that employees would save the time and expense of travel between home and office and that employers would save the expense of providing offices. Further momentum for this approach came from the US federal law on air pollution control; it stipulates that companies with more than 100 employees must contribute to decreasing commuter traffic by car.

Liveable cities are cities where home and work lie close together, and where compact green neighbourhoods support active living and increased productivity. We may assume that requirements for quality and comfort will be maintained if not raised. Such requirements can only be met, in the long term, with sustainable building, building that is as flexible, exacting and contextual as it is resource-friendly and efficient. To achieve this, architects must familiarize themselves with ecological assessment and planning.

5 Living and Working in the Information Age: Integrated Building

Work in the information age and in the industrialized countries of the future will be characterized by:
– Time-sharing and regrouping for smaller tasks
– Integration and overlapping of computer and Internet links
– Fulfilling ecological and economical requirements

The labour market will become more flexible through time-sharing if a large volume of work continues to migrate to other countries or if "full employment shared by many" becomes the ultimate goal. In a time of growing economic globalization, it does no good merely to offer incentives to the employed and government charity to the unemployed. Wages will rise only in areas with above-average work performance. In fact, wages and salaries will stagnate on a broad basis, and may even decline.

O. Giarini's and P. M. Liedtke's report on "Work in the future" to the Club of Rome (1998) may well turn out to be true.

The report puts forth a "multi-layer work model" as an essential requirement to achieve a new policy of full employment. In this model the first layer or level of productive activity prescribes that each member of society capable of gainful employment is assigned a minimum of paid productive work (approx. 20 hours of work / week = subsistence minimum).

The second level of productive activity (gainful employment) is flexible, enabling those capable of gainful employment to decide for themselves whether and to which extent they wish to be employed.

The third level, finally, comprises activities without measurable market value, e.g. volunteer work (education, health, social services etc.).

The essential characteristic of this model is that there would be no remuneration for inactivity or unemployment. Instead, occupation would be supported (social policy = employment policy).

If several people share one task, working at a "fixed" workplace will become equally uncertain; time-sharing means that some of the work will be done at home or that several employees will share one workplace.

According to W. J. Mitchell, the automated rooms and buildings of the future will be locations where bodies meet bits, where digital information is translated into visual, audio, tactile or other sensory forms and, conversely, where physical action is recorded and transformed into digital information. Designing these programmable locations is not simply a matter of installing cables in walls and electronic devices in rooms; on the contrary, these electronic technologies will merge with and disappear into the fabric of the building through miniaturization. Sensors will be omnipresent, buildings and computer interfaces will be interchangeable.

Architects of the future will continue to design rooms, both real and virtual, for various uses. They will be challenged to think of the visual and physical environment from new perspectives in response to increased density. Functionality, structural stability, resource conservation and aesthetics will continue to be guiding principles. Functionality will be as dependent on software and interface as on floor plans and building materials. Stability will no longer be solely the result of load-bearing systems but also a matter of the logical integrity of the computer systems. All these factors will influence construction and aesthetics, opening new dimensions.

5.1   Living Areas

In the future, housing will no longer be exclusively for "living" but will also function as a workplace. Hence it will accommodate data networks and quiet areas appropriate for work. Responding to these demands, architects Jockers + Partner designed a project for EXPO 2000, organized under the theme "Living and Working on the Information Highway" *(Figure series 77)*. Within this flexible workplace structure, work can be conducted at home in a telebox or at a nearby telecentre. The telecentre is linked to a media centre with communal services. The whole building complex is connected to a high-performance telecommunication network.

Other demographic trends will affect architecture. For example, the need for environmental protection and resource conservation will lead to increased building density as people move back into the city. Distances between home and workplace will consequently diminish, supporting the development of tele-workplaces.

Another important consideration is the growing percentage of elderly people in the population. Futurists predict not only a higher life expectancy, but life expectancies of up to 150 years. Hence, homes will have to "breathe", that is, they will be flexible in size and room partition: small in the beginning, then larger, then smaller again. As well, to improve the quality of life, urban areas must become greener than they are at present.

Bertrand Goldberg proposed years ago that residential buildings offer additional services geared towards singles communities. His idea was to develop large apartment towers in which one could live out one's entire life. In other words, this would be housing "from cradle to grave". These apartment towers, or "apartment office towers", would offer all amenities and services for daily life (medical clinics, shopping,

77.1
The residential area on the former Nordwolle site in Osnabrück is under renovation for EXPO 2000. The theme, "Living and Working on the Information Highway", focuses on new forms of telework at home. Model photograph of a competition design, architects: Jockers + Partner

77.2
The telecommunication net links buildings to the information highway.

Innovative living for elderly people
– Control of life rhythm
– Alarm link to service centre
– Monitoring of functions in home, service

1 Low/high speed data link (Teleworkplaces)
2 Language transmission
3 TV, video transmission
4 Process control technique, European Installation Bus (EIB)
A Seniors' service centre
B Telecentre, Telework
C Mediacentre

155 Mbit/s - LWL connections
155/622 Mbt/s - LWL connections

Service centre
– Data collection, telemetrics
– Representation of telecentre operating status

External link
– Telecom
– Satelite links
– Private links

entertainment, school, home, workplaces, etc.). When we apply Mitchell's fiction to this concept, such a "machine" is not so far-fetched – if work were brought into the home via network links, travel were to occur in cyberspace and all other needs were to be satisfied on location. Yet these utopian visions give rise to profound doubts, as we have seen.

The human psyche rejects a flood of stimuli and information; many people increasingly experience the need to switch the "screen" off. Too much information deconstructs our psyche. Isolation, a much-feared side effect of telework, is not only a psychological danger; excessive stimulation is a danger as well. People who spend too much time on the Internet will sooner or later perceive the world as a loose association of largely random phenomena. Consequently, they will no longer be able to distinguish between what is important and what is unimportant. Life in the real world, writes Clifford Stoll, one of the leading spokesmen of the new "back-lash movement", is immeasurably more interesting, important and richer than anything one might find on a computer screen. ("Leave your home! Meet your neighbours again! Plant your own tomatoes! Switch your computer off, for heaven's sake!")

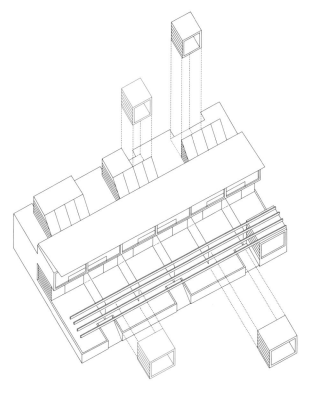

77.3
In single-family homes, telework takes place in a mobile "telebox", which can fit into different locations in the home and is adaptable to the user's individual needs.

77.4
The telecentres offer not only tele-workplaces, but also administrative services (secretarial services, conference rooms) that are offered in the free market.

77.5
Within the home, telework may also take place in office modules, such as the home office (Bisterfeld and Weiss).

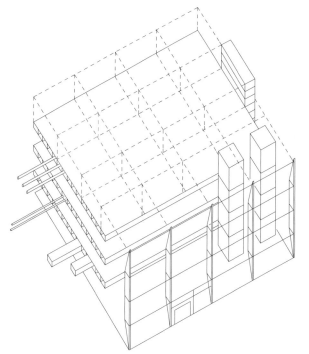

We can therefore assume that many old values will endure, with some adaptation to information age environments. Many of the systems that Bill Gates is having installed in his new home (as described in his book, *The Road Ahead*) are not only inspired by his leadership role as president of Microsoft. Savings in energy and in resources are another principle at work in the design. Bill Gates's home is constructed, like other homes, of wood, glass, concrete and stone. However, the installation of silicon microprocessors and memory chips gives it certain attributes that will soon define millions of homes. The entertainment system in this house, for example, anticipates the future use of media. The technology also meets the requirements of daily life (heat, comfort, convenience, security). The Bill Gates house, which offers a variety of entertainment options – which relaxes, and also stimulates creativity – is equipped in such a manner that the technology serves the home and not the other way around. The physical space is designed with generous proportions: a reception hall, large living areas as well as smaller additional rooms, a small cinema, bedrooms with adjoining bathrooms, etc. The Gates house differs from the palaces of past centuries in that the design is based on function and comfort rather than on the projection of power.

Anyone entering the home is presented with an electronic pin, which connects them to all electronic services of the home. This pin will more or less "tell" the home who is where; the house will use this information to "meet the requirements" of the user. When it is dark outside, the pin will cause a moving zone of light to accompany its wearer. Unoccupied rooms will be unlit. Music, too, will move with the guest from room to room, if desired. Movies and news will similarly travel around the house on screen walls. Telephone calls are automatically transferred to the handset nearest the guest. This technology is unobtrusive and kept in the background but readily accessible. Remote controls are used to manage the entertainment system in the user's immediate surroundings.

The remote control extends the capabilities of the pin, so that the house not only identifies and locates the visitor, but is also able to receive commands from the guest. The remote control activates monitors in the rooms to display whatever one wishes to see. The menu offers thousands of pictures, recordings, movies and television programmes. Unobtrusive consoles in individual rooms allow the guest or user to give specific instructions. The information system of the house, controlled by the pin, is programmed to indicate whether the user has permission for specific activities.

In the evenings, lamps are automatically dimmed when the TV or a screen wall are on. When the house is occupied during the daytime, it automatically matches inside brightness to that of the outdoors. All systems in the house can effectively save energy with the help of regulation and control systems. The energy consumption in private households can thus be reduced through data networks and corresponding control systems, especially during peak hours. Another positive effect is that in the Gates house, the Internet continuously delivers information about local traffic conditions, useful in the morning before leaving for work.

Bill Gates is not a believer in Mitchell's prophecy that robots will do all household chores in the future. At least, he hasn't equipped his own home for this eventuality. Instead, the key concepts that inform the design are responsiveness to individual needs and ready access to information.

All these technologies should not be dismissed as science fiction; they are practical and in some instances already in use. At the trade fair Ambiente Electronica in 1991, Philips Consumer Electronics demonstrated how designers and architects envision the home of the future.

Entertainment electronics have become less and less sensual over time as the "overbred" electronics culture expresses its functionality through minimization and reduction. A deficit in form is sometimes the unfortunate result. Media and media consumer goods lead to new attitudes and interiors. The invention of the radio, for instance, changed the layout of living-rooms; in the same way, the home cinema is inspiring new room layouts and furniture items.

While modern electronics have adapted to our rhythm of life, their external appearance has become dissociated from our environment. Ambiente Electronica exhibited six media rooms illustrating a new symbiosis between entertainment electronics and interior design. *Figures 78 to 83* show design proposals by:

Ron Arad, Imagination Room
Massimo Iosa-Ghini, Living-room with image bands
Coop Himmelblau, Moveable kitchen
Matteo Thun, Bathroom
Philips Corporate Industrial Design, Home office
Elizabeth Garouste and Mattia Bonetti, Bedroom

78
Imagination room, Ron Arad
This is a quiet place for imagination and meditation, for contemplating media-captured art in all its complexity: imaginary museum, private gallery and video screen combine on a display wall to present a shifting electronic exhibition. Ron Arad: "My room displays electronic reproductions on the wall. Instead of leafing through the pages of a book or magazine, the user can change the "painting" at the push of a button."

79
Living-room,
Massimo Iosa-Ghini
The pieces re-interpret traditional models: table, sofa, cabinet, carpet. The result: a new line of furniture to elegantly "clothe" the new entertainment media. The TV cabinet – abandoned as passé – makes a surprising comeback (now with wide-screen TVs). Massimo Iosa-Ghini: "When present in all rooms of a house, the electronic idol loses its symbolic force and is reduced to the level of a light switch. It is condemned to a complete loss of identity."

80
Moveable kitchen,
Coop Himmelblau
The result is futuristic functionality. The kitchen is the centre of action, a workshop for the senses. With video cookbook, electronic controls and information media, cooking can be experienced not only standing by the stove but also sitting in the chair. Coop Himmelblau: "Mobile architecture. The medium extends the concept of mobility. The "meal-time" is a piece of furniture, horizontally and vertically mobile. The unreality of media turns into a comprehensible reality."

81
Intelligent bathroom,
Matteo Thun
The vision continues, all the way to a video wall displaying rolling waves: the moving image as an element in interior design. For his media room, the designer has selected a comic-strip style of drawing instead of impersonal high tech. His media steles are fantasy creatures with names. Matteo Thun: "Check your body. The bathroom fixtures are partners in a sensual body cult. High touch. Communication with objects, rooms, the world around us is exciting and fun."

82
Home office, Philips Corporate Industrial Design
This poetic set demonstrates that the home office need no longer be separate from the rest of the house. The new interactive communication and information systems, from telefax to visual display phone to PC, deliver a surprising degree of freedom and flexibility inside the home and interactively with the world outside. Philips Corporate Industrial Design: "We are no longer tied to our desk. Working at home is flexible and relaxing. The technology once again gives us the freedom to choose our work environment and to re-evaluate our work habits."

83
Bedroom, Elizabeth Garouste, Mattia Bonetti
The bedroom: an idyll regained, not only for sleep and love, but also for daydreams enhanced by electronic images. Television and video are windows into real and surreal worlds, into present and past and the world of invented stories. Elizabeth Garouste and Mattia Bonetti: "For our bedroom we have selected a dream, a room without borders, darkness and unreality. Close your eyes and fall asleep with a child's fantasies, weightlessly, on an imaginary planet."

84
Residential development on Genter Strasse, Munich, architect: Otto Steidle + Partner, Munich
The supporting framework and almost temporary character of the development signal its openness to change: the residents have already taken advantage of options for simple renovation and extension.

Regardless of whether one is attracted to these design proposals or not, they offer a first insight into how architects and designers currently interpret "living in the future". (Beyond that, the old adage applies: Taste is, well, a matter of taste).

Living in the future is associated with the principles of resource efficiency and environmental protection. Flexible housing design for a dense urban setting has been under development for some time. Some 25 years ago, Otto Steidle + Partner designed a residential complex in the Genter Strasse, Munich, whose supporting framework and almost temporary character reflect a receptiveness towards change *(Figure 84)*. As a result, the inhabitants have taken advantage of the many options for easy renovation and extension.

Built between 1971 and 1973, this residential complex was designed before the advent of requirements for low-energy construction. Legislation was in place by the time Rödiger Kramm and Axel Strigl designed subsidized housing for Frankfurt's Bonames neighbourhood. Passive solar utilization was the basis for the architectural concept. The buildings are oriented on a north-south axis, closed on the north side, where service areas such as kitchen, bath and entrance are located, and open on the south side for living-rooms, winter gardens and loggias. These rooms allow for year-round utilization of environmental resources. For reasons of energy efficiency the buildings are compact, achieving a good ratio between exterior surface and walled-in space.

Options for interior variations were anticipated with the relevant zoning. *Figure 85* shows the dense urban site; *Figure 86,* two typical floor plans. In *Figure 87,* one can clearly see the standard configurations for two-, three- and four-person households. For each example, a modified floor plan for optimal use is given. *Figure 88* shows the corresponding cross-section,

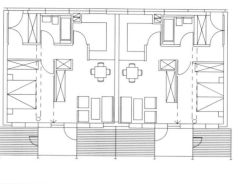

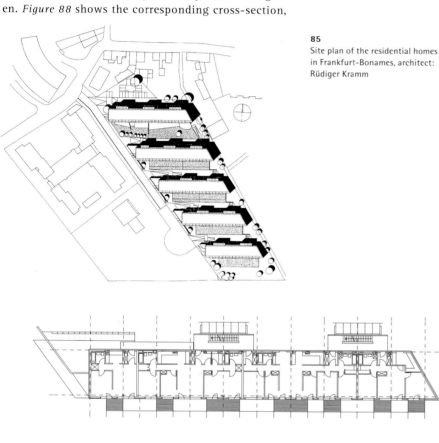

85
Site plan of the residential homes in Frankfurt-Bonames, architect: Rüdiger Kramm

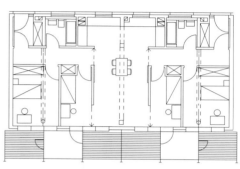

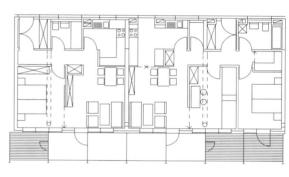

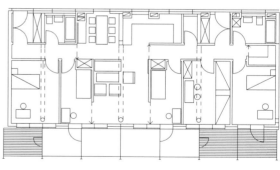

86
Ground plans

87
Floor plan options

while *Figure series 89* offers an overview of the whole complex as well as a view of the north and south façades.

The principle of living area distribution in each unit is based on a ratio where each person has up to 45 m² in living space, with another 10 to 12 m² for each additional occupant. All units enjoy direct access to the outside – at ground level on verandas or in tenant gardens, at the upper levels on balconies, loggias or in winter gardens. The traditional master bedroom has been omitted in favour of identically proportioned individual rooms for each member of the household. The kitchens are live-in areas with open transitions to the living-rooms. Fixed floor plans were avoided to gain flexibility in the arrangement of rooms. Individual rooms can be merged according to user needs. In this complex, rooms can be utilized as needed, and adapted to age and family structure.

Here, one building houses apartments for diverse household types and age groups in a socially compatible manner. One room for common use, traditionally the living-room, measures approximately 18-20 m².

When needed, this room can be opened up to include two adjoining rooms. Each row has one communal room for child care, which also serves as a meeting or guest room, or for communal gatherings. Four houses, each four storeys high, were erected in rows. The fifth building has three storeys. Local traffic has access along a dead end street. Parking (naturally ventilated) is available underground below the units. The open areas between the rows are used as tenant gardens and reserved for the ground floor units. These gardens are not, however, open to the general public.

This building project aimed for an architectural concept with the lowest possible energy consumption: buildings with a specific heat energy consumption of 25-60 kWh/m²a. The actual annual energy requirements are currently approximately 50 kWh/m²a, meeting the target set for low-energy buildings. In addition to the measures for reducing heating energy requirements (compactness, façade design and orientation, thermal or heat storage), heating is provided by conventional low temperature heating with distribution system. A fully modulated condensing boiler supplies additional heat during peak hours. Humidity-regulated exhaust systems ventilate the living areas via the bathrooms. To achieve a more efficient energy supply, a small combined heating and power unit, operated by the municipal works, is used as well; this supplies electricity and thermal energy.

88
Section

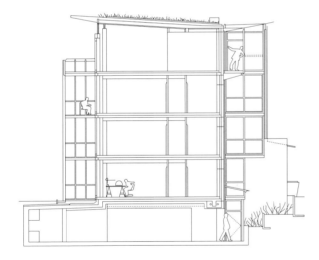

89
Elevations: north façade (above),
south façade (left),
general construction work

5.2 Working Areas

According to trend research, there will be three fundamentally different types of work in our society in 10 to 15 years.

Traditional work, "old work", will continue to exist, but will command much lower wages. There will be a decline in workplaces with guaranteed salaries, working hours and responsibilities, where jobs can be ergonomically described and taught, because they involve more or less the same activity day after day. As in all industrial labour, the individual workers are replaceable. Service-sector work will suffer a similar fate.

The truly interesting work, "new work", will be work "without a job". None of the former habits of work will continue. A new independence will prevail within companies. "New workers" will be located partially in and partially outside the company conglomerate. When they are in the company, they will have to be able to fulfil multiple functions. Companies of the future must be prepared to restructure in order to adapt to a changing world market. The remuneration for "new work" will no longer be fixed, rather, it will consist of a basic remuneration, team bonuses and individual productivity bonuses.

"New workers", also called "symbol analyser" according to Robert B. Reich in *The New Economy,* are people who recognize problems, analyse them and find solutions; they work alone or in teams, the members of which change in accordance with the task. Fast reactions, the ability to connect, innovation, team spirit, articulateness and broad knowledge of the world, paired with a healthy measure of human understanding and intuition as well as a distinct and integrated personality will be the most sought-after attributes. New workers must be able to deal with complexity; above all, they must be willing to participate in a continuous learning process, reflecting the existential nature of modern economics.

Due to increased flexibility, new workers will be masters of their own time. The shift from fixed work hours set in an annual timeframe is necessary to compensate for the rise and fall in demand and to create a better economic balance for the company. New workers are employees in an economy of ideas. The knowledge of complex tasks in a company resides in the minds of a few, making them even more valuable to the company.

Futurists assume that new workers will no longer merely secure places of employment but will have to ensure that work is generated in the first place. Skilled labour in industrialized societies will become increasingly scarce owing to the use of modern information tools and the globalization of markets. Furthermore, a work market is emerging, which is formed by a population of illegal immigrants who belong to an underpaid black-market economy, which the state is no longer able to control. These workers have become an integral facet of prosperous societies, which naturally has an effect on the labour market.

The current migration of work off-shore is in essence a return to an economic structure that seemed to have gone out of fashion with colonialism, although we may ask how many years or decades will pass before the countries now categorized as threshold or developing nations will catch up to the industrialized nations (equal wages, expectations and social- and welfare legislation etc.).

Profits are optimized by the low wages paid in many countries and are partially realized in industrialized countries through the presence of still available cheap labour. These shifts in the global economy have led to the creation of new types of work, which Matthias Horx *(Trendbook 2)* describes as follows:
- Flexists and complexists
  (Professional revolutionaries who help corporations to practice flexibility and complex thinking)
- Media navigators
  (Those who search for, condense and qualitatively process information)
- Designers
  (Small-scale entrepreneurs who emerge out of the structural crises in apprentice trades)
- Ritualists
  (Experts in universal rituals)
- Future-positivists
  (People who counteract arguments such as: "Can't do that", "I've always done it like that", "It's not my responsibility")

Work either takes place at home or in highly flexible buildings. These locations are primarily sites of information, information processing, knowledge expansion and creativity, and are thus locations where information is given value. Office buildings have been located in expensive, central business districts, reflecting the power and prestige of the corporations. In the future, headquarters will remain where they are today – in the inner city with easy access. A large sector of employees, however, will be relocated to suburbs, where places of work can be developed with much less effort and still meet the standards and provide the comfort required for people who pursue demanding intellectual work. This trend also satisfies the ecological need for shorter distances between home and work, giving employees more free time (instead of spending hours in traffic jams), creating a better integration of life and work in an urban setting and putting a stop to the flight from the cities. The city of the future will be a city of short distances.

Well-qualified recruits for the new type of work will be in short supply for some time. To attract the best workers, corporate architecture must reflect the image and status of the company. It is therefore not only important that workers be comfortable with the building, the exterior of the building must project confidence as well.

A central challenge in the development of new buildings will be whether and to what extent the use of these buildings can be redefined depending on demand and market situation. So that new uses can be quickly and easily realized, more component buildings will be developed, which can be sized up or down like a building block system. Office design will be judged primarily by its ability to accommodate a range of uses and to react flexibly to any changes in use. *Figure 90* shows a range of requirements. Of all new office buildings in the future, a maximum of 50 % will be owner-occupied, possibly considerably fewer. On the other hand, more office buildings will be developed by investors and will be either entirely leased or a combination of owner-occupancy and lease arrangements. The ownership and initial development of a building will also determine its uses.

Room configurations for different use requirements are shown in *Figure 91;* one new type that can already be defined is the reversible office. Reversible office buildings must accommodate all imaginable types of rooms in their structure; the building is thus not fixed to one specific type of room or space. The increase in office rental space and the demand for greater flexibility as well as rapid modifications for utilization mean that this type of office will be more and more in demand. Reversible offices integrate, as shown in *Figure 92,* cellular offices with inward-oriented office areas, combination offices, group rooms and small open plan areas. The building depth resulting from this constellation is approximately 15 m *(Figure 93).* The reversible building structures allow for areas dedicated to research and the manufacture of small components, as well as the usual office areas.

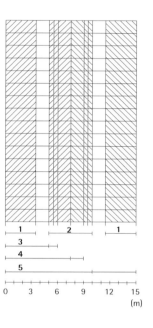

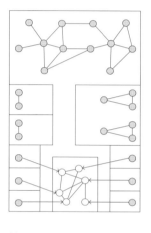

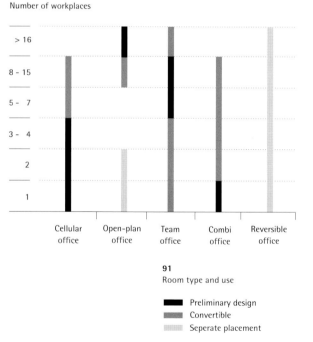

90
Dependencies between type of office building and use

92
Reversible structures with approximately 15 m depth

- ◉ Fixed workplace
- ○ Flexible workplace

93
Basic structure of area module for different layouts

1 Combi office
2 Common zone
3 Self-contained office
4 Linear team office
5 Team office

├─┤ Minimum
├─┤ Maximum

91
Room type and use

- ■ Preliminary design
- ■ Convertible
- ▦ Seperate placement

Number of workplaces

	Criteria	Examples/ Definitions
Table 2 Criteria for the Evaluation of the Office Principle		
Organizational criteria	Necessity of spatial flexibility	Qualitative modification of group sizes Qualitative task changes with changes in surface / area (function) Technological influences (technological flexibility) Humanizing the workplace (standard) Different composition of work stations (changing work process) Promotion
	Intensity of future communication relationships and new forms of co-operation	Within and among groups / departments / areas With external / company-owned posts With external / foreign posts
	Type of future work procedures at various workplaces	Individual work / group (team) work Visualization needs Percentage of work in meetings and conferences Use of media (devices) Transparency of work
	Application of progressive leadership approaches	Project management Co-operative management
	Confidentiality	Team colleagues Colleagues in other teams Visitors
	Percentage of workplaces requiring a high degree of concentration	Acoustic and visual sensitivity to disruption
	Optimal utilization of administrative services / organization	Central office technology Dedicated messenger-, mail- and supply service per floor Archival services, secretarial services
	Shared use of depositories [hard drives] and monitors, from several workstations	
	Absenteeism	
	Number of visitors	
Economic criteria	Area-utilization ratio	Economic viability of utilization and secondary areas Viable area standards
	Building costs	
	Operating costs	Energy dependency
	Savings in organization expenses	Flexibility / adaptation costs Organization costs
	Effort for planning	Time, expenses, deconstructing resistance
Criteria relating to employees	Attractiveness of workplace conditions	Optical effect and comfort aesthetics
	Relation to outside world	Window distance
	Optimal air quality	Window opening / fresh air Temperature / cleanliness / smokers
	Lighting	Natural daylight, artificial light
	Acoustic and visual protection against interruption	sound-absorbing finishing elements, lighting systems, glare protection
	Demand for individuality in work environment	

Aside from the home office and the reversible office building, other types of workplaces are currently under discussion:

– **Nomadic office**

Working at any location worldwide with the help of a portable telephone linked to databases (via the Internet) and to the "home computer". Project leaders and team members communicate exclusively by computer.

– **Virtual office**

Working in a virtual office that has no recognizable corporate image (e.g., the First National Bank, a bank with no subsidiaries and offices). In the virtual office, information processing takes place on-line by telephone, fax and data-processing systems.

– **Market office**

Working in the market office means using a type of office where administrative tasks are centralized and shared by several people. Different professional sectors share spacious structures for accommodation and work; the interiors must be extremely flexible to create the necessary work areas. In addition, interior spaces are created for the exchange and development of ideas and concepts, and the formation of teams to generate new projects.

– **Festival office**

Strategy meetings and workshops with specific goals take place over the course of several days at festival sites to underline the importance of the event. In addition to large meeting rooms accommodating up to 100 people, work is supported by all available information and communication technologies. User friendliness, reliability and facilities for relaxation characterize the festival office.

Economic activities are already becoming decentralized. Managers and experts are increasingly dispersed across the entire globe and co-ordinate their activities by phone. The mobility of capital has increased enormously. On the other hand, there is also a trend towards centralization, mainly in the area of production, because production processes are ultimately based on the use and transformation of materials. Industrial sites continue to depend on local resources, and whether the necessary goods and labour are available. Furthermore, the development of the modern telecommunication infrastructure still favours urban centres over medium-sized towns and remote areas. In addition, profitable information work goes hand in hand with high investment costs. Yet, in the end, many opposing forces will influence the urban and regional development in a complex and socially differentiated manner, and will also impact site patterns for industry, trade and living. Cyberspace communities will play a key role in the new economic order emerging together with the new infrastructure.

6 Comfortable Rooms: Quality Building

Standards of comfort grow out of a range of conditions. The determining factors are generally categorized in the following way:
– Thermal comfort
– Hygienic comfort
– Acoustic comfort
– Electromagnetic compatibility
– Visual comfort
– Influence of colours
– Influence of surfaces and materials
– Avoidance of contaminants

Ideal conditions in a comfortable room, primarily defined by room temperature, can lead to optimal performance. *Figure 94* shows average performance levels for different temperature conditions with different forms of ventilation:

Option 1 – All natural ventilation
Option 2 – Supplementary ventilation and night cooling
Option 3 – Supplementary ventilation with active cooling
Option 4 – Supplementary ventilation and cooling to room temperatures of 26° C in summer

Ergonomists have observed that human performance is negatively influenced by room temperatures above approximately 28° C or below approximately 18° C. The values indicated in *Figure 94* are complemented in *Figure 95* by the maximum room temperatures for different ventilation and cooling options in a building with optimal insulation and good solar protection in summer. Performance can also be adversely affected by direct or indirect glare when working on PCs, high or very disruptive noise levels, poor ventilation and insufficient exhaustion of air pollutants and odours, lack of visual contact with the outside, electromagnetic fields affecting occupants, and so on. Below we have outlined once again some criteria for comfort in rooms, to highlight the parameters for qualitative building in the information age.

94
Human performance as a measure of "climate comfort" for different ventilation systems and temperature conditions

Option 1
All natural ventilation
Option 2
Supplementary ventilation and night cooling
Option 3
Supplementary ventilation with active cooling
Option 4
Supplementary ventilation and cooling to room temperatures of 26° C in summer

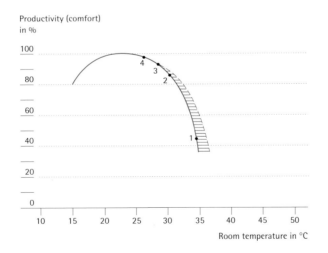

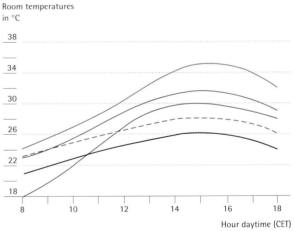

95
Maximum room temperatures with different ventilation and cooling options in general office areas

——— Fresh air
——— Option 1, natural ventilation
——— Option 2, supplementary vent.
– ··· Option 3, supplementary ventilation + cooling
——— Option 4, climatization according to DIN 1946 Part 2

6.1   Thermal Comfort

Thermal comfort is achieved when the occupants find the temperature, humidity, air movement and heat radiation in their environment to be ideal and wish for neither warmer nor cooler, drier nor more humid air. An overview of experimental results regarding the influence of room or ambient temperature on accident frequency and performance levels during tasks carried out while sitting is shown in *Figure 96*: thermal comfort exists only within a small range of temperature fluctuation, this being at the same time the optimal thermal conditions for intellectual performance, presuming that other influencing factors are also ideal (air velocity, humidity, surface temperatures, clothing, health, age, degree of activity).

Thermal comfort and air quality in a room are influenced by the occupants, depending on:
– Activity
– Clothing
– Duration of time spent in room
– Thermal and chemical density
– Number of occupants

Thermal comfort and air quality are also influenced by the room itself, depending on:
– Surface temperatures
– Air temperature distribution
– Heat sources
– Contaminant sources

Finally, they are influenced by ventilation and air-conditioning systems, depending on:

– Temperature
– Air velocity
– Humidity
– Air change rate
– Air purity
– Noise (noise levels / frequencies)

In addition, *Figures 97.1* and *97.2,* based on Grandjean, show comfort zones for ambient air temperatures, room temperatures and relative room humidity respectively. Air-conditioning systems directly influence the air temperature, air velocity, and relative air humidity of a building. Building design protects against direct sun radiation; ventilation and air-conditioning systems have no influence on it. In areas where people spend significant amounts of time, the combined ratio of air temperature and radiation temperature of surrounding surfaces must be taken into consideration. The local temperature is called perceived temperature or, sometimes, operative room temperature; it was not sufficiently considered in the past. Perceived temperatures are usually measured at 0.1 m and 1.7 m above floor level; for the calculation of local radiation temperatures, surface temperature and surface factors are weighted according to their irradiation zones.

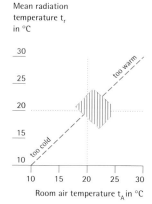

Mean radiation temperature t_r in °C

97.1
Comfort zone in the t_r / t_A- schematic according to Grandjean
t_r = mean radiation temperature
t_A = room air temperature
Based on air velocity 0 to 0.2 m/s; relative humidity 30-70 %

97.2
Comfort zone for the pair of variables:
t_A = room air temperature
φ = relative room humidity φ
(Leusden and Freymark)

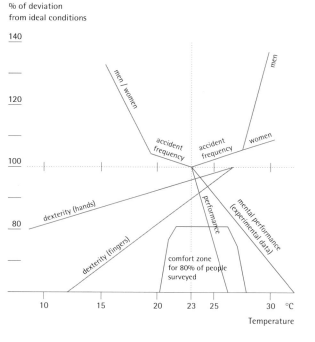

% of deviation from ideal conditions

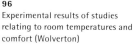

96
Experimental results of studies relating to room temperatures and comfort (Wolverton)

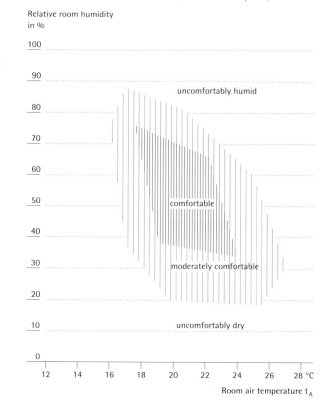

Relative room humidity in %

Room air temperature t_A

In *Figure 98,* operative, that is, perceived room temperatures are shown in relation to outside temperatures. A rise in the perceived temperature is acceptable during the height of summer for short periods. The heat gain (cooling requirement) for rooms is frequently defined less by outside temperatures than by interior thermal loads. If these loads are short term, the perceived room temperature may rise to 26° C with outside temperatures below 29° C. Perceived room temperatures ranging from 20° C to 22° C are acceptable with certain ventilation systems (e.g., floor-to-ceiling ventilation, displacement ventilation). The vertical temperature coefficient is another important factor for thermal comfort. This coefficient must not exceed 2 K per metre of room height. The room temperature at 0.1 m above floor level should be no less than 21° C to avoid discomfort (heat demand at ankle point). One-sided warming or cooling of the human body through uneven temperatures in the surrounding areas can lead to thermal discomfort.

Thermal comfort is greatly influenced by air movement within a space. The limits for air movement in the comfort zone depend upon the air temperature and the turbulence quotient of the air flow *(Figure 99)*. Perceived room temperatures ranging from 20° C to 22° C still provide thermal comfort if the air velocities indicated in the figure are not exceeded. The three curves each represent the limits of velocities measured over a given period of time for each degree of turbulence. Maximum air movement is necessary for convective heat and molecular transport; this occurs naturally as a result of free convection at a heat source. The upper limit for relative humidity in the air, while maintaining overall comfort, is approximately 70 % to 75 %, with low room temperatures. The lower limit lies between 35 % and 40 %; some short-term deviation to even lower values is acceptable.

98
Range of perceived temperatures (DIN 1946, German code for room ventilation, Part 2)
Prerequisites:
Activity levels I and II
Light to medium clothing
Acceptable during short-term additional cooling loads
Recommended range
Acceptable (e.g. displacement ventilation)

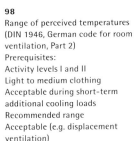

||| Acceptable during short term additional cooling loads
||| Recommended range
||| Acceptable e.g. for displacement ventilation

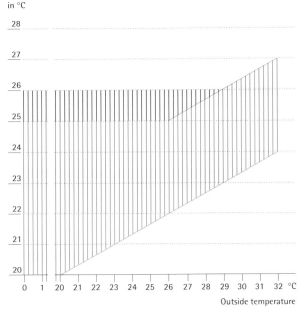

Perceived room temperature in °C

99
Comfortable average air velocities as function of temperature and turbulence quotient in air. Values apply to activity level I and heat-transmission resistance of clothing of approx. 0.12 m² K/W. With higher activity levels and heat transmission resistance, boundary values can be determined (VDI 2083, Form 5).
The 40 % curve applies also to turbulence quotients > 40 %.

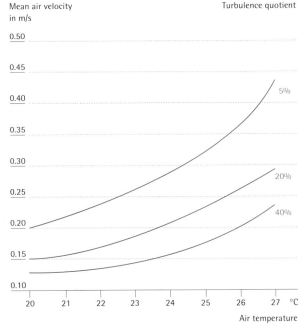

Mean air velocity in m/s

Turbulence quotient

Air temperature

6.2 Hygienic Comfort

The air quality in a room is determined, on the one hand, by the quality of intake air and, on the other hand, by air-contaminating factors such as room usage. Intake air consists mostly of outside air, rarely of recirculated air. Recirculated air should be avoided whenever possible and be used, if at all, only in situations with low levels of pollution or, if necessary, due to thermal loads. Outside air intake should ensure sufficient filtration of pollutants. Natural ventilation can produce this condition if heat loss is kept low in winter and heat gain equally low in summer. *Figure 100* indicates how frequently secondary ventilation and cooling (possibly humidification) are used during standard office hours in Central Europe; *Figure 101* illustrates the necessary CO_2 reduction in occupied rooms for different air change rates and *Figure 102* shows outside air flow rates per person for different acceptable CO_2 concentrations. The carbon dioxide scale (according to Pettenkofer) indicates the rise of exhaled CO_2 in closed rooms and would be of little consequence were not CO_2 content the indicator for impoverished air quality in rooms, as indicated by odours and evaporation. When the CO_2 content rises above 0.1%, the air is qualified as being poor (0.1% = 1.000 ppm). Toxic effects of CO_2 occur when levels exceed 2.5%. In heavily occupied and poorly ventilated rooms, this CO_2 level may be achieved rapidly, ventilation with the highest possible air change rate being the only remedy. Constant air change (approx. 4 ac/h) maintains the CO_2 content in heavily occupied rooms at approximately 0.14%, a level subjectively perceived as poor air quality, but which is, objectively, not dangerous. The outside air flow rates per person indicated in *Figure 102* for different acceptable CO_2 concentrations and different

exothermic heat levels caused by activity, show boundary values, wherein the boundary value 3 (threshold limit value or lower toxic limit) describes the maximum workplace concentration which must not be exceeded under any circumstances. Further air pollution can arise from the processing of organic and inorganic elements such as:

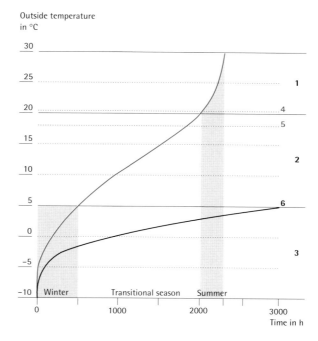

Outside temperature in °C

100
Frequency of secondary ventilation with cooling and humidification, respectively; period of natural ventilation

1 Supplementary ventilation (+cooling)
2 Natural ventilation
3 Supplementary ventilation (+humidification)
4 Daily average 7 a.m. to 7 p.m., office days
5 Daily average 24 hours, office days
6 Daily average, throughout the year

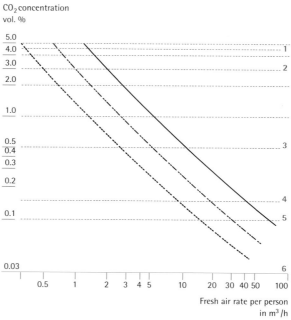

CO_2 concentration vol. %

102
Fresh air rate per person for different permissible CO_2 concentration levels (Reinders)

— Strenuous work, 400 W heat transmission
–– Light work, 200 W heat transmission
···· Sitting, 100 W heat transmission

1 Exhaled air
2 Shelters
3 Industrial MAK-value
4 Maximum for offices
5 Pettenkofer value
6 Fresh/outside air

CO_2 content in %

Air change ac = 0

l=1.0
l=1.0
l=12
l=4.0
l=12

Time in minutes

Fresh air rate per person in m^3/h

101 (far left)
CO_2 content in densely occupied rooms, e.g. classrooms (approx. 1 person / m^2) for different air change rates

- Gases and vapours (CO, CO_2, SO_2, NO_X, O_3, radon, formaldehyde, carbon-hydrogen)
- Odours (e.g. microbial by-products or organic material; human, animal and plant odours; evaporation from building materials and work processes)
- Aerosols (inorganic dust, such as fibres and heavy metals; organic dust, such as carbon-hydrogen compound and pollen)
- Viruses
- Bacteria and spores (legionella, gas-gangrene bacillus)
- Fungi and fungal spores (e.g. germs causing humidifier fever, humidifier lung)

Generally, intake air should have outside air quality, unless, of course, the outside air is polluted. To create hygienic room air conditions, it may suffice to keep windows open or to open them when necessary for intensive air change (when possible without the loss of heat or cooling energy). This air change as a result of natural ventilation or the influx of air via a ventilation system guarantees the filtration and transport of pollutants and odours. A naturally ventilated room, or a ventilation system, is all the more successful in exhausting pollutants the greater the ventilation efficiency:
- Ideal mixed flow: ventilation efficiency ≤ 1
- Intensive natural ventilation through openable window elements: ventilation efficiency approximately 1
- Displacement flow (ventilation from bottom to top): ventilation efficiency > 1.

As a general rule, all sources of contaminant emissions should be avoided in construction with regard to building components, jointing compounds, paints etc. Sources of the worst contaminants are:

- Insulating paints
- Adhesives of all kinds
- Floor coverings
- Suspended ceilings
- Jointing compounds
- Insulating materials
- Pre-fabricated materials
- Wood preservatives
- Raised floors

In addition to these hazardous materials, installation techniques play an important role because materials used for heat and sound insulation have both documented and hidden risks. High concentrations of artificial mineral fibres are mainly the result of inexpert handling. Very real danger exists when fibre particles penetrate ventilation ducts or when building components – for instance, suspended ceilings, lightweight partitions, floating screed – sway from time to time.

6.3 Acoustic Comfort

The expression "acoustic comfort" chosen for this section is an uncommon one that appears neither in technical publications or workplace guidelines, nor is it necessarily included in the curricula of polytechnic institutes or universities. This is due mainly to the fact that the term encompasses more than physical parameters to which we usually refer in the natural sciences. Although acoustic comfort is difficult to qualify, there are at least some cases where acoustic discomfort can be clearly defined. Acoustic discomfort exists, for example, near low-flying airplanes or at extremely loud rock concerts. These conditions are experienced as jarring because they produce a very high noise level; on the other hand, soundless and sound-absorbing rooms are equally uncomfortable acoustically. We usually inhabit rooms that are neither one nor the other extreme, that is to say, rooms that may well be acoustically comfortable. Here are some notes pertaining to definable parameters in the physical sense:

Unpitched sound

Unpitched sound consists of the mechanical oscillations and waves of a medium (in this case, air). When unpitched sound occurs within a frequency range of 16 Hz to 16 kHz, one speaks of audible sound. Like footfall sound (or impact sound), unpitched sound is partially radiated as airborne sound.

Tone

Tone is a pure sinusoidal oscillation of specific strength and frequency; in contrast to tone, noise or that which is perceived as noise, is the result of random and aperiodic oscillations.

Loudness

The loudness in a room is the perception of tones in frequencies recognized by the human ear. The perceived sound is usually expressed in sound pressure levels, that is, the dual pressure created by sound oscillation in addition to frequency.

Sound pressure

Sound pressure is a measuring parameter for loudness.

Sound power level

The sound power level is a parameter of sound energy and is the product of sound pressure, sound velocity and the cross-sectional area vertical to the oscillation direction.

The sound pressure level used for the evaluation of rooms is the SPL (logarithmic ratio between sound pressure and sound power level) in which the numbers brought into relation with each other are sound pressures. The reference sound pressure for all evaluations has been established to be the lowest sound power level perceived by the human ear for a frequency of 1,000 Hertz. This SPL is $2 \cdot 10^{-4}$ microbar. For individual room categories, SPLs are indicated which lie between approximately 25 dB(A) and 65 dB(A), as a rule. SPLs of 25 dB(A), required for studios, concert halls, theatres and opera houses, create absolutely quiet rooms.

Rooms for sedentary activities, such as offices, conference rooms and the like, should have an SPL of approximately 35 dB(A), regardless of room size and number of occupants; these values can be far exceeded for industrial halls. In the latter, physical protection must be provided (headsets, ear plugs etc.). Measurements taken by acoustics experts are of concern since they indicate that more traffic translates into a doubling of noise levels every ten years. Our most sensitive organ is exposed to continuous stress, and this may have serious implications not only on the ear itself, but on the whole organism. The consequences have been documented as stress-related illnesses (concentration problems, sleep disorders etc.). In the information age, undisturbed environments are of paramount importance, and buildings must therefore provide surroundings where sound and noise are not perceived as unpleasant.

6.4   Electromagnetic Compatibility

Electromagnetic compatibility is defined in Europe by a code for the functional capability of electrical appliances and electrical systems; a conformity approval symbol (CE-symbol) identifies appliances that have been approved. The electromagnetic compatibility defines, firstly, the degree of interference the appliance itself is permitted to give off. Secondly, it defines the levels of interference from other appliances or environmental influences that the appliance must be able to handle. The aim here is to avoid interference among several appliances or any impediment to their functions, which is especially important when large data-processing systems are used.

While electromagnetic compatibility refers to appliances, electromagnetic environmental compatibility is used in the context of humans and animals. At issue are possible health hazards as a result of electric, magnetic or electromagnetic fields. Assessment is hampered by the absence of proven scientific data indicating how much humans are influenced by electromagnetic fields. It has been established that high levels are definitely harmful. The current discussions focus on the degree and type of health hazards created by such fields. In relation to electricity, data-processing installations, cable systems etc., three different types of fields are described.

Electrical fields

Electrical fields arise from supply voltage (volt/m). They have a source and a sink and can be shielded by simple means (protection through plants, metal strips etc.).

Magnetic fields

Magnetic fields form when electricity flows through a conduit (ampère/m). In contrast to electrical fields, magnetic fields do not have a source or a sink; rather, they are closed circuits and can therefore not be shielded. Shields simply lead to field distortions or to the dissolution of the field. These measures require complex technical efforts (e.g. thick metal plate covers of soft iron).

Electromagnetic fields

Electromagnetic fields are created by the radiation of electromagnetic waves. Examples are radio reception, television reception via antennae, radio engineering, mobile phones. The health risk potential posed by electromagnetic fields is not yet clearly established; however, recommendations have been formulated, for example, to use mobile phones for only half an hour each day. Mobile phones operate in the microwave range; their transmission performance of approximately 2 W is radiated immediately at the head of the user. Wireless telephones have an effect similar to mobile telephones, but the transmission performance is noticeably smaller and therefore presumably less dangerous. Long-term experience exists only in the area of radiated electromagnetic waves – for example, in the operation of sending stations. There, statistics prove that health hazards exist when people are exposed to electromagnetic waves over a long period of time or, respectively, when electromagnetic waves are very strong.

In the area of electrical and magnetic fields, which occur whenever electric energy is transferred, electrical fields can be viewed as relatively unproblematic based on current knowledge, with the exception of the immediate vicinity of high-voltage lines. Magnetic and electromagnetic fields in buildings occur in areas where high electrical performance is transmitted (transformer stations, low-voltage main distributions, busbars, main supply routes). These fields are indeed a serious concern; the primary concern is, however, how long a person is exposed to these fields. Today, we think twice before locating a workstation or a desk near magnetic fields. Government literature on the subject defines boundary values for this scenario in each country.

Boundary values

Biological effects of low-frequency, electric and magnetic fields are above all assessed by the density of the created structure-borne currents flowing through a specific area. Such impact currents occur naturally. Many organs in the human body exhibit impact current densities of approximately 1 mA/m². In the heart and the brain, they may reach up to 10 mA/m². Acute health risks caused by electric and magnetic fields can be avoided when long-term impact current density is no greater than 2 mA/m². This value lies within the range of natural impact current densities. This value is guaranteed in electric field forces below 5 kV/m and in magnetic flow densities below 100 T for 50 Hertz.

Typical field forces and flow densities for different household appliances are shown in *Table 3*.

The listed boundary values are general recommendations, primarily for households, and are based on recommendations resulting from international tests. The following overview shows how low the boundary value issued by the radiation protection commission was set:

Impact current density
in mA/m²

>1000	Noticeable damage possible Additional heart contractions Ventricular flutter
100 – 1000	Health hazards possible Changes in excitability of central nervous system Stimulation thresholds
10 – 100	Good confirmed effects No health hazard Optical sensory perception Accelerated healing of bones
1 – 10	No confirmed effects No confirmed reports on individual discomfort
2	Boundary value established by radiation protection commission
<1	No confirmed biological effects

Table 3
Max. allowable field strengths/
magnetic flux densities

Electrical fields strengths in buildings in V/m;
readings taken at 30 cm distance from device

Boundary value est. by radiation protection
commission for population at large 5000

Boiler	260
Stereo receiver	180
Iron	120
Fridge	120
Hand mixer	100
Toaster	80
Hairdryer	80
Evaporator	80
Colour TV	60
Coffee-maker	60
Vacuum cleaner	50
Clock (electr.)	30
Fields acting on house from the outside	20
Electr. stove	8
Lamp	5

Representative values of magnetic flux
densities emitted by household appliances at varying distances
measured in microtesla (μT) standard distances are highlighted

	3 cm	30 cm	1 m
Hairdryer	6 – 2000	0.01 – 7	0.01 – 0
Electr. razor	15 – 1500	0.08 – 9	0.01 – 0.3
Can opener	1000 – 2000	**3.50 – 30**	0.07 – 1
Drill	400 – 800	**2 – 3.5**	0.08 – 0.2
Vacuum cleaner	200 – 800	**2 – 20**	0.13 – 2
Mixer	60 – 700	**0.60 – 10**	0.02 – 0.2
Electr. discharge lamp	40 – 400	**0.50 – 2**	0.02 – 0.25
Microwave	73 – 200	**4 – 8**	0.25 – 0.6
Soldering bit	105	0,3	< 0.01
Radio (portable)	16 – 56	1	< 0.01
Stove	1 – 50	**0.15 – 0.5**	0.01 – 0.04
Washer	0.8 – 50	**0.15 – 3**	0.01 – 0.15
Iron	8 – 30	**0.12 – 0.3**	0.01 – 0.03
Dishwasher	3.5 – 20	**0.60 – 3**	0.07 – 0.3
Immersion heater 1 kW	12	0.1	< 0.01
Toaster	7 – 18	**0.06 – 0.7**	< 0.01
Monitor (colour)	5.6 – 10	**0.45 – 1**	< 0.01 – 0.03
Dryer	0.3 – 8	**0.08 – 0.3**	0.02 – 0.06
Kettle 1 kW	5.4	0.08	< 0.01
Computer	0.5 – 3	**< 0.01**	
Fridge	0.5 – 1.7	**0.01 – 0.25**	< 0.01
Clock (AC)	300	2.25	**< 0.01**
Slide projector	240	4.5	**0.15**
Heater	10 – 180	0.15 – 5	**0.01 – 0.25**
Transformer	135 – 150	0.60 – 1.05	**0.24**
Television	2.5 – 50	0.04 – 2	**0.01 – 0.15**
VCR	1.5	< 0.01	

6.5   Visual Comfort

Visual comfort exists when the perceptive faculties in the human brain can operate without any interference. Incorrect distribution of light density in a room, glare, poor colour matching and inappropriate interior design all inhibit perception. On the other hand, when perception is in no way inhibited, the basic senses of the eye, such as vision, speed and contrast sensitivity, are optimized. Optimal working conditions can be achieved by harmonizing the light density conditions in the working environment, starting with the light density conditions at the workstation. A stable perception field for workstations, where vision is especially important, should include contrast sensitivity as a criterion. *(Figures 103.1 and 103.2)*.

Visual comfort also depends on sufficient light in the area of visual focus and the avoidance of glare, be it direct, indirect or daylight glare. The light and temperature of colours in lighting systems for rooms are additional criteria. Lit rooms should also exhibit sufficient shadow effects to enhance the plasticity and three-dimensionality of objects and surfaces. Last, but not least, visual comfort means visual contact from the inside out and from the outside in. This topic is more thoroughly explored in Chapter 11.

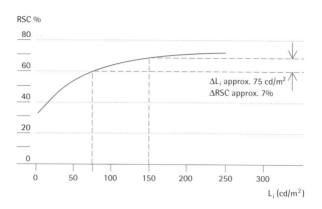

103.1

Contrast sensitivity (RSC in %) dependent on interior field light density (Li in cd/m²)

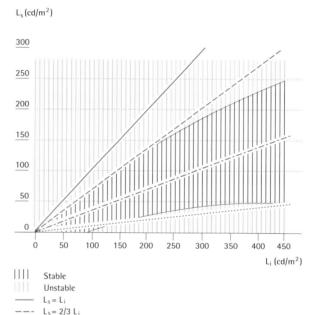

103.2

Stable / unstable field of perception for surrounding light density L_s dependent on the interior field light density L_i

6.6 The Influence of Colours

Dr. Leonhard Oberascher,
Eco-Psych. Salzburg

Colour, as a basic design element, has a strong influence on the impression and behavioural effect of the architectural environment and thus contributes to the psychological and physical well-being of users in a room. We experience colour as a fundamental quality in our visual perception: surface colours – mainly perceived as an inherent quality of the object – are the visible "skin" of the environment. From the overall impression (that is, the composite image of texture and colour), the eye derives the condition, material characteristics and utility of an object (thus a yellow-red fruit signifies ripeness and "usually" readiness for consumption).

Colour and form together determine the overall shape, or gestalt, of an object. Colour is therefore not, as is often assumed, a superficial aspect, but rather a fundamental element in "giving shape". To give shape means to give meaning. Colour therefore not only influences the optical appearance of an object but also its meaning, effect and various uses. The task of design is mainly to create a harmony between the possible colour functions and the intended object functions (or to create a defined relationship between the two). Colour can fulfil the following functions:

- Indicative function
- Symbolic function
- Aesthetic function

In its indicative function, colour clarifies (together with the surface texture) the invitational character, utility and function of an object by indicating its visual validity, condition (e.g. hot or cold), material characteristic (e.g. wood, stone, metal, etc.), purpose and functional structure. Colour thus suggests the real qualities and functions of an object.

In its symbolic function, colour communicates imaginary object qualities. It projects values (e.g. the red of a sports car can communicate speed and power); it can also take on a random symbolic meaning (e.g. the same red in another context can represent socialism, postal services or a red-light district).

In its aesthetic function, colour mainly serves as a decorative element or for formal composition. Since aesthetic behaviour is largely independent of use, the evaluation of colours in this context is less according to their functional use than according to their affectivity and expression. The decisive aspect herein is the formal aesthetic relationships between different colours, as judged by contrast, harmony, field size and distribution.

All three colour functions listed above are important for the relationship between colour effect and a sense of comfort and well-being. Its value is not only determined by the function of the room, but also to a great degree by the relevant needs and preferences of its occupants. Psychological studies have shown, however, that these rarely match the ideas of the designers. A conservatively inclined user will prefer a beige ambience, not because these colours are intrinsically beautiful or because the composition is balanced in an aesthetic sense, but because these colours express the user's deep-seated associations with "comfort", "reliability" and "earthiness".

The complex influence of colour and its use on psychological and physiological well-being cannot be reduced to simple recipes; rather, it can only be usefully evaluated within the framework of an inclusive system: human beings, community environment. A thorough evaluation includes:

- Cultural factors (different colour cultures)
- Milieu factors (group-specific colour preferences and significance)
- Individual disposition and preferences (personal associations with colour)
- Function and meaning of the room (relation to colour function and meaning)
- Colour-form relation (influence upon *Gestalt* effect)
- Colour-material relation (influence upon material impression)
- Factors given by and in the surrounding environment (relation of the colour to the landscape, urban surroundings, historic and stylistic reference).

Colour and physical well-being

There is a common opinion that colour has immediate physical impact on the human organism. Two concrete questions are addressed here:

The colour-excitation hypothesis

Does colour influence the overall physiological condition of humans? Are warm colours (red, orange, yellow) stimulating, and cold colours (blue, turquoise, green) calming? Are we more stimulated by intensive (strongly hued) colours than by subtle colours?

Küller and Mikelides point out that the results of studies carried out over the past 50 years give few answers to these questions because they looked mostly at the effect of coloured light or of isolated colour areas, but not at actual rooms. The physiological effect of the entire visual environment was first studied by Küller (1976, 1986) in two rooms with different degrees of visual complexity. One room was designed in different colours and patterns, while the other room was uniformly grey. The test candidates who spent three hours in each room were observed using an EKG and heart rate. The results showed that the colours and patterns of the first room clearly stimulated brain activity, that is, they produced a measurable physiological state of excitation, while at the same time lowering the heart rate, which was assumed to be a compensatory autonomous-nervous reaction to a high degree of stimulation. These findings were further supported by verbal statements made by the test candidates about a sensory overload in the first room. It took up to three hours after the text before a feeling of relative control was achieved. Mikelides (1989) compared the effect of two rooms uniformly painted in red and blue, respectively. The assumption that red is cortically more stimulating than blue was confirmed in EKG readings. Küller and Mikelides conclude from the impact on heart rate and brain activity that colour and complexity of visual environment have a far greater influence on humans than had been previously assumed. This supports the approach of using colour in design as a means of achieving some control over the general excitability of humans (Küller, 1991). However, it would hardly be possible or desirable to use colour as a form of compensation for boring and monotonous tasks. Instead, such use of colour would create additional stress, evidenced by the paradoxical decrease in heart rate.

In conclusion, we can state that intense colours, independent of hue, as well as high visual complexity (e.g. through pronounced colour contrasts) are in general physiologically stimulating, while subdued colours, such as grey, display the opposite effect. A comparison of different hues with the same intensity shows that red activates much more strongly than blue.

The hue-warmth hypothesis

In general, hues between yellow and red are associated with 'warmth' and those in the blue to green range with "cold". Can we derive from this that the colours in a room influence our climatic well-being? Does a red room, for example, require less heating for our comfort than a blue room?

Küller and Mikelides note that a general relationship between room colours and climatic well-being could not be confirmed in experiments. According to Mikelides (1989), temperature estimates in a red room and in a blue room are equally close to the actual temperatures. While the ideas of warm and cold colours influence our assessment of interior spaces, they seem to have no impact on actual thermal comfort. Nevertheless, the characteristics associated with room colours do influence our psychological well-being. It is quite plausible, for example, that we perceive opti-

cally "cold" rooms as repellent and unfriendly, while "warm" rooms appear cosy and friendly.

Colour and psychological well-being

In addition to collective and individual colour associations and the resulting psychological impact in a room, there are a number of other factors which are important in the context of colour and psychological well-being:

Colour – an aid for order and orientation

Colour generally facilitates a better "readability" of the visual environment by imprinting it with a visible structure: the eye automatically integrates surfaces and areas of the same colour and differentiates areas of contrasting colours. Pronounced contrasts in brightness, hue or saturation create enhancement or isolation; related colours create homogeneity and integration. Colour as a room-structuring element is principally a means of creating lucidity, safety, orientation and order as well as helping to represent specific room functions and action processes. Visual lucidity, order and comprehensibility promote a feeling of spatial control and are hence an important contribution to well-being.

Colour – a territorial marking and status symbol

Colour identification can visually indicate territorial claims, hierarchical structures and status. Waiving the use of such symbols appears to have a negative effect on the sense of insecurity.

Colour – an aid for identification

In the role of conspicuous identification common to all corporate design, colour can be an essential contribution to the creation of a "visual" identity, or "branding". The high recognizability of colour instils confidence and boosts well-being.

Colour – a symbol of lifestyle

Next to the colours of clothing and cars, home fur-

nishing and interior decorating colours are important indicators and expressive means of personal lifestyle. Together with material and surface-texture characteristics, colour communicates specific societal value. Positive effects on the psychological well-being of room occupants are more likely when the colour scale reflects personal value perceptions and aesthetic preferences and lies within the acceptable range of group-specific value and style orientation.

Colour – an expression of trend orientation

Variety and change are a basic human need. Trend colours are the result of a collective desire for colour change. They are a symbolic expression of the predominant orientation in taste, and their main purpose is to demonstrate that one belongs to an idealized group (usually promoted in the media), which represents the zeitgeist. The change in collective colour preferences underlines that the relationship between colour and psychological well-being is not static but rather one that must be evaluated in the context of the era and the culture.

Generalized recommendations for the use of colour can only be conditional. Basically, one should take care that the room or object functions communicated with the choice of colour support the intended room or object functions or at least avoid being in conflict with them (e.g. if orientation and safety are an important concern, the aesthetic function of colour may have to be secondary to this primary function). With regard to the physiological impact of colour, the range of colours chosen should reflect the occupants and their activities. (The use of pronounced colour contrasts and highly stimulating hues can be assumed to be counterproductive to the well-being of the users of an operating theatre, or anyone under stress.) Furthermore, cultural, group-specific and individual preferences should be considered as much as possible in the choice of colours.

Another indicator for the formulation of general colour design recommendations is found in concepts developed in the field of environmental psychology which seek to explain aesthetic environment preferences. Kaplan & Kaplan postulate an accepted evolutionary need for meaning and order. The need for familiarity and the desire for innovation complement one another. Preference for a specific environment situation depends on the following dimensions:
– Coherence (degree of cognitive organization of a scene)
– Readability (degree of categorical distinctness of the elements present in the environment)
– Complexity (number and variety of these elements)
– Mysteriousness (degree to which the scene promises the discovery of additional information to the viewer)

Laboratory exercises concerning "Experimental Color Design", conducted by the Space Laboratory at the Technical University of Vienna (under the direction of Dr. L. Oberascher), open up far-reaching confrontation with the phenomenon "Colour" in the context of architectural design. Practical work and experimenation are held in a relationship of 1:1. The methodology allows for the aesthetic and psychological effects of color, as they are experienced in reality, to be analyzed experimentally and to be guaged with a large degree of reliability.

Based on this, the following general recommendation can be formulated: a use of colour in design that is oriented to human needs should principally aim to achieve a balanced relationship between stimulation and reassurance, order and variety, relatedness and contrast. Colour should, on the one hand, integrate, order and explain and, on the other hand, it should offer another means of active interaction with the architectural environment.

7 In the Environment or with the Environment: Contextual Building

Information age buildings will be adaptable to changing spatial needs, organizational structures and production processes involving technical expansion. In other words, the ideal and "quasi-intelligent" buildings of the future will "breathe" and will have modifiable room dimensions. Furthermore, the ideal office and production building will have an exterior surface and building structure designed to harness the environmental resources of each season (sun, light, wind, rain, etc.) with minimal need for secondary and external energy to operate the building. The future office will have a room depth of approximately 15 metres, accommodating all basic structures for office organization in a reversible space module.

Future buildings, particularly office buildings, will not only be designed and constructed in accordance with floor-plan efficiency and economic viability, but above all with ecological compatibility and resource economy in mind. In the architectural design of a building, exterior surfaces and structural components such as thermal storage will therefore play an essential role, as will the secondary technical services (heating, cooling, ventilation, electricity, information supply etc.). *Table 4* summarizes the basic principles and planning measures for ecological building that should be applied to all projects, while *Figure 104* outlines principles pertinent specifically to buildings for the information age. The following examples illustrate how such principles can be translated into contemporary solutions and to what degree this kind of architecture is already harnessing natural resources.

Principles	Measures			Table 4
	Buildings	Open spaces	Supply and disposal	Principles and Measures of Ecological Planning
Adaptation to natural and social factors at site	Integration into eco-system depending on sun and wind	Minimal sealing	Proximity to home, services and culture	
	Zoning of ground plans	Few topographical changes Maintain existing vegetation Compact buildings	Reduced personal traffic Link to public transportation	
	Minimum area consumption		Link to low-emission energy carriers	
Energy savings	Passive use of solar energy	Harnessing climate-regulating effects of vegetation and water surfaces	Create closed cycles when possible	
	Heat conservation Heat recovery Winter gardens + solar energy use		Waste – raw material Rainwater Grey- and cooling water	
			Waste heat – energy	
Protecting resources and raw materials	Using environmentally friendly materials Avoiding toxicity	Create green belt Integrate parking into green area	Substitute potable water	
			Avoid waste	
	Low-energy production and processing		Heat-power coupling	
			Minimize emissions	
Create high-quality and humane interior and exterior	Influence micro-climate with building surface	Enrich green area with plants and trees compatible with location	Utilize surfacewater (Rainwater)	
	Planted façades and roofs	Create "relaxation" areas	Compost organic waste to improve soil	
	Sun protection Interior design Ergonomic workplace design	Stimulating environment		

Variable heat protection / sun protection

1 Open
  U = > 2.0
2 Partially closed
  U = > 2.0
3 Fully closed
  U = < 1.4

Wind / light indirect

Solar energy / light / wind direct

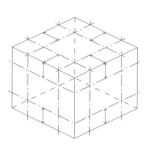

104
"The Intelligent House"
The information age building "breathes"; it adapts to changing spatial needs, organizational structure and technical expansion. It has an exterior surface and building structure designed to harness environmental resources. The building consumes fewer resources and utilizes the local supply of raw materials.

7.1 Building in Green Spaces

Administration Building in a Park:
German Federal Foundation for the Environment, Osnabrück

The unusual shape of this building, designed by E. Schneider-Wessling, Cologne, developed in response to the site: a park-like setting surrounded by two three-storey villas. The shape also expresses an energy-conscious approach to architecture and is, therefore, an outward manifestation of the Foundation's mandate.

105.1
German Federal Foundation for the Environment, Osnabrück,
site plan, architect:
Erich Schneider-Wessling

The glass building fits seamlessly into the park. It follows the contours of the trees, encircling the imposing 160-year-old beeches. This design not only accentuates the trees but also successfully converts an open space into a sheltered courtyard *(Figure 105.1)*. The façade, a fully glazed wood and aluminium construction, is complemented by a grid which functions as a trellis for plants in the summer, providing shade. Additional glass panels can be used to transform the grid into winter gardens, which then act as buffers in the sense of creating a double-skin façade *(Figure 105.2)*.

The radial arrangement creates rooms in dynamically narrowing and widening suites with ideal floor plans for flexible office organization. "Sun catchers" above the centre of each ring allow natural light to penetrate deeply into the building. There is little need for artificial light *(Figure 105.3)*. The lobby, staircase and secondary rooms are placed along the north side; short communication paths reduce traffic inside the building, create compactness and offer a high degree of flexibility *(Figure 105.4)*.

The circular design creates a compact building with an excellent relationship between exterior skin and volume. The planners dispensed with an underground garage or basement to preserve the old existing tree growth. The fully glazed façade features high-insulation windows (triple-glazed, argon-filled; U-value 0.8 U W/m² K). Natural, user-controlled ventilation ensures hygienic air conditions. The exterior façade and the "light towers" guarantee excellent natural lighting with a minimum illuminance of 300 Lux during 80 % of office hours.

105.2
The glass building is integrated in the park, framing a stand of 160-year-old trees.

105.3
The "sun catchers" light the interior.

105.4
Extended to the inside, the gratings cover a perimeter service duct that facilitates flexible room partitioning.

Solar collectors for warm-water generation are installed on the roof; a photovoltaic system to generate electricity can be retrofitted at any time. These systems help reduce the primary energy requirement. From the start, the project was geared towards low-waste construction with recyclable materials, including recycled concrete in the structural walls, foam glass insulation below the floor and in the roof, Isofloc insulation from recycled paper in the dividing walls and biodegradable natural fibre carpets as well as floor coverings made from recycled material. Natural paints were used throughout for finishing.

Approach to Urban Planning: "Buildings in Fields", Bergwachtstrasse, Munich

Developed for an open competition by the architectural team HouseLab together with architects Paul Schlossbauer, Klaus K. Loehnert and Irene Burkhardt, this project was awarded first prize in 1995.

The original character of the agrarian landscape, defined in parcels and access lanes and resulting in long gently curving fields, is still visible alongside the built-up community. The fields have been incorporated into the urban development rather than being swallowed up by the architecture erected on them. The designers made every effort to overcome the polarization of city and nature *(Figures 106.1 to 106.3)*.

The project model seeks above all to create a contemporary urban texture, reinterpreting familiar local structures and attempting to understand their basic forms. In this way, the field pattern became the foundation for urban planning. The outcome is an economical and extremely flexible structure open to future developments.

The design is intended more as a method than a permanent form. The narrow, east-west oriented "fields for building" and "fields for planting" alternate in defined sequences, forming rows. That is, the rows are alternately assigned to vegetation or to architecture. Nature and architecture are thus given more or less equal weight, complementing one another. The linear structure shown in *Figure 106.3* faces south, allowing for open corridors through which air can circulate. Good ventilation is guaranteed in this design, which takes advantage of the westerly and south-westerly winds predominant in the region, while natural cooling is provided by moist vegetation and trees near buildings.

106.2
"The relationship between urban space and nature", site plan

106.3
Masterplan for "Buildings in Fields"

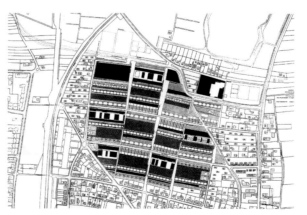

106.1
"Fields for building",
Morphology of the location
architects: HouseLab,
Klaus K. Loehnert,
Paul Schlossbauer

This urban model – an interplay of house types and free forms – creates a social topography for specific locales whose full spectrum from privacy to public openness delivers the framework for burgeoning communal living. The parallel rows of built-up and open spaces create two contrasting views: in the north-south direction, the planted areas overlap and merge to form lively colourful images; in the east-west direction, planted areas protectively frame the separate rows *(Figures 106.5)*. The northernmost of these thematically aligned spaces symbolizes contemplation and emphasizes the beauty of "designed" nature. The centre row with flower meadows creates space and openness for play and recreation, while the end row is dedicated to gardening, culminating in the adjacent nursery, orchards and more intensely private gardens. Seasonal changes in the landscape were a further influence on the design.

Longer rows of houses occupy the "fields for building", spanning the distance between sidewalks and cycle paths *(Figures 106.5)*. The two- to three-storey

homes are characterized by a deliberately simple, very basic building structure. The partial wood construction allows for pre-fabrication and reduces construction time. None of the models have predetermined front or rear sides. Within each unit as well, the living space can be freely assigned owing to utilization-neutral floor plans. Furthermore, all models benefit from proximity to public green spaces as well as the privacy enjoyed in gardens, on balconies, and in courtyards, winter gardens and atria.

106.4
Membrane houses in park setting (Photomontage)

106.5
Spatial sequence for building in fields

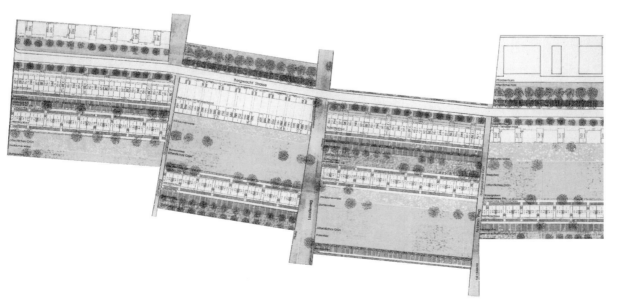

- Public green area
- Common green area
- Private gardens
- Street area
- Public space
- Parking area
- Private lane
- Green belt
- Tennant gardens
- Meadow

Ecological Housing Complex:
Housing Complex Waldquelle, Bielefeld

This project by architect Hans Friedrich Bültmann, previously documented in *Faktor 4* by Ernst Ulrich von Weizsäcker, Armory B. Lovins and L. Hunter Lovins, is an excellent example of contextual building in a green environment:
Between 1993 and 1996 an open, growing housing complex was realized on a plot approximately 53,000 m² in size. The complex integrates offices and professions that are compatible with a residential area. There are nearly 100 apartments; some are private apartments while others are rental units. Initially, the city awarded a contract to create a building scheme as a generic ecological plan. Once the ecological outline had been established, and prior to the building phase, the Ecological Building Group Waldquelle (EBG) was founded. Some three years of teamwork by the architect and the inhabitants ultimately led to what we see today as a built town *(Figure 107)*.
The current and future inhabitants of the complex are shareholders of the EBG and represent a wide social and cross-generational spectrum ranging from student to single mother to independent entrepreneur. The EBG Waldquelle formulated, by collective and democratic consensus, the concrete, legal and financial bases for the purchase of the property and for construction, as follows:

Urban development, structure and neighbourhood sociology
- Integration of residential area into urban space
- Planning and development in consultation with inhabitants
- Back-fill and demarcation
- Building on the neighbourhood boundary and density
- Integration into existing network of paths
- Ensuring quiet by avoiding through traffic

- Integrating the typical characteristics of the exterior space
- Linking and interpenetration of existing and planned green systems
- Limited private roads to minimize sealed surfaces
- Open village structure (no fences or borders)
- Living, working and recreation at one location
- Enlivening the neighbourhood with residential models for all age groups
- Sociological and societal blending as people of different lifestyles live side by side
- Integration of workplaces (trades, crafts, art, services)
- "Demobility", that is, avoiding the use of personal vehicles
- Self-sufficient neighbourhood, a stable structure

107
"Waldquelle" ecological housing complex
Architect: H. F. Bültmann

The following ecological approaches and characteristics played an essential role in the development of the project:

Water supply and disposal
The goal was to achieve a closed, natural water cycle on site, low consumption of water as a raw material and minimal pollution or any other toxic stress on water. Surface sealing was avoided whenever possible.

Potable water supply
The neighbourhood has its own central water supply from wells in the north section of the property. Ground water is used exclusively for cooking, hygiene and laundry (requirement: approx. 140 litres/person/day).

Surface water
Surface water is allowed to seep into the ground on site; the sandy ground makes this feasible. Run-off from roofs can be collected by each household for watering plants and gardens. The group decided not to install a water system. Washing machines and dishwashers are mostly supplied with water from the warm-water system (potable water quality).

Sanitary waste water
All buildings are outfitted with composting toilets (e.g. Terra Nova). Human waste is composted together with kitchen and garden waste in a specially ventilated container in the basement. There is no need for flushing with water. The compost is used in the gardens; there is no unpleasant odour.

Natural sewage treatment plant
Grey water is processed in a natural treatment plant (vertical, intermittently fed, reed treatment plant) located on the south side of the property. The treated water can seep into the ground on site; the water cycle is closed.

Energy supply
The association of owners and tenants aimed for minimal consumption of electricity and heating energy. An integrated concept for energy production and supply envisions the use of conventional energy carriers such as gas as well as regenerating energy sources. This concept is intended radically to lower the total energy requirements of the neighbourhood. In this way, CO_2 emissions will actually be cut in half (CO_2 emission approx. 1.3 tonnes/person/year). By using gas stoves, warm-water dishwashers and washing machines as well as energy-efficient lamps, electricity consumption is significantly reduced.

To generate energy, a small combined heat and power station has been installed, which guarantees high energy efficiency (approx. 90 %) through power-heat coupling. This power station supplies both electricity and energy for heating and is operated and with town gas. During low heat requirement periods, the C.H.P station is switched off and the total electric energy requirements are supplied by the city network. The use of solar and wind energy can be retrofitted in the medium term, while in the long term (10 to 20 years) the aim is to supply energy from hydrogen installations. In addition to the thermal energy supplied by the C.H.P. station, a peak-load boiler is also available.

Building materials
The parameters for the building materials were driven by ecological demands and the principles of resource-efficient building. Pollutants in manufacture and installation were rigorously avoided. The thermal transmittance quotients for the reduction of thermal energy requirements were:

– Exterior walls $\quad$ U-value = 0.4 $\quad$ W/m^{2}K
– Windows $\quad$ U-value = 1.5 $\quad$ W/m^{2}K
– Roofs, ceilings $\quad$ U-value = 0.2 $\quad$ W/m^{2}K
– Basement ceilings $\quad$ U-value = 0.35 W/m^{2}K

All opportunities for using natural insulating materials were explored and fully implemented. Concrete, metal, plastics and fibre cement panels were avoided as wall materials. Another aim was and is the avoidance of not only aluminium and PVC, but also polystyrene.

Traffic

With regard to traffic, the following measures were introduced and executed:

- Gradual reduction in the number of individual cars through car-sharing, car-pooling and other communal use
- Promoting alternatives to transportation by car by improving local public transportation
- Prevention of unnecessary transport through collective shopping and shopping within walking distance

Waste

The concept of handling waste includes limiting waste in the first place, and, of course, waste disposal. Limiting the amount of waste created can be an individual as well as a communal effort. Disposal of sewage begins with the compost toilets, complemented by the now-standard recycling of paper, glass, plastics, etc.

All three examples demonstrate that we are already capable of achieving much in building in an ecologically sustainable manner, depending on circumstance and task. Contextual building also means that the focus needs to be re-established for each case.

7.2   Building with Wind

The interest in wind energy for ventilating buildings and urban areas has been revived in response to growing demands for energy conservation and the harnessing of local natural resources whenever possible. In the spirit of the current debate on returning to fully or partially wind-powered ships, planners will be encouraged to consider wind as a source of energy in the planning of buildings. Working with natural air streams is, however, not only a question of reducing energy requirements in building operation, but often a question of thermal and hygienic comfort as well (see chapters 6.1 and 6.2.)

Low or extremely tall buildings, buildings with low or extreme depth, can usually be naturally ventilated by using outside air flow. Natural ventilation requires a driving power capable of moving air through a building either by pressure or by suction. Pressure differentials at the built envelope (steady-state and turbulence-induced fluctuating differentials), caused by wind and thermals, are the chief means for meeting this need. Several manufacturers offer complex façade systems which create these conditions, partially or completely, with special constructions.

Building with wind is not a subject for standardized design solutions; it must instead be addressed at the earliest stage in each new project and be integrated into the planning process. Design factors and building location result in vastly different air flow conditions. Layout must take into account not only aerodynamics but also acoustics, fire safety regulations and emissions. In recent years, advances in computer technology allow the simulation of internal air movement on the basis of known boundary condi-

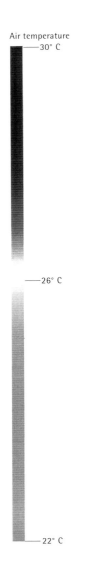

Air temperature
—30° C

—26° C

—22° C

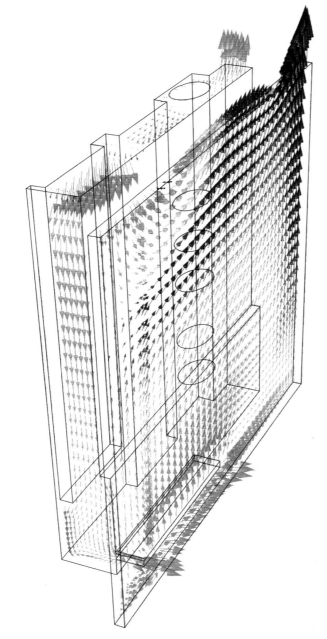

108
Computer simulation
Air flow in the double façade of a
12-storey building

tions *(Figure 108)*. This method is not applicable to air movement on façades (e.g. double-leaf) where pressure differentials caused by natural wind at openings and joints are the decisive factors. The flow action is also greatly influenced by the surface and texture of the surrounding terrain and the structure of the built environment. Neighbouring buildings can completely alter the pressure, velocity and turbulence fields near a building.

Similar to the nature of problems encountered in weather forecasting, geometric details such as parapets, roof overhangs and roof pitch, as well as small differences in wind direction, can significantly change the course of air flow on a façade. Currently, there are no economically viable calculation procedures for accurate and detailed prediction of the velocity field, the pressure field and the transport of contaminants near buildings.

At the outset, several factors must be analyzed and their effects considered to reliably predict the use and effects of wind in construction:

– Wind comfort and ventilation efficiency
Analyses of turbulent air movement in pedestrian areas of cities; air flow into buildings

– Static wind-load stress
Forces released by the effects of wind; these forces elicit some torsion but little or negligible motion from a built structure

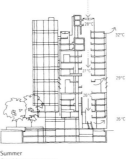

Summer
Outside temperatures

Section of
Spiegel high-rise
Arch.: Prof. Friedrich

– Dynamic wind-load stress
Eddies present at built structure – aperiodic, random pressure variations

– Recirculation turbulence
Separation of air flow from building; eddy formation with characteristic frequencies

– Wind-load stress on façade components
Wind forces acting upon façade components on the wind and the leeward side of a building

– Atmospheric boundary layer
Representation of actual wind velocities at different heights

The following are examples of the different options for handling the effects of wind.

Skyscraper
The urban core of Frankfurt, already dominated by skyscrapers, will soon see its skyline expanded yet further. Two basic questions arise in connection with the new project:
1. What impact will it have on comfort in the pedestrian areas, especially in terms of the frequency of gusts and the development of pockets sheltered from wind, or conversely, pockets with strong air movement?
2. How effective is urban ventilation of exhaust fumes in low wind areas?
The answers are determined by analysing wind conditions in the built environment. The basic factors are:
- Regional wind system
- Wind statistics
- Wind in urban corridors (caused by urban heat "pockets")
- Formation of inversions
- Wind flow patterns in the urban core

Figure 109 shows the flow of cold air from the Taunus Mountains across the Nidda Valley towards the city. The wind statistics in *Figure 110* illustrate the seasonal variation in distribution of wind frequency and direction in downtown Frankfurt am Main. The relative parameters are measured, recorded and to some degree visually displayed in a wind tunnel study.

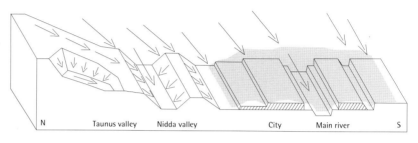

109
Cold air flowing into the city of Frankfurt as a result of the local wind system (source: Georgii)

⟶ Downward current
⟶ Descending valley breeze
⟶ Local wind system
▭ Blanket of smog

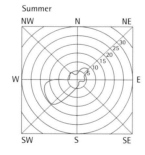

Spring

Summer

Fall

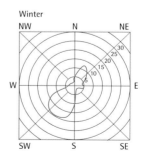

Winter

110
Seasonal variation in frequency distribution of wind direction in downtown Frankfurt am Main (in %)
(source: Wachter)

111
Model of building and
surrounding built environment,
design stage

Figure 111 shows the model of the planned building and the projected conditions in the surrounding built environment. In wind tunnel studies, a turbulence intensity profile is established to study the parameters of the site. The localization and visualization, as well as the quantification of ground wind field, are tested by a sand erosion method. A uniformly deep layer of sand is used to demonstrate how the sand gradually erodes when wind velocities increase and to predict where erosion will take place. *Figures 112.1 to 112.6* show the increasing erosion resulting from an increase in wind velocity.

In addition to these preliminary studies, exact pressure measurements are often taken on building models to determine accurate parameters for simulation calculations based on pressure coefficients for different wind velocities and wind directions. The wind-load stress on façade components (open or closed façades, opaque or transparent) can be evaluated in relevant wind tunnel studies. For this purpose, larger models or computer simulation are often chosen. When studying large models and very deep buildings, the air movements are often made visible with smoke. By this means, designers gain not only insight into the actual conditions, but are also able to pinpoint areas near a building where critical situations may arise.

Multi-Purpose Hall

In response to a competition for a convention and exhibition hall, Schulitz + Partner interpreted the competition theme "Man – Nature – Technology" as a clear mandate to design a building that would meet the following criteria:

- Positive evaluation of ecological building materials
- Minimal material consumption for resource efficiency
- Use of regenerative energy carriers
- Optimal use of daylight
- Minimal artificial ventilation and cooling and optimal natural ventilation

The architectural concept reflects the diversity of the site. The building faces north, opening onto a tree-lined boulevard; to the west and east, the site is bordered by an access road and another convention hall, while the south side forms the boundary between the fairgrounds and a service-building block. The moderate height of this block acts as a transition to the adjacent residential area.

Supporting framework

The trussless covering of the hall (spanning 105 x 240 m) and resource efficiency were achieved primarily by minimizing the use of material. *(See also Section 8.2.)*

112
Example of enlarged eroded areas
due to progressive increase in flow
velocity, wind tunnel study
The wind velocities were raised to
the following values at 2-minute
intervals:
Projection 1   2.45 m/s
Projection 2   2.88 m/s
Projection 3   3.37 m/s
Projection 4   4.01 m/s
Projection 5   4.89 m/s
Projection 6   6.22 m/s

Natural lighting

The generous openings in the roof near the arched girders guarantee optimal daylight with low heat loss. Regularly placed bands of skylights along the length of the hall create an even, wave-like daylight quotient curve. The average value of the quotient is higher than 17 %, while direct heat gain is reduced with solar protection glass. The orientation of the main façade to the north provides optimal daylight penetration when sun radiation is low (diffuse light); additional glare protection measures are not required. The south façade has a smaller glass surface ratio and is fitted with external shading in the form of adjustable, rotating horizontal louvres. The west façade provides passive, natural shading with the help of a planted trellis connected to the cantilevered components of the external supporting framework. In winter, this same façade is used for passive solar heat gain. The east façade is largely shaded by the adjacent hall and does not require planting for shade.

Natural ventilation

In Hannover, wind velocities average 3 to 3.5 m/sec. *Figures 113* and *114.1* to *114.3* indicate wind direction frequencies with velocities below 5.4 m/sec and the frequencies of average wind velocities and average temperatures for three seasons. The highest wind velocities occur when temperatures are approx. 15° C; therefore, during transitional periods and in summer,

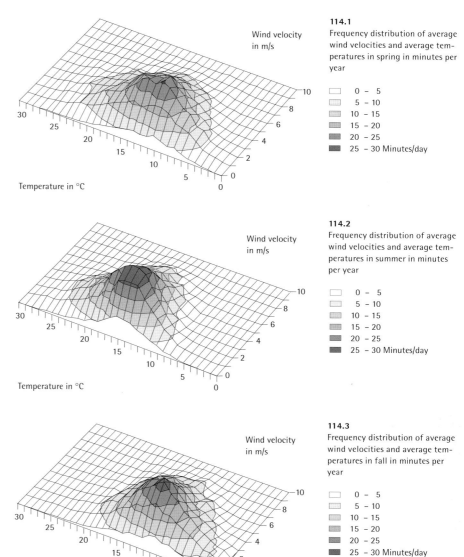

114.1
Frequency distribution of average wind velocities and average temperatures in spring in minutes per year

- 0 – 5
- 5 – 10
- 10 – 15
- 15 – 20
- 20 – 25
- 25 – 30 Minutes/day

114.2
Frequency distribution of average wind velocities and average temperatures in summer in minutes per year

- 0 – 5
- 5 – 10
- 10 – 15
- 15 – 20
- 20 – 25
- 25 – 30 Minutes/day

114.3
Frequency distribution of average wind velocities and average temperatures in fall in minutes per year

- 0 – 5
- 5 – 10
- 10 – 15
- 15 – 20
- 20 – 25
- 25 – 30 Minutes/day

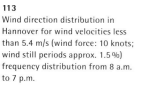
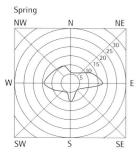
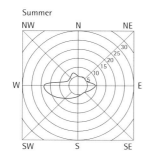

113
Wind direction distribution in Hannover for wind velocities less than 5.4 m/s (wind force: 10 knots; wind still periods approx. 1.5 %) frequency distribution from 8 a.m. to 7 p.m.

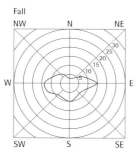

temperatures are best suited for directly ventilating the large hall space. The structure and orientation of the building *(Figure 115)* are designed for long-term natural ventilation, especially during set-up and strike periods (before and after events), during idle periods and to some degree when the hall is fully used *(Figure 116.1)*.

The arched roof takes advantage of thermals and serves to ventilate hot air in summer owing to the formation of strong negative pressures on the surface. To guarantee natural ventilation even with the glare or shade protection in place, vents have been installed on the closed sections of the roof. These vents are combined ventilation and smoke exhaust openings. Natural ventilation occurs through these openings in combination with the openable vertical glass surfaces in the façades. A detailed wind tunnel study established that by opening the roof vents according to wind direction and velocity, together with the openable windows in the vertical glass surfaces, fresh air can freely circulate through the entire hall *(Figures 116.2* and *116.3)*.

115
North-west elevation of multi-purpose hall
Arch.: Professor Schulitz + Partner

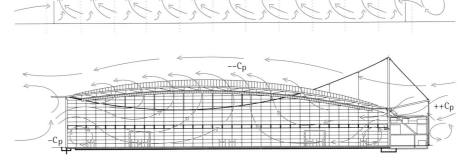

116.1
Flow conditions on building
Oncoming wind from
east-north-east

116.2
Flow conditions in the hall
Oncoming wind from
east and west

116.3
Flow conditions in the hall
Oncoming wind from south

++Cp strongly positive pressure
gradient
- Cp slightly negative pressure
gradient
--Cp strongly negative pressure
gradient

Table 5 shows the operability of the hall depending on daytime and season; set-up and strike phases constitute the majority of operation time.
A comparison between this example and Fairhall 26 illustrates how similar prerequisites and requirements can lead to very different architectural solutions.

Table 5 Types of operation dependent on time of operation and season	Time of operation	During trade fairs	Other events	Set-up and strike phases	Hall closed
	I **Winter** < +5°C	Mechanical ventilation	Mechanical ventilation	Ventilation and heating with circulating or ambient air	Ventilation and heating with circulating or ambient air until readings fall short of boundary value
		Outside air cooling	Outside air cooling		
		Façade shield air Heat from central mains supply GAS/WW	Façade shields air Heat from central mains supply GAS/WW		
		Air volume up to 760 000 m³/h	Air volume depending on event up to 760 000 m³/h	Air volume approx. 300 000 m³/h	
	II **Transitional season** + 5°C to + 22°C	Ventilation, in part natural with some mechanical	Ventilation in part natural with propulsion jet with some mechanical	Ventilation in part natural, supplemented by ambient air for heating	
		Ventilation as supplement	Ventilation as supplement		
		Outside air cooling Heat from central mains supply GAS/WW	Outside air cooling Heat from central mains supply GAS/WW		
		Air volume varies	Air volume varies	Air volume varies	
	III **Summer** > + 22°C	Mechanical ventilation	Mechanical ventilation	Natural ventilation Low winds supplemented with thermals	Natural ventilation as needed
		Cooling from central mains supply	Cooling from central mains supply		
		Air volume up to 760 000 m³/h	Air volume up to 760 000 m³/h		

Fairhall 26, Hannover

Thomas Herzog + Partner employed a three-part design *(see Figures 117)* for Fairhall 26. In its original version, the building was to be lit exclusively from above by means of a roof glazed in insulating glass, supported by an integrated lighting grid to ensure even lighting throughout the hall. Time pressures led to a design with reduced openings. Instead, the suspended roof was almost completely covered by tension bands and wood panels. The concept of natural and mechanical ventilation for the hall, as well as natural lighting, is shown in *Figures 118* and *119*. Despite cost restraints, the architect and his planners succeeded in designing an outstanding example of architecture and engineering – a completely new type of hall was created.

Wing Tower

English architect Richard Horden (TU Munich/London) proposes an even more complex approach to finding new solutions for building with wind. Here is his commentary:

"The large buildings of recent years, such as huge congress centres, skyscrapers, large sport stadiums, etc. create a curious circumstance where the weight per square metre of a building may be only slightly less than the wind pressure present during a wind storm of medium force. And there are even more extreme examples such as the geodesic dome created by Buckminster Fuller or the shell structures designed by Nervi, Frey-Otto and others, with area weight distributions of 0.5-0.2 kN/m². By comparison, the wind pressure in an average storm is approximately 1 kN/m². Textiles began to be used more frequently in architecture in the seventies and eighties.

117
Hall 26, German Fair AG, Hannover
Arch.: Herzog + Partner

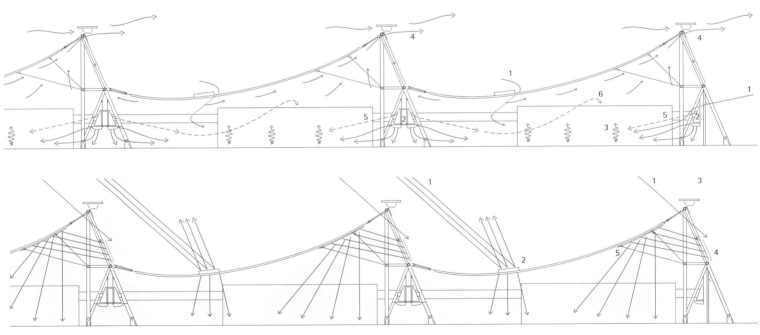

118 (top)
Principle of natural and mechanical ventilation of hall

Cooling:
1 Natural intake air through façade louvres
2 Glass air tunnel with displacement vents on bottom side for cooled air
3 Thermal lift from internal heat sources
4 Natural ventilation through roof openings

Heating:
5 Mechanical distribution of heated intake air through wide-angle nozzles
6 Outgoing air ventilated through lateral ventilation

119 (bottom)
Principle of daylighting

1 Direct sunlight
2 Insulating glazing with light grid, reflected sunlight
3 Diffuse daylight
4 Deflection slats for redirecting daylight
5 Mirrored ceiling

Aerodynamics is now an important factor in the calculations carried out for contemporary structures."
Until recently, architects tended to view wind as a force acting upon, not with, the building. Because modern buildings can and should be lighter to achieve resource efficiency, the classic function of architecture to protect against the forces of nature is gradually changing into an approach where nature is actively harnessed for the operation of buildings. Roofs will no longer cower beneath a threatening sky, but open towards it, welcoming energy in the form of wind, water and sun. In 1995, 1.3 billion people travelled by plane. This is approximately one-fifth of the world's population. The aeroplane is now seen as one of the safest means of transportation, and it is based on a technology built on the principles of aerodynamics.
With the Millennium Tower project in Glasgow *(Figure 120.1)*, Richard Horden translated the active use of wind power in architecture from theory into practice. The 100-metre high panoramic tower houses a restaurant with exhibition rooms at the base and a cockpit for 30 persons at the peak. The dead-load weight of the aluminium tower modelled on a wing cross-section is a mere 200 tonnes and rotates on an oil film. The tower revolves non-stop in the primary wind direction, reducing its aerodynamic resistance *(Figure 120.2)* by rotating at an angle to the wind. An anemometer and a weather satellite monitor local and distant wind conditions to calculate the optimal rotational angle of the tower per time unit and to avoid fast rotations. The tower is so constructed that its stability is maintained even during lateral wind impact in the event of a failure of the rotational mechanism. The overall aerodynamic profile and the movement of the wings create vibration at the peak. By comparison to conventional structures, the Wing Tower has approximately 25 % less weight, which ultimately translates into savings in construction.

To sail before the wind is in fact to sail at an angle to the wind. In aeronautics, 300 tonnes and more can be lifted into the sky. Here, too, aerodynamics is the driving force. The same applies to race cars, such as in Formula 1 racing, where spoiler wings create pressure acting against the car greater than the weight of the car itself *(Figure 120.3)*. All these discoveries were used in the development of the Wing Tower to ensure that when velocities are high, the tower leans into the wind using the force acting against it to reduce the stress load created by it.

Figure 120.4 shows the peak of the Wing Tower, where two wings create this effect. The wing in front creates a down-current (spoiler); the wing at the rear, an up-current. This reduces the torque caused by the air resistance of the tower. The stabilizing wings (winglets) on the side lower the vibration in the panorama cockpit.

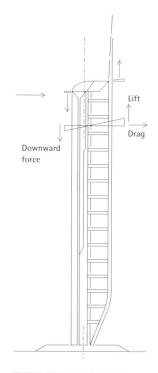

120.1
Model of Millennium Tower, Glasgow
Arch.: R. Horden Ass.

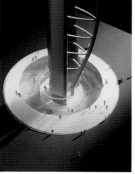

120.2
The Wing Tower rests on an oil film and revolves at a carefully calculated angle to the wind to reduce aerodynamic resistance.

120.3
Forces acting on the Wing Tower

120.4
Peak of the Wing Tower
The use of additional wings placed at the panorama level of the Wing Tower was studied for more wind power: the down-draft of the forward wing and the up-draft of the rear wing are designed to reduce the torque produced by oncoming winds.

Students of architecture and structural engineering supervised by Richard Horden, P. Heppel, Ludwig Ilg and Klaus Daniels studied concepts for a 1,000-metre-high "super skyscraper" called K.1. Aside from developing new technological concepts, the main objective was to inspire an interdisciplinary approach. To architects, the search for technological options is and should always mean researching and developing a new architectural language. Hence the task was put to the students with the following question: How does one build a skyscraper using wind?

Figure 121 illustrates Richard Horden's approach to the concept study for K.1. With the aerodynamic properties of a Frisbee in mind, the students studied various forms of rotation, which were subsequently tested in a wind tunnel for air resistance and the ability to create a torque in relation to oncoming wind. Horden's idea was to design the physical forms aerodynamically and to create a lightweight tower with a dissolved volume. The disc-shaped levels fulfil both supply and disposal functions in the manner of autonomous organisms, harnessing environmental energies whenever possible *(Figure 122.1)*. The sky offers a wealth of energy in the form of sun and wind (cooling from wind and from solar energy; electricity from wind turbines) and water (collected rainwater and condensation). Possibilities were also explored for utilizing temperature and air pressure variations over a height differential of 1,000 metres.

A particular problem in extremely tall buildings is the fact that elevator shafts take up an enormous amount of usable space. For K.1, cable cars were envisioned as direct linkages between levels, while elevators would serve exclusively for access to specific floors. The analogy to the Zugspitze cable car in the Alps underlines the technical feasibility of this solution. (The cable car on the Zugspitze covers a height of 2,000 metres in 10 minutes, whereby a span of more than 1,300 metres is travelled across a freely suspended rope between the last pole and the summit.) The concept study for K.1 demonstrates the options open to architects in the future when one thinks in terms of environmental energies as well as in terms of the new dimensions of urban density.

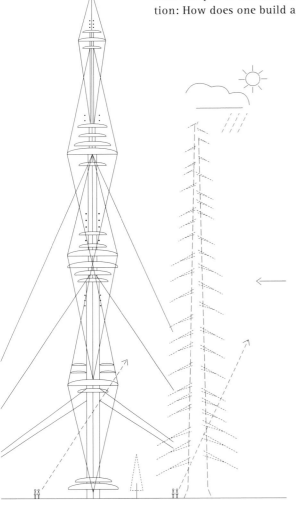

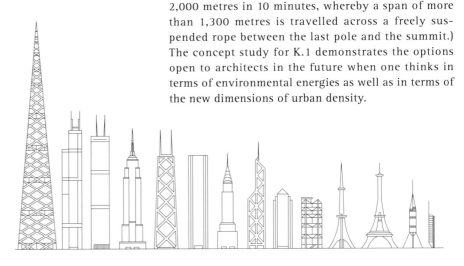

121
The concept study K.1 investigates new options for skyscraper construction using aerodynamic forces.
K.1 draws energy directly from the sky like a mammoth tree.
(Arch.: R. Horden Ass.)

Traditional architectural design was to a large extent determined by gravity. In this century, water, sun and wind are increasingly utilized through new technology. In the future, weightlessness and the use of lifting forces as well as reduced loads will dominate architectural design. The transition from light to light is already evident in *Figure 122.2,* on the one hand interpreted as "light-tech" in the sense of natural light and, on the other hand, in the sense of "light-weight technology".

122.1
Disc-shaped "building body" on K.1

7.3   Building with the Sun

There is such a wealth of literature and documentation on building with the sun. To avoid repetition, the following short treatment of the subject focuses on two specific projects.

Revolving Solar House HELIOTROP®, Freiburg

The revolving solar house shown in *Figure 123.1* (architect: Rolf Disch) is an attempt to develop a new concept of architecture where ecology, energy, efficiency, construction, technology and design are brought together. The result is a house for qualitative living, for "keeping house" and for "sustainable management".

HELIOTROP®, with a usable area of approximately 180 m², is tree-house and solar power station in one. Dynamic simulation calculations predict a heating energy requirement of only 21 kWh/m²a, without taking into consideration the active solar installations which can lower the requirement to zero. HELIOTROP® is an "energy-producing" house; it can generate far more electricity than it uses and is able to feed the excess energy into the public net. The design satisfies the following demands:

122.2
Energy concept of the K.1 building bodies

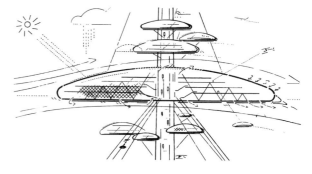

Light	**Light**
Light and nature	**Light and Technology**
Considerations:	Considerations:
Solar	Access and safety
Airflow	Maintenance, Materials
Aerodynamics	Structures, active and passive
Sonics	Construction methods
Thermal	Weight distribution
Pressure	Building mobility
Precipitation	Fluids systems
Condensation	Air/gas systems
Permeability	Sonics, Convection
Reflectability	Electricity, Electromagnetics
View	Communications
Glare	Adapatability, Comfort
Light-Day	Personnel movement systems
Light-Night	Freight handling
Light-Colour	Waste, Recyclability
Light-Shade	Exhaust and intakes

- Maximum use of solar energy (active in summer, active and passive in winter)
- Rainwater utilization
- High level of comfort
- Comfortable interior climate with high daylight quotient and high level of visual comfort
- Excellent residential value with options for orientation (sunny orientation, panoramic view, height)
- High design standards: sequencing of rooms, variable room divisions and flexible use
- Use of ultra-modern wood construction techniques and wood materials for solar energy and CO_2 storage *(see Figure 123.2)*
- High market, image and identification value through recognizable form and design

An electric motor (120 W) can rotate the entire tree-house 360° *(Figure 123.3)*. Cubicles are grouped around a central column, spiralling upwards; access into the rooms is achieved directly from the column or through adjacent rooms. Floor plans in *Figure 123.4* suggest the different uses to which the rooms can be put; *Figure 123.5* shows the view of the outside from the living room. The biaxial solar panel has an aperture surface of 54 m² with a peak performance of approximately 6.6 kW.

123.1
Revolving solar house HELIOTROP©
Arch.: R. Disch

123.3
The driving ring

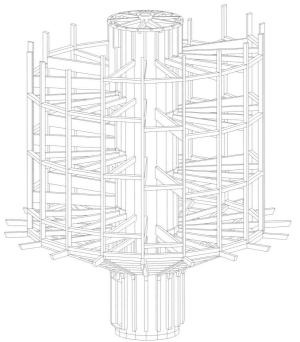

123.2
Isometric drawing of the wood structure

The total weight of the house, including installations and stairs, is approximately 100 tonnes (central column: 17 tonnes). The house rests on a foundation base of only 9 m² (sealed surface). Wall, roof and ceiling insulation achieve transmittance values of 0.1 to 0.13 W/m²K. *Figure 123.6* shows a detail of a typical wall section with adjacent window. Thermal-insulating triple glazing achieves a mean U-value, including frames, of 0.6 W/m²K. With krypton or xenon fillers, this can be lowered to 0.4 W/m²K. The remaining heat energy can either be generated from evacuated tube collectors or flat plate collectors, installed at the parapets in combination with a latent heat storage unit.

Rainwater can be collected on the roof and used as service water. Household waste water is treated, as far as the site allows, in two sewage treatment basins and is then collected in a pond in the garden for re-use as dishwashing and laundry water.

This revolving solar house is an intriguing structure, which satisfies almost all requirements for ecologically correct building. Its clever technology and simple construction may make it a highly successful export, not only to countries with sufficient solar supply, but also for regions with cold winters.

123.5
View outside from living room

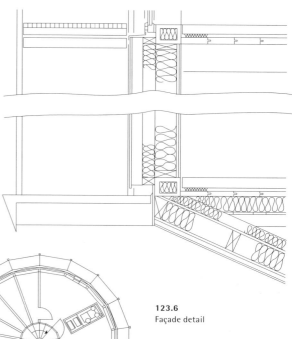

123.6
Façade detail

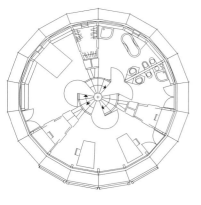
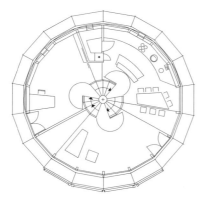
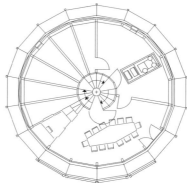

123.4
Floor plans

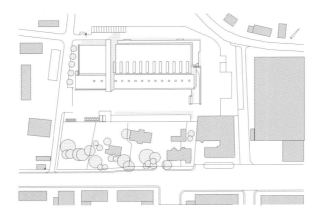

124.1
Werkhof Schöntal, site plan
Arch.: T. Hotz

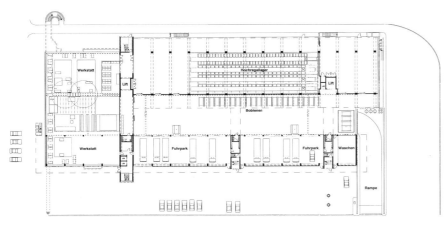

124.2
Floor plan of ground floor

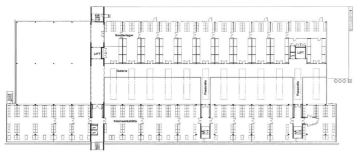

124.3
Floor plan of first floor

Werkhof Schöntal, Municipal Works Winterthur

The municipal building designed by Zurich architect Theo Hotz has been awarded the 1996 Constructec-Prize. This European award for industrial architecture is given not only for architectural design, but also in recognition of a combined achievement in architecture, construction and technology.

Figure 124.1 shows the site plan with the building and its orientation. One is struck immediately by how well the building is placed in its urban landscape with a pronounced north-west and north-east façade (upper and right section of building). The floor plans are organized such that areas with less daylight and, in transitional seasons and winter, those sections with little or no direct sunlight, are used as a high-rise warehouse *(Figures 124.2 and 124.3)*. Rooms benefiting from the natural environment – the car park, small workshops, main workshop, offices and casino – are located on the south-east and south-west sides.

All building sections are steel constructions or concrete component structures with rear-ventilated curtain walls and large, partially frameless glazing.

Considering the use to which the building is put, the special requirements for sun protection and energy efficiency as well as lighting and comfort are satisfied by the fact that the main façades are responsive to environmental conditions. The offices and work areas facing south-east *(Figure 124.4)* are effectively shaded by large mobile louvres for photovoltaic solar energy use. The façade details *(Figure 124.5)* show the main components. The workshops on the south-west side are equipped with shading units that redirect daylight.

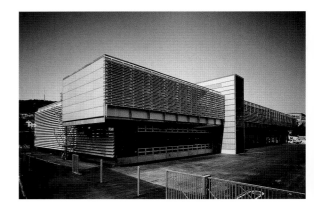

124.4
South elevation

7.4 Building Near Water

In addition to the photovoltaic installation (energy performance approx. 40,000 kWh/a) a flat plate collector system of 20 m² for warm water supply is installed on the roof. The flat plate collectors conduct heat energy into the solar storage unit (total 2,000 l), raising the total annual heat energy yield to approximately 16,000 kWh/a. The technical system is complemented by a combined heat and power station, gas-motor driven, with a thermal performance of 310 kW. A heat pump powered by the radiation heat of the gas motor is also installed (heat output approx. 50 kW), and a gas boiler completes the system.

This building demonstrates that excellent design and the demands for high integration, on the one hand, and engineering to minimize energy consumption, on the other hand, can be very compatible.

Building near water, living with water, living on water – these have many implications, especially when one considers all types of bodies of water on which or near which one could live. Building near water as an idea is presented in this section by discussing a specific design concept: one developed by Richard Horden for London, supported by a study conducted by students at the Eidgenössische technische Hochschule, Zurich (architecture) and at the engineering school in Lucerne.

Building above water is nothing new, as the sixteenth-century example in *Figure 125* illustrates. The city of London has decided to take a new look at this option by holding an international competition.

The Peabody Trust, a foundation active in social housing, created the Millennium Project to celebrate the 200th anniversary of its founding father. A bridge-cum-building designed by Horden Associates initiated the project. International architects also designed bridges for other locations throughout London. Horden's design is illustrated in *Figures 126.1* to *126.3:* the bridge features shops, small galleries and restaurants on the upper floor, as well as

125
The old London Bridge, model photo

124.5
Façade details

residences with private entrances for small families, artists and students on the ground floor. The bridge would serve as an active link between St. Paul's Cathedral and the new Tate Gallery, which is being installed in the former Bankside power station.

The 200-metre-long central arcade has roughly the same length as the famous Burlington Arcade on Piccadilly Circus and provides a sheltered pedestrian walkway over the Thames with a marvellous view. The upper promenade level of the bridge will be almost completely transparent so that patrons in the restaurants and stores on this floor can enjoy the view of London's skyline with the Tower Bridge to the east. The glass-covered middle section is designed as a green space, partially planted with trees – a reference to the grand glass buildings of Victorian times. Restaurants and seating areas tempt visitors to pause and enjoy the unique experience of the river area at the heart of the city. The commercial allocation for the upper level is an important element of the whole concept. Although a bridge with residential units is not subject to direct land-use costs, a project of this kind is nevertheless open to comparatively high building costs. Hence the commercial use of at least part of the bridge was a financial requirement, and furthermore helps to keep the rent low for the ground-level apartments. The bridge is designed to be more than simply a connection across the river: it also serves as a major link for a monorail system.

The construction of the bridge would begin with projecting steel framework trusses on two sides. To minimize disruptive construction in the downtown core, the bridge can be largely prefabricated, using the river as a transportation route *(Figure 126.4)*. Once the support structure of the bridge is in place, the prefabricated residential units and all toilet cores for shops, restaurants, etc., will be inserted into a 8-metre grid. Finally, the bridge can be clad and finished on the interior.

The bridge is to be clad mainly in glazing with integrated photovoltaic elements. The glazing is geared, on the one hand, to react to the brightness, weightlessness and transparency of the river and, on the other hand, to create an architecture that allows users to experience the surrounding environment. Finally, measures are taken to achieve a maximum in energy efficiency in the often foggy river area. At this point, the student group began its study to make the bridge

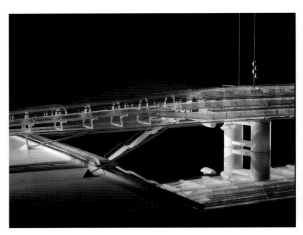

126.1 – 3
A habitable bridge across the
Thames, R. Horden Ass.,
model photos

into a self-sufficient building which would utilize the energies available in its immediate environment.

Figures 127.1 and *127.2* show wind velocities and wind frequencies in London; they illustrate that wind velocities are predominantly around 4 m/sec, from all directions. The data are based on measurements taken 10 metres above ground. Following an estimate of energy consumption (heat energy, electricity), indicated in *Figures 128.1* and *128.2,* the group calculated how much electricity might be gained with photovoltaics, tide energy and wind energy *(Figure 128.3).* A schematic and percentages of energy supply and consumption are shown in *Figure 129;* it illustrates, symbolically, the options for generating energy (left: wind power, photovoltaics, pipe turbine for tidal power stations, thermal use of river water via heat pump; right: energy consumption for electricity, cooling energy, heating energy, warm water).

Conceptual diagrams for the use of energy from tides given a tidal range of approximately 7 metres are shown in *Figure 130.1,* while *Figure 130.2* schematizes the structure of a pipe turbine, which could be housed in a tide-caisson (flooding of one or several

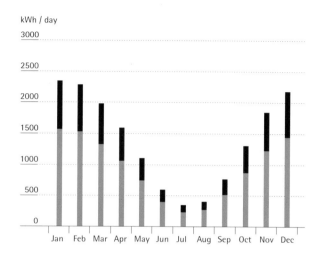

128.1
Daily requirement of heating
energy and corresponding supplies
over the course of a year

■ Heat from river by heat pump
■ Electrical energy for heat pump

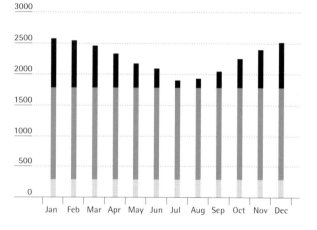

128.2
Daily electricity requirements over
the course of a year, plotted for
different consumers

■ Heat pump
■ Lighting
□ Cooling

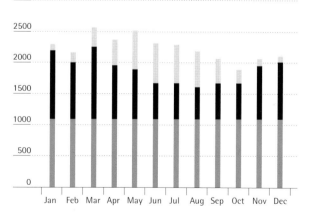

128.3
Daily production of electricity
from environmental sources over
the course of a year

■ Wind energy
■ River flow
□ Photovoltaic

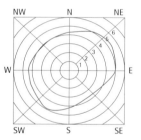

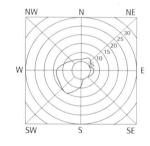

127.1
Wind velocity distribution at
London Heathrow airport (10 m
above ground) (in m/s)

127.2
Wind direction distribution at
London Heathrow (in %)

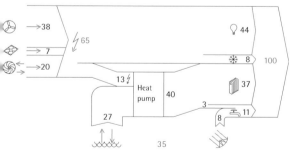

129
Annual energy balance
(Parameters in %)

↯ Electricity
⊘ Wind energy
⊗ Photovoltaics
⊗ Turbine
♀ Consumer

River as heat source
▥ Heating
⬒ Warm water
⬓ Solar collector panels
❄ Cooling

water basins in the pylon area of the pillars, energy gain from turbine during low tide and from run-off).
Figure 131.1 plots initial ideas on how wind energy could be used in this project. It soon became clear that the slender pylons designed by Horden would need to be much taller (approx. 55 m) to accommodate sufficiently large wind power wheels for generating electricity *(Figure 131.2)*. The sketch of a wind wheel shows a rotor diameter of approximately an

urban planning perspectiv22 metres. This solution is not only problematic from e but also with regard to noise emission. The concept is therefore more appropriate to a rural setting. Photovoltaic surfaces and warm water collectors round out the whole concept. The photovoltaics achieve a peak performance of approximately 35 kW for a total electricity requirement of approximately 200 kW *(Figure 132.1)*.
The use of hydro power (with an average water speed of approx. 2.2 m/sec and without utilizing the tidal differences) with 26 turbines at 2 metres each would be impractical.

130.1
Energy source water
Concept of tidal power station

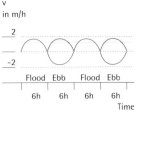

130.2
Bevel wheel tube turbine

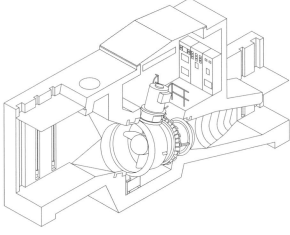

131.1
Energy source wind
Bases for harnessing wind energy

The relation of height to wind velocity determines the required hub height.
The wind energy potential may vary greatly even during relatively stable average wind velocities throughout the year.

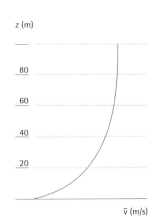

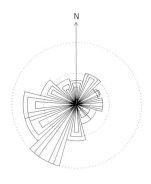

The wind rose diagram taken from the European Wind Atlas shows the distribution of wind directions, average wind velocity and average wind energy (v³) and helps to determine the best orientation as well as the (potential) yield of the wind power station.

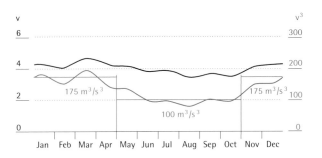

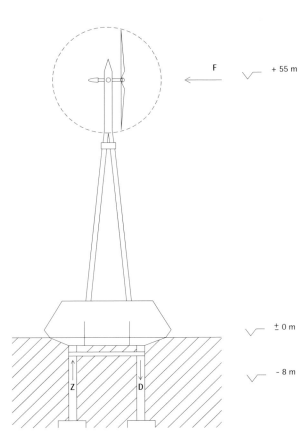

131.2
Study (detail) of a wind power station
Problems:
– Dynamic load
– Assembly, height
– Accessibility; service
– Eddy formations

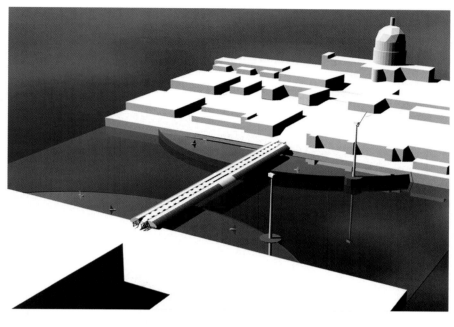

Public areas such as restaurants can be partially cooled by drawing fresh air from directly above the water surface near the pylons and blowing it into rooms that require cooling. Furthermore, the aerodynamic profile of the bridge would seem to create a tendency for a slight negative pressure at its top side, thus naturally ventilating the rooms located on the upper level. *Figure 132.2* shows the design developed by the students in a computer-assisted design (CAD) study.

132.1
Energy source sun
Electricity from photovoltaic elements

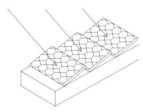

Radiation intensity
W/m^2

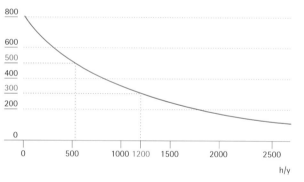

132.2
Building on water
Student group design
Visualization: Odilo Schoch

Seminar participants:
Reto aus der Au
Christian Bertschinger
Erich Brun
David Buholzer
Kjell Droz
Michael Gruber
Pascal Gysi
Daniel Holenweg
Jörg Karow
Sabine Kaufmann
Thomas Lehmann
Andrea Rhyner
Marcel Scherrer
Raphael Schmid
Thomas Schmid
Odilo Schoch
Jörg Senn
Roelof Steekenbrink
Stefan Thöne
Elena Ucan
Britta Vodicka
Puis Widmer

Seminar leaders:
Andrea Compagno
Klaus Daniels
Richard Horden
Ludwig Ilg
Dan Nguyen Dai
Miro Trawnika
Andreas Vogler

to 132.1
The required minimum radiation irtensity of 300 W/m^2 is available for 1,200 hours/year, the average irtensity is approximately 500 W/m^2 for 512 hours with an effeciency coefficient of 10 %.

Energy potential with photovoltaics: 60 kWh/m^{2}a
Area available on façade:
1,400 m^2
Total electric power capacity:
84 MWh/a
This corresponds to 10 % of the total energy requirement.

8 Heavy or Light? Resource-Conserving Building

Heavy and light structures date back to the beginnings of human architecture: "heavy", in building, is associated with nature – caves – permanence; "light", on the other hand, calls to mind materials like wood, bamboo, straw, fabric – and non-permanence.

Heavy building can be resource friendly when heavy materials are manufactured, installed and, if possible, recycled on location. In fact, heavy building has advantages in specific cases. Until modern times, the history of architecture in the West has been dominated by mass and weight.

In the twentieth century, the concept of architecture is no longer determined by weight, but rather by weightlessness (lightness) and limited material consumption. This is directly linked to the demand for flexibility, re-allocation of use, reduction of both waste and "material avalanches" and, finally, recycling. New building materials should be manufactured without creating huge amounts of waste and without consuming huge amounts of raw material (the "ecological backpack"). The following discussion centres on energy savings and resource efficiency and illuminates some aspects pertinent to planning buildings for the future.

8.1 Building with Mass: Storing Thermal Energy

One reason for building with mass is to create a positive ambient climate with the least amount of technology. Storage capacity, night cooling, delayed use of incident solar energy – these are familiar expressions in today's architectural vocabulary. A quick review of the significance of storage behaviour in buildings suffices. To efficiently use the properties of building mass in the future, one should be aware that the primary function of thermal storage in modern buildings is to reduce cooling loads (heat gain in the building) or to delay the effect of solar heat gain (passive solar utilization).

Thermal storage in buildings is usually geared to reducing the heat load caused by exterior or interior gains without resorting to the use of cooling energy supplied by electrical or gas motors or other technology. In these cases, the momentary loads are so changed by the storing elements that the heat-gain time function changes into a cooling-load time function. The room, as a unit, absorbs radiant heat at the interior surrounding walls, through windows (diffuse and direct solar incidence), from artificial lighting and from occupants, machines, etc. – all of which have an effect. How far radiant heat penetrates walls or storage components depends on the wall construction and the duration of the radiation.

Surfaces are in a constant state of reciprocal radiation exchange; depending upon air and surface temperatures, a convective heat transfer is effected from the surface to the air and vice versa. A rise in room temperature triggers a reduction in the cooling load from thermal storage. A fall in room temperature triggers an increase in the cooling load owing to heat release. The accuracy achieved in computation and simulation procedures is now at a level that the results relating to diurnal processes can be applied in the design stage of a building to predict how rooms will react to specific stress criteria and to specific storage behaviour in any given climate.

The following room types or buildings are distinguished relevant to thermal storage:
– Very low thermal mass
– Low thermal mass
– Medium thermal mass
– High thermal mass

Buildings with very low thermal mass usually have a total mass of less than 200 kg/m² of floor space. The low and medium thermal mass rooms or buildings are those whose thermal mass is in the range of 200 to 600 kg/m² of floor space. When the total mass of a room or building is greater than 600 kg/m², we speak of high thermal mass structures.

To study storage capacity and the resulting perceived room temperatures, different types of rooms are observed in computer simulation under otherwise identical conditions *(Figure 133):* room options 1 and 3 have low thermal mass; options 3 and 4 have medium thermal mass; while options 5 and 6 have high thermal mass. For all options, for both power and data installations (a must for modern buildings), hollow floors or narrow mesh floor trunking systems were assumed.

133
Room types with different surrounding structures

Dimensions:
Orientation :	South
Floor space:	21.0 m²
Occupants:	2
Room height:	2.90 m
Lighting:	158 W
Ceiling suspension (void):	0.15 m
Machines:	315 W
Balustrade height:	0.70 m

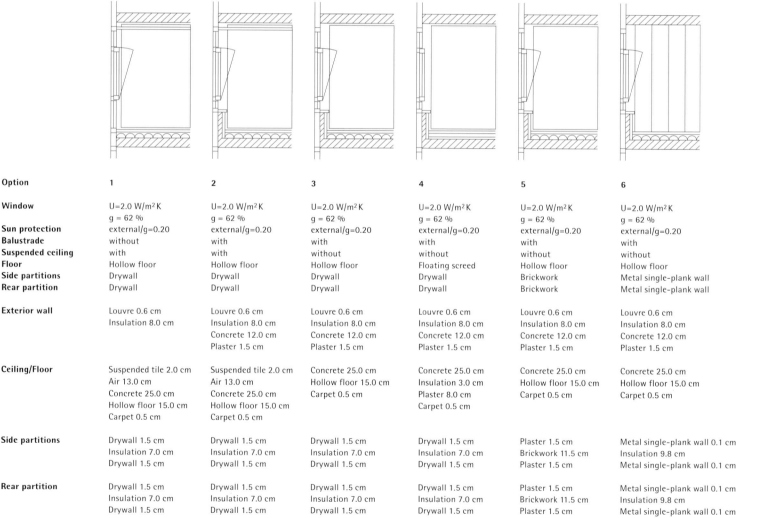

Option	1	2	3	4	5	6
Window	U=2.0 W/m²K g = 62 %	U=2.0 W/m²K g = 62 %	U=2.0 W/m²K g = 62 %	U=2.0 W/m²K g = 62 %	U=2.0 W/m²K g = 62 %	U=2.0 W/m²K g = 62 %
Sun protection	external/g=0.20	external/g=0.20	external/g=0.20	external/g=0.20	external/g=0.20	external/g=0.20
Balustrade	without	with	with	with	with	with
Suspended ceiling	with	with	without	without	without	without
Floor	Hollow floor	Hollow floor	Hollow floor	Floating screed	Hollow floor	Hollow floor
Side partitions	Drywall	Drywall	Drywall	Drywall	Brickwork	Metal single-plank wall
Rear partition	Drywall	Drywall	Drywall	Drywall	Brickwork	Metal single-plank wall
Exterior wall	Louvre 0.6 cm Insulation 8.0 cm	Louvre 0.6 cm Insulation 8.0 cm Concrete 12.0 cm Plaster 1.5 cm	Louvre 0.6 cm Insulation 8.0 cm Concrete 12.0 cm Plaster 1.5 cm	Louvre 0.6 cm Insulation 8.0 cm Concrete 12.0 cm Plaster 1.5 cm	Louvre 0.6 cm Insulation 8.0 cm Concrete 12.0 cm Plaster 1.5 cm	Louvre 0.6 cm Insulation 8.0 cm Concrete 12.0 cm Plaster 1.5 cm
Ceiling/Floor	Suspended tile 2.0 cm Air 13.0 cm Concrete 25.0 cm Hollow floor 15.0 cm Carpet 0.5 cm	Suspended tile 2.0 cm Air 13.0 cm Concrete 25.0 cm Hollow floor 15.0 cm Carpet 0.5 cm	Concrete 25.0 cm Hollow floor 15.0 cm Carpet 0.5 cm	Concrete 25.0 cm Insulation 3.0 cm Plaster 8.0 cm Carpet 0.5 cm	Concrete 25.0 cm Hollow floor 15.0 cm Carpet 0.5 cm	Concrete 25.0 cm Hollow floor 15.0 cm Carpet 0.5 cm
Side partitions	Drywall 1.5 cm Insulation 7.0 cm Drywall 1.5 cm	Drywall 1.5 cm Insulation 7.0 cm Drywall 1.5 cm	Drywall 1.5 cm Insulation 7.0 cm Drywall 1.5 cm	Drywall 1.5 cm Insulation 7.0 cm Drywall 1.5 cm	Plaster 1.5 cm Brickwork 11.5 cm Plaster 1.5 cm	Metal single-plank wall 0.1 cm Insulation 9.8 cm Metal single-plank wall 0.1 cm
Rear partition	Drywall 1.5 cm Insulation 7.0 cm Drywall 1.5 cm	Drywall 1.5 cm Insulation 7.0 cm Drywall 1.5 cm	Drywall 1.5 cm Insulation 7.0 cm Drywall 1.5 cm	Drywall 1.5 cm Insulation 7.0 cm Drywall 1.5 cm	Plaster 1.5 cm Brickwork 11.5 cm Plaster 1.5 cm	Metal single-plank wall 0.1 cm Insulation 9.8 cm Metal single-plank wall 0.1 cm

133.1
Room temperatures following five days of good weather in summer
Weather data from TRY (TRY region 8)
Room temperatures are indicated as perceived temperatures (from DIN 1946 / part 2), under consideration of building component and surface temperatures.

—— Fresh air
━━ Option 1
– – Option 2
- - - Option 3
···· Option 4
—— Option 5
–·– Option 6

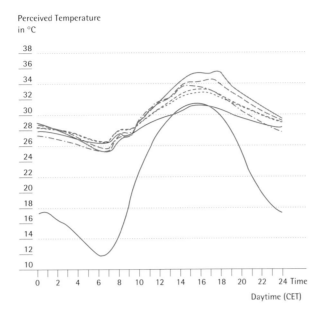

Perceived Temperature
in °C

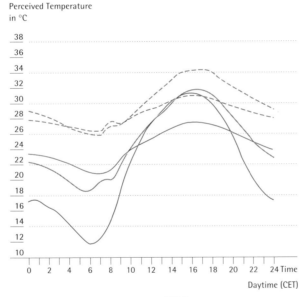

Perceived Temperature
in °C

133.2
Room temperatures following five days of good weather in summer
Comparison: with/without night ventilation
Weather data from TRY (TRY region 8)

—— Fresh air
– – Option 2 (without NV)
—— Option 2 (with NV)
– – Option 5 (without NV)
—— Option 5 (with NV)

NV = night ventilation
(air change 3.0 1/h
from 5 p.m. to 8 a.m.)

The curves in *Figure 133.1* indicate the outside temperatures and the room temperatures for the various options (facing south). Without ventilation or air-conditioning systems, temperatures range from 36° C to 31° C, depending on the thermal mass of the room; low storage capacity increases room temperatures by up to 5 K.

The storage capacity of a room can be significantly improved by ventilating the space with outside air during the night. *Figure 133.2* represents the temperature patterns for option 2 (low thermal mass) and option 5 (high thermal mass), with and without night cooling. In the case of the light storage capacity room, the maximum room temperatures are reduced by approximately 2 K, and for the high storage capacity room, by a further 4 K. Option 5 achieves maximum daytime room temperatures that are very comfortable to nearly comfortable.

During the simulation and final assessment, it is important to determine how frequently specific room temperatures are exceeded over the course of a year; that is, whether a building or a specific room in a building exhibits room temperatures significantly above 30° C for more than 100 to 200 hours per year. *Figure 134* charts temperature statistics for May to September for the room options presented above. It clearly shows that option 5 results in very favourable conditions: the room temperatures rarely surpass 29° C, even without night cooling.

Many high storage capacity buildings have already been documented; *Figure 135* shows an office building which may surprise some in being a high thermal mass building.

Frequency, number of hours
in h

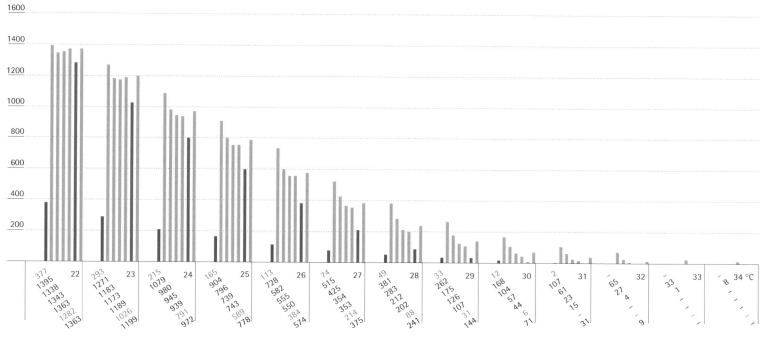

377		293		215		165		113		74		49
1395	22	1271	23	1079	24	904	25	728	26	515	27	381

1600
1400
1200
1000
800
600
400
200

377
1395
1338
1343
1363
1282
1363
22

293
1271
1183
1173
1189
1026
1199
23

215
1079
980
945
939
791
972
24

165
904
796
739
743
589
778
25

113
728
582
555
550
384
574
26

74
515
425
354
353
214
375
27

49
381
283
212
202
88
241
28

33
262
175
126
107
31
144
29

12
168
104
57
44
6
71
30

2
107
61
23
15
31
31

65
27
4
9
32

33
33

8
34 °C

Frequencies in h

135
Example of high storage capacity building:
Office building of HL-Technik AG, Munich, west elevation
architect:
Dr. Ralph Hammann, Munich

View of atrium (stone floors, masonry walls, plastered ceilings)

134
Room temperatures from May to September
Weather data from TRY (TRY region 8)
Number of hours when temperature is greater than indicated temperature from 7 a.m. to 6 p.m. (daily)

▌ Fresh air
▌ Option 1
▌ Option 2
▌ Option 3
▌ Option 4
▌ Option 5
▌ Option 6

8.2   Building Without Weight: Light-Tech Architecture

The importance of mobility and flexibility in modern society and modern economic systems was discussed in Part 1. Buildings should "breathe" – they should be flexible and adaptable to different types of use; they may even be de-constructed and re-constructed.

Responding to the demands for low material consumption and for a new architectural language, some architects began turning to light construction as early as 1950 – "the world is becoming lighter" was the theme. Television images of astronauts in space demonstrated zero gravity; architecture without mass can now be experienced in cyberspace, where one can walk through walls and ceilings in virtual reality.

Building without mass, according to Richard Horden's interpretation, means:

– Intelligence instead of mass
– Less material = less energy consumption = lower costs
– Flexibility
– Speed
– Mobility

136
The design of a glass cube in London demonstrates a new form of expression for a weightless, light architecture.

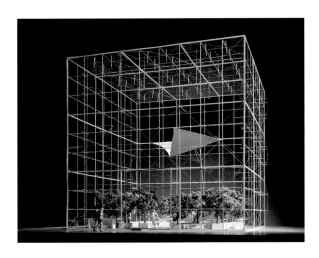

Intelligence instead of mass
Stone and brick building construction is based on the layering of stones or bricks, joined chiefly by their weight and the resulting friction. To achieve the same stability with less material and less weight, we must break down the course of forces. Structurally, material is needed where force and torque occur. Tensile forces can be handled in a material-efficient manner with steel ropes. The buckling load, the critical load for a column, is the factor determining the cross-section in the measurement of pressure elements. Tubular cross-sections are the obvious answer. Avoiding moment in the first place is the key to light building. For this, truss girders were developed in the last century and thin-skin and membrane structures in this century.

Engineers have directly contributed to construction that is more cost and material efficient. Increasingly precise calculation processes and computer simulation have helped engineers to realize these ideas. A wide-span, weight-bearing concrete bowl can now be accurately reduced to a few centimetres for calculation purposes. Lighter and more open structures can be realized with wire-grid bowls and textiles.

The trend towards material-efficient building has sparked a movement in architecture where load-bearing supports are replaced by tensile elements as the main structural component – a development in which transparency substitutes for the solidity associated with architecture.

The glass cube project at Stag Place in London *(Figure 136)*, designed by R. Horden Associates together with engineers Ove Arup + Partners, is an example of how material consumption can be lowered through intelligent analysis of forces: the structure is inspired by the light rigging used on sailboats. The glass cube with 15-metre long sides is based on a 50-mm steel construction reinforced with compression members. The play of light created by the "rigging" on the glass and floor surfaces reflects the semi-transparency of the trees planted inside the glass cube (light[weight] = light[optics] = construction).

The same can be said of the multi-purpose hall discussed in Section 7.2 (architects Schulitz + Partner, construction RFR, Paris). *Figure 137* illustrates how form can save material: the hall with an open-span width of 105 metres was intended as a steel structure; this high-performance and fully recyclable material would have been ideal. The optimal geometry for minimal material use is found in catenarian curves and arches. The parabolic curvature of the upper and lower boom results in a combination of arcs and carrier cables. Material savings increase with greater construction height. To bring such height in harmony with low hall volume and the specific requirements for use, the lifting of the carrier cable above the pillar is transferred to the outside with rear bracing. This corresponds to a restraint above the support negative moment or, respectively, to a shortening of the effective span width. The penetration point is spatially disentangled by doubling the pressure arcs; simultaneously, this solution allows for integrated natural lighting in the structural design of the primary support framework.

The roof surface is held down against wind suction with a tension cable above the arcs. Uneven roof load stresses are absorbed by conventional arc trusses created by linking the secondary girders to diagonal struts and by braces at the joints between girders and principal framework arcs. This construction gives the supporting framework a clarity; the free course of the carrier cable emphasizes the openness and generosity of the structure. The roof areas near the secondary girders are covered in trapezoidal metal plates to reduce weight. The hall is cross-braced on one side in the service zone with compression diagonal struts and bilaterally strut-braced. The fixed point at the middle of the hall is defined by the pronounced angle of the column pairs. *Figures 138.1* to *138.3* show computer simulations and details, illustrating the construction and some technical installations.

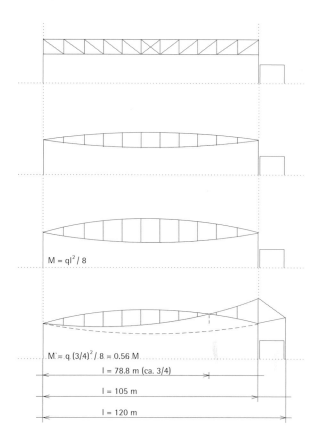

$M = ql^2 / 8$

$M' = q \, (3/4)^2 / 8 = 0.56 \, M$

l = 78.8 m (ca. 3/4)

l = 105 m

l = 120 m

137
"From heavy to light construction":
Material savings through form and design (Prof. Schulitz / RFR)

138.1
Computer simulation of multi-purpose hall

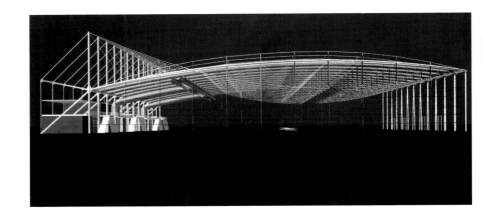

138.2
Main elevation

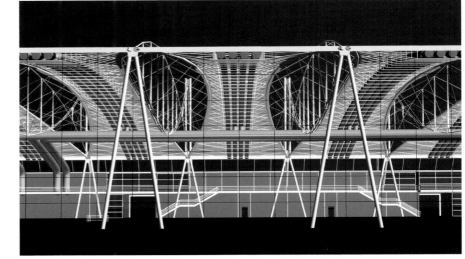

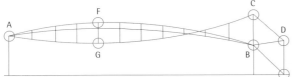

138.3
Hall and construction details

A Front connection, post, girder
B Rear connection, post, girder
C Top deflection point for
   suspension cables
D Bottom deflectionpoint for
   suspension cables
E Base for suspension cables
F Suspended support, top
G Suspended support, bottom

A

B

C

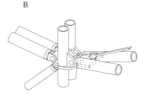

D

F

A

B

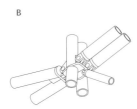

C

E

G

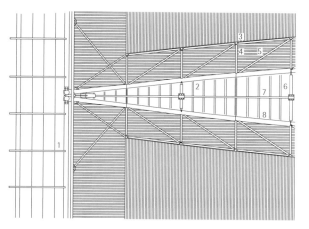

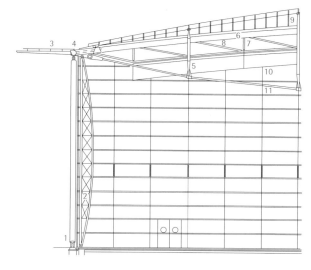

Section
1 Forward post
2 Secondary post
3 Overhanging cantilever beam
4 Perimeter beam
5 Suspended support
6 Arched truss
7 Compression arch
8 Diagonal and vertical rods
9 Wind lift bracing
10 Suspended acoustic ceiling
11 Suspension cable

Roof view
1 Edge girder
2 Roof glazing
3 Arched truss
4 Vertical rod
5 Diagonal rod
6 Horizontal rod
7 Suspension cable
8 Compression arch

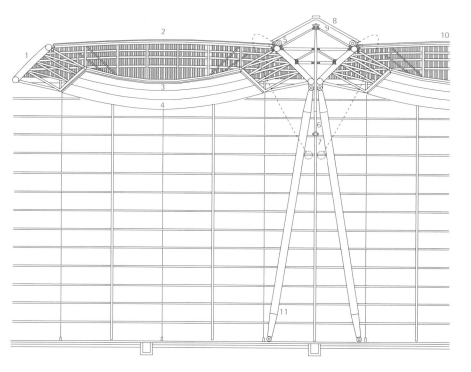

Façade, plan view
1 Arc, tube
2 Top girder
3 Bottom girder
4 Suspended acoustic ceiling
5 Sun protection, shade
6 Suspended support
7 Suspension cable
8 Roof glazing
9 Wind lift bracing, 2 round
  steel rods
10 Compressible polymer water-
  proof lined roof sheeting,
  mechanically fastened; non-
  compressible rock wool
  insulating panels; trapezoidal
  steel plate
11 Front post, 2 tubes

139
Typical building procedure for
light construction
Architect: R. Horden Ass.

Less material = less energy consumption = lower costs

Light building directly impacts building costs and also allows speed in construction and dismantling. With good planning, modifications can be straightforward. Additional cost savings exist for grey energy and production and transportation costs, in combination with reduced energy consumption. Light building goes hand in hand with a breakdown of the force trajectory: where traditional architecture tends to build "against" these forces, today's component-based approach works "with" the forces. The lighter these components are, the greater the speed and safety of their use and application on a building site.

Figure 139 illustrates this approach through the example of a boat-house; *Figure 140* shows the object after completion. The boat-house was originally planned with a base area of 123 m², expanded to 164 m² shortly before construction began and ten years later to 218 m². The design of the light aluminium support framework was based on Rodney Marsh's Tornado catamaran model.

Flexibility

Flexibility has become a fundamental demand on modern architecture, a demand that is rarely fulfilled. Modular light building offers a solution with flexible room design, variable relationships between interior and exterior and adaptable room sequences. All elements are readily interchangeable, a basic property supported by the low weight of the building materials.

Wall components, especially exterior components, can be added or replaced to keep energy consumption at the lowest level possible with state-of-the-art technology. Light construction is especially advantageous for allocating existing buildings to new uses or expanding existing structures. *Figure 141* shows the connecting details of the featured boat-house.

Speed

Light construction is generally synonymous with speed. This results from both the dry construction method in component building and the faster handling of light materials and building components. Light, prefabricated materials are more easily transported and hence "kinder" to the environment even en route to their destination.

Mobility

When we look at a typical construction site today, we may be excused for doubting that we live in the space

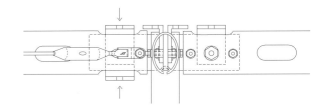

140
The light aluminium framework of
the boat-house drastically reduces
the time required for construction.

141
Connecting detail of the boat-house framework
Simple details deliver a high
degree of flexibility.

age: heavy transport trucks deliver construction materials right into crowded downtown areas. At the site, construction workers work in a limited area, often in dangerous conditions and exposed to all kinds of weather. During construction, not only is the immediate environment affected by noise, dust and traffic, often the entire infrastructure of the city suffers.

Despite pressures of time and cost, the building industry still follows practices that are time and labour intensive, involving the individual manufacture of thousands of partially standardized or completely unstandardized parts. All this in an age where robots assemble a car in half an hour.

In light building, large components – possibly even whole structures – are prefabricated. Prefabrication can make the building process more effective, more efficient and safer. The use of prefabrication is already well established in other industries. (For example, when you buy a car, you're not faced with a convoy of delivery trucks with parts and labourers who assemble it in your garage.) Quality in architecture need not be compromised by using mobile units; this is demonstrated in the following examples.

Intelligence and responsible handling characterize the work of Jörg Schlaich + Partners, Stuttgart. The firm is known for buildings designed according to the principles of low material and energy consumption combined with low cost. Whether it's an addition to an older building to improve its structure and utility or light building in a rural setting, the motto is: light construction has never been more pertinent and more necessary than today, from an ecological, sociological and cultural point of view.

Jörg Schlaich: "Light building is material efficient, because its aim is to optimize the strength of materials and to avoid resource waste. Light construction is easily disassembled; the components can be reused. Light construction puts the brakes on entropy and, more than any other approach to construction, fulfils the requirements for sustainable development.

"Light construction is also a sociological necessity. It creates employment, because light-component construction requires finished, labour-intensive details, which go hand in hand with a greater effort in planning and manufacture. Mental effort replaces physical effort; time and craft once again take over from the die press – the joy of building instead of pounding. As long as our economic system identifies work time with cost, pays only the transportation costs for raw materials and ignores the real costs (ecological backpack), light buildings will remain more expensive than functionally equivalent massive buildings. Hence, light construction runs the risk of being seen as elitist. It is true that only banks, insurance companies and some museums can afford light architecture at present; it is still a rarity in residential and everyday industrial construction. Builders and architects bask in this elitist light (in stark contrast to the spirit of the pioneers of light construction: Buckminster Fuller, Wladimir Suchov, Frei-Otto), displaying a kind of 'construction exhibitionism' and seemingly oblivious that 98 % of our built environment is calling out for their attention. Their attitude and actions are, therefore, in the deepest sense anti-social."

Jörg Schlaich doesn't mince words – he knows what he's talking about. The objects he has designed, either on his own or in collaboration, follow guidelines that reflect his principles. In sum, these principles are:

– Building structures become heavier the greater their span width (permanent load). The logical response is to avoid large spans in the first place or to "outwit" this law of nature with engineering ingenuity.
– Bending-stressed components are to be avoided in favour of purely axial tension and compression members
– Tensile-stressed building components must be utilized efficiently (high tensile stability, low raw density).
– Unfavourable pressure stresses in tensile areas must be transformed with pre-tension.

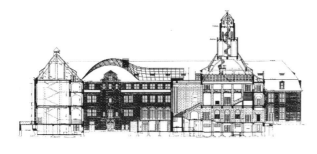

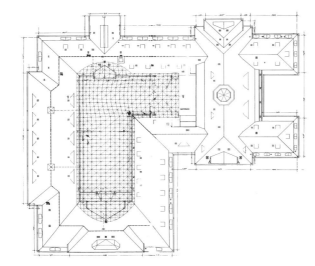

142.1
Hamburg City Historical Museum
(Architects: von Gerkan, Marg +
Partner and Schlaich/Schober)
Section and view of roof

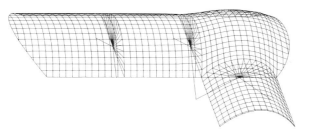

142.2
Three-dimensional representation
of the roof structure

– Light plane structure elements should be designed as double-curved areas with pure axial stress (membrane stress).

Figures 142 and *143* illustrate typical examples of projects created by Schlaich, Bergermann + Partner, Stuttgart, who base their work on the rules listed above.

Twenty-five years ago, Behnisch/Frei-Otto designed the trendsetting roof for the Olympic Stadium in Munich, initiating a movement to develop and translate architecture by using textile membranes. Buildings with textiles membranes are more common today; their longevity fits the needs of changeable buildings. This may signal a new era in building, which may fundamentally change life in our variable climate. In this area, the future has only just begun.

An example for this new building type is the Arena Misericordia in downtown Saragossa: the arena, built nearly 200 years ago, has traditionally been used almost exclusively for bullfights, which meant that it

142.3
The barrel vault, stiffened with spoked wheels

142.4
The hub of a spoked wheel

was used only on certain days in the summer season. The goal was to open the arena to more cultural and athletic events in a resource-efficient manner. To protect participants and spectators from the influences of weather year round, some sort of roofing or covering was required. Werner Sobek and Rudolf Bergermann designed a textile roof, which covers the arena in two sections without supports.

It was essential to introduce only a few new forces into the old building structure. The design goal was therefore to utilize all sections of the roof for load displacement. A solution was achieved by creating a reclining "spoked wheel", which is very efficient in load displacement (e.g. the wheel rim principle in bicycles). The outer pressure ring (ø 83 m) accommodates steel cables (similar to spokes in a wheel), which end in an inner ring (similar to a hub). The "hub" consists of two ring cables (ø 36 m), one above the other, splayed with compression bars.

The mobile inner roof spans the round opening created by the hub of the outer roof. It consists of a hub as well as 16 upper and 16 lower cables, which are

143.1
Pedestrian bridge at Lake Max-Eyth, Stuttgart, site plan
Architects: Schlaich Bergermann + Partner

143.2
Completed suspension bridge

143.3
Bridge over the Neckar River: guyed masts with deflection sheaves for main cables

144.1
Sol y Sombra – Sun and shade were the determining factors for the design of a new roof for the Arena Misericordia in Saragossa. Architects: Schlaich Bergermann + Partner

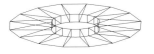

144.2
The load-bearing structure of the outer roof:
a spoked wheel with open hub

144.4 – 8
The inner roof in motion

attached to the upper and lower ends of the 16 compression bars; these, in turn, are connected to the "hollow hub". Central node and spoke cables form an autonomous stable primary system, whose support properties once again correspond to that of a spoked wheel. *Figure 144.1* to *144.12* series shows the building and how the roof functions.

Developments in construction that solve problems facing us today cannot be overrated. The examples presented in this section illustrate the existing options. As Jörg Schlaich says: "The dedicated engineer is attracted to light construction, because it, more than any other approach, addresses and challenges his knowledge, ability and experience, while engaging his imagination and intuition. In light construction the engineer can create appropriate and aesthetic expressions through intelligent and efficient structures, thus making a cultural contribution."

144.3
The sliding casings on one of the lower cables in a test run: the outermost slide bush is entering the coupling block.

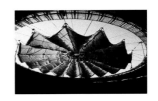

144.12
A wide gutter of transparent polycarbonate is suspended below the joint between outer and inner roof.

144.9 – 11
View into the centre of the inner roof in motion; opening or closing requires only two to three minutes.

8.3 Building with Renewable Raw Materials: Wood and Paper

Building with renewable raw materials means using the trees, bushes, grasses, etc., growing in the area where the building is being constructed.

In Europe, the principal renewable resource for building is wood (thatched roofs have become a rarity). Only forest management can guarantee wood as a sustainable resource. "The only chance of saving the world's forests is the use of wood in construction." (Julius Natterer, ETH, Lausanne). Today, wood is used not only by a select circle of architects searching for ecological approaches, but also by those who have made a splash with wood as a working material (Frei-Otto, Thomas Herzog, P. Kulka, Dieter Schempp – to name but a few German architects).

Of all building materials, wood requires the least amount of energy to manufacture, transport and distribute, including costs arising from environmental damage. Furthermore, wood has excellent insulating properties and is therefore an ideal material for low-energy houses. The more natural and untreated the wood, the better its capacity for recycling or even separation into its component parts after several applications or, ultimately, combustion.

Architects, engineers and the forest industry have revitalized wood construction in the wake of increasingly critical environmental conditions. Wood houses are low-tech buildings with high-tech performance. Where wood block and framework buildings used to be typical of wood construction, contemporary wood architecture features a technically advanced yet still traditional block-type approach as well as innovative concepts. These are skeleton construction, panel construction, frame construction, wood construction in the stacking method, as well as wood-concrete composites.

The skeleton construction as a frame system offers, with clear lines and weight-bearing pillars, the greatest freedom for room layout. In panel construction, the prefabricated panels become systems for individualized home design, typical of prefabricated homes. Frame construction is visually a continuation of the familiar framework (Tudor style) buildings yet also related to panel construction; it presents creative options for a variety of interior design requirements.

Stack construction or batten stack construction, developed chiefly by Julius Natterer, is less well known. Building components are massive, two-dimensional elements consisting of solid timber planks. The planks are stacked vertically and nailed together; they are the primary load-bearing structure for walls, ceilings and roofs. Board stack elements are used in thicknesses of 8 to 12 cm for walls and 12 to 24 cm for ceilings. Optimal thicknesses are 24 to 33 mm, as this dimension can be handled by many wood-processing plants. As a result of the large wood mass of the board stacks, their thermal storage capacity is comparable to brick; thermal transmittance quotients are, however, significantly better. Furthermore, this technology delivers good sound-proofing values, while the fire safety classification of this material is that of a half-hour fire wall. Greater thickness in the elements can even produce fire resistances of 60 to 90 minutes. Modern board stack construction can, when necessary, be combined with wood and concrete in the ceiling areas to create wood-concrete ceilings. In this process, a covering concrete is added on top of the board stack ceiling with additional impact soundproofing and chipboard or poured screed.

For these ceilings, the tensile zone lies in the wood and the pressure zone in the concrete; thus, the load-bearing capacity of the ceiling can be greatly multiplied. Contrary to a concrete ceiling, this method economizes in the area of dead weight, the stress of the ceiling (kg/m^2) being approximately 50 % of that present in conventional concrete ceilings.

Finally, to exemplify contemporary wood construction, here are some images (Figures 145.1 to 145.3) of a building designed by architect Dan Badic & Associates, Morges (Switzerland) for the ETHL (Eidgenössische Technische Hochschule, Lausanne) in Ecublens: the cupola was erected in only three months from boards joined together by screws (board stack construction).

Paper Tower

Paper, as we know, is made of wood. Hence the paper tower of the Swiss Pavilion *(Figures 146.1 to 146.4)* is an interesting example of recyclable light building with a renewable raw material for dry regions (or for interior construction).

The landmark of the Swiss Pavilion at the 1992 Expo in Seville was the paper tower with an outside diameter of 13 metres and a height of 33 metres. To build to such a height with paper presented several material and technical problems; the most challenging was the considerable tensile and compression stresses at the base caused by wind pressure, which had to be absorbed by the light construction and its connecting parts. The basic concept, which led to sufficient sta-bility, was achieved by crossing the edges (running towards the inside) of each prism-shaped tower element exactly at the central axis of the tower.

The tower consisted mainly of corrugated cardboard, which was used for vertical and horizontal bracing to ensure overall stability. Without these corrugated cardboard components, the tower could not have been erected to this height; it would have collapsed. The volume percentages of the building materials were:

– Cardboard   79.26 %
– Wood   20.22 %
– Steel   0.52 %

Roughly one-third of the original components were assembled in Switzerland from 1,348 elements, stacked into 17 storeys and disassembled for transport to Seville. The property of the corrugated cardboard to absorb significant pressure because of its large surface ratio meant that it could be utilized as a bracing material and for short-term loads (e.g. wind). On the other hand, the light, glued paper construction was extremely susceptible to creep. To keep the creep within permissible limits while under constant stress, it was necessary to fit the panels with a light wood frame; the sides of the individual prisms were additionally braced with steel tensile rods to guide the tensile stresses present in extreme wind from node to node.

According to the express wish of architect V. Mangeat, who originally planned the tower, it was to have been designed in a more ephemeral manner. The Basel engineering firm of Walther, Mory, Maier, Bauingenieure AG took on the task of construction and detailing and was able to overcome the inherent transitoriness of the tower to some degree through material processing. After the exhibition, the paper tower was recycled (environment-friendly recovery) – the tower had been conceived from the very beginning as biodegradable.

145.1
Spherical cupola for an auditorium at the ETH in Lausanne
(25 m x 25 m)
(Prof. J. Natterer)

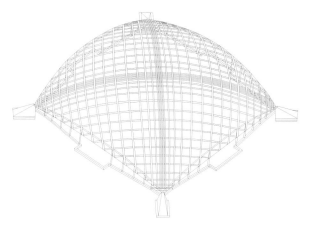

145.2
Axonometric drawing of supporting structure

145.3
The edge beam at the main intersection

Setting and deforming measurements were taken over the course of the exhibition period to determine whether there are application options under certain conditions for this type of construction. As a result, the recommendation was made that it could be used without trouble for short-term light buildings in specific regions: those with a sufficiently warm and dry climate (water absorption of cardboard panels over approx. nine months: nearly 40 %).

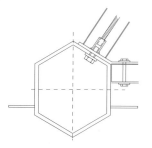

146.1–3
Paper tower,
Swiss pavilion, EXPO 1992, Seville
Architect: V. Mangeat,
Construction: Walther, Mory,
Maier, Bauingenieure AG, Basel

146.4
Details of the construction

9   The New Skin: Efficient Building

The multi-layered glass structure developed in the early eighties by architect Mike Davis (Richard Rogers Partnership, London) draws on the surrounding environment, responding to the seasons and individual user needs. The basic design is illustrated in *Figure 147*. This "polyvalent wall" provides sun protection, insulation, daylight, glare protection and ventilation – all in one structural element. In Mike Davis's original concept, sensors respond to whether a room is occupied.

The polyvalent wall lets sunlight penetrate for passive heating in winter; in summer, it provides a shield against glare and heat. It opens for daylight when indoor light is insufficient and the room is in use, while taking into account the level of heat penetration. In the outer skin, it transforms radiation from the sun into electricity, contributing to power requirements. Finally, it produces ideal surface temperatures for optimal thermal comfort in the room. It is not surprising that the polyvalent wall has been nicknamed the "chameleon of glass technology". Unfortunately, the design has never been successfully executed.

Nevertheless, Davis's proposal and his vision of an ideal glass skin has made an impact on the glass industry of the industrialized nations. It has been an inspiration to move towards a new definition of glass surfaces in buildings, and to provide solutions for minimizing energy consumption and improving resource conservation.

Façades used as envelopes are architecturally challenging; as well, they are designed to fulfil a number of functions for which appropriate solutions must be found. It is crucial to search for the ideal façade in the planning phase of a project, and to create a new design if necessary. For residential building, there are some ready-made solutions; for all other applications, it is accurate to say that no two façades are alike.

In the creation of glass façades, a host of factors play essential and sometimes decisive roles. Lighting technicians, heating engineers, services engineers, aerophysicists, architects, building physicists, façade consultants, building climatologists – these are the experts involved in shaping the layers that form the boundary between interior and exterior.

The principal factors that characterize a façade are:

Light transmission factor
The light transmission factor is the percentage of daylight that penetrates a glass surface or window pane from the outside.

Total solar energy transmission g-value/b-factor
Total solar energy transmission is taken in the range of visible light and infrared radiation. The shading coefficient b describes the percentage of energy permeating a double pane.

147
Polyvalent wall designed by Mike Davis (Richard Rogers Partnership, London)
1 Silica weather skin and deposition substrate
2 Sensor and control logic layer, external
3 Photoelectric grid
4 Thermal sheet radiator / selective absorber
5 Electro-reflective deposition
6 Micro-pore gas-flow layer
7 Electro-reflective deposition
8 Sensor and control logic layer, internal
9 Silica depositions substrate and inner skin

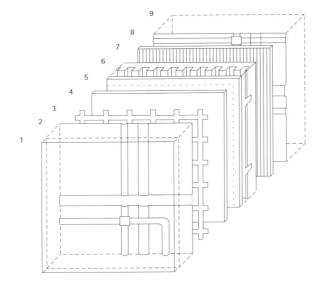

Thermal transmittance U-value
The thermal transmittance of a pane indicates how much energy is lost or gained through the surface, depending on the temperature differences between inside and outside.

Diminution factor
This factor measures the percentage of incident radiant energy that passes through a shading element.

Other factors in the evaluation of glass panes measure:
– Light reflected towards the outside
– General colour reproduction values
– UV permeability
– The selectivity factor

9.1 Insulation

Since the majority of buildings are residential, thermal transmittance, measured as U-value, is often given the highest priority. This is indeed appropriate if we focus exclusively on residential architecture.

Figure 148 charts the accumulation of solar radiation on roof surfaces in Central Europe. While solar heat gain is desirable in residential spaces up to an outside temperature of 20° C (approx. 50 % of total incident heat energy throughout the year), the situation may differ considerably in office and production buildings: high interior heating and cooling loads, which contribute indirectly to heating the building with electricity, are typical in these buildings. It is quite common that such buildings require heating only when outside temperatures fall below 0° C. Hence the importance of establishing the true energy requirements of the building and determining whether the structure is not in fact over-insulated; i.e., the heat volumes generated inside the building are not sufficiently emitted to the outside, such that the building requires mechanical cooling.

For residential building, harnessing solar energy is desirable in winter and in transitional seasons. Only ten years ago, the U-values of good window combinations were in the range of 3.0 W/m²K. Today, we are discussing U-values of 0.7 to 1.2 W/m²K, and recent developments produce even lower values. This advance is further supported by window elements with transparent insulating materials and multi-layered

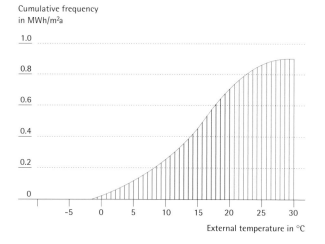

Cumulative frequency
in MWh/m²a

External temperature in °C

148
Accumulation of radiation on roof surfaces

|||| Direct energy potential
|||| Low energy potential
|||| Barely usable energy potential

walls, massive exterior walls with U-values of approximately 0.7 W/m²K. While U-values of less than 1.0 could only be achieved by installing multi-layered pane combinations with air chambers, the newest insulating glass panes on the market are similar to older models; these panes, however, are filled with noble gases and low E-layers.

Figure 149 illustrates the annual thermal energy requirements with the latest pane combinations in comparison to standard insulating glass. The insulating glass with the highest cumulative heat flow (110 – 180 kWh/m²a depending on the orientation) is a pane with a low U-value of 3.0 W/m²K. It produces considerable heat loss, which is a precursor to energy consumption. By contrast, selectively coated panes filled with a noble gas demonstrate heat gains and, even with a northern exposure, little heat loss.

Clearly, the problem of creating panes that prevent heat loss or where heat loss is so minimal that interior heat sources (occupants, lighting, diffuse radiation) suffice for heating, has been more or less solved. The challenge now is to apply these combinations to all new projects.

9.2 Shading

A central difficulty in the use of solar energy in many building types is controlling the radiated flow on windows and glass façades. Energy and light requirements rarely correspond to the solar supply. This creates either overheating on sunny days (U-value too low, g-value too high) or, in the case of insulating glass, unsatisfactory yields from solar energy on days when heating is required. While mechanical shading systems respond to the fluctuations in solar transmission, they are often high-maintenance and therefore expensive solutions. In practice, insulating glazing with low U-values (approx. 1.0 to 1.6 W/m²K) is often combined with higher heating requirements and adjustable shading systems (external louvres, awnings, etc.), which are activated when necessary to prevent overheating in rooms. *Figures 150.1* to *150.3* illustrate the interaction: different g-values (variance resulting from shading systems) lead to different room temperatures and a great range in specific temperature limits.

The Fraunhofer Gesellschaft - Institute for Solar Energy Systems has been a pioneer in working with the glass industry to create ideal products for the consumer market. Currently, a worldwide effort is under way to develop "switchable" light transmission in windows through electrochromatic or gasochromatic coatings. In electrochromatic panes, the transmission can be influenced by adding ions between layers. Typically, these systems consist of five layers *(Figure 151.1):* two conducting electrodes, one ion-conducting layer, one ion-storage layer and the active layer (e.g. tungsten oxide). These systems are expensive to manufacture; furthermore, they exhibit unstable switching behaviour as well as temperature variation. At the same time, these developments seem to represent an important new orientation in glass manufacturing and design.

The main characteristic of gasochromatic panes is that the protons necessary for tinting the tungsten oxide layer are derived through a catalyser directly from the gas phase. For colour stripping, exposure to

149
Annual energy balance of windows (thermal energy requirements)
Calculation based on insulation guidelines, Fraunhofer Gesellschaft Institute for Solar Energy Systems

South
East/West
North
A   Two selective coatings
    and xenon filling
B   Two selective coatings
    and crypton filling
C   Insulating glass (double)
D   Two selective coating
    and argon filling
E   Insulating glass (triple)
F   One selective coating,
    optimized

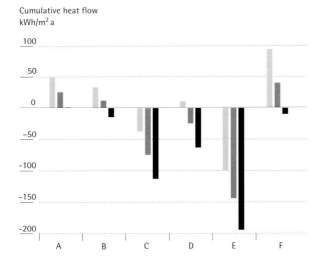

Cumulative heat flow
kWh/m² a

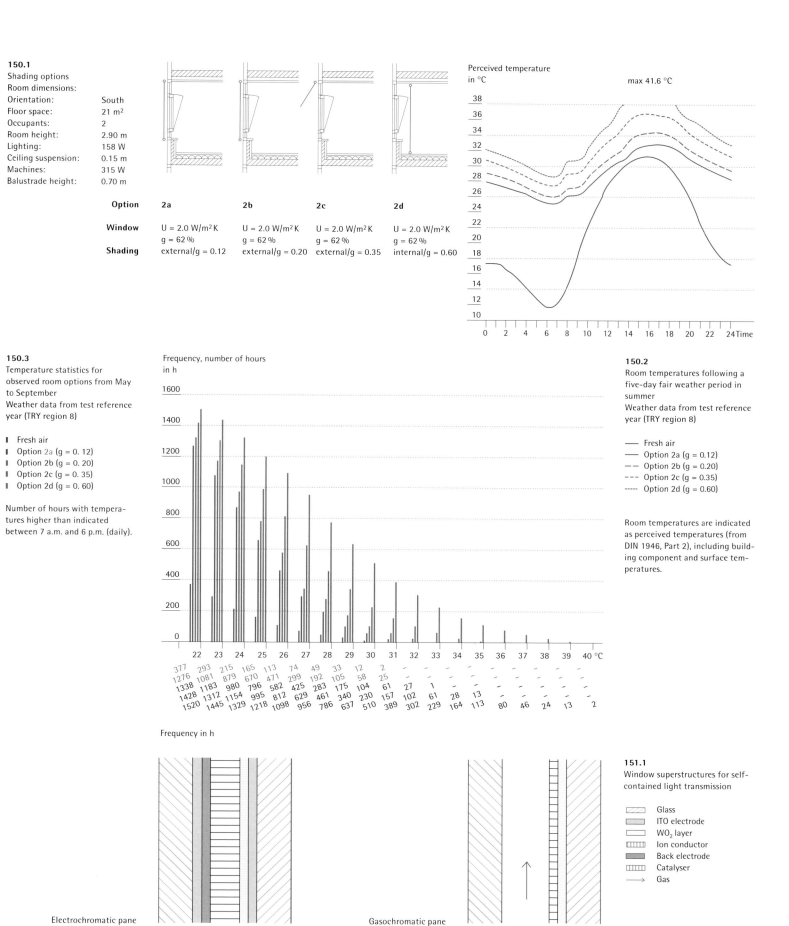

150.1
Shading options
Room dimensions:

Orientation:	South
Floor space:	21 m²
Occupants:	2
Room height:	2.90 m
Lighting:	158 W
Ceiling suspension:	0.15 m
Machines:	315 W
Balustrade height:	0.70 m

Option	2a	2b	2c	2d
Window	U = 2.0 W/m²K g = 62 % external/g = 0.12	U = 2.0 W/m²K g = 62 % external/g = 0.20	U = 2.0 W/m²K g = 62 % external/g = 0.35	U = 2.0 W/m²K g = 62 % internal/g = 0.60
Shading				

Perceived temperature
in °C   max 41.6 °C

150.3
Temperature statistics for
observed room options from May
to September
Weather data from test reference
year (TRY region 8)

▮ Fresh air
▮ Option 2a (g = 0. 12)
▮ Option 2b (g = 0. 20)
▮ Option 2c (g = 0. 35)
▮ Option 2d (g = 0. 60)

Number of hours with temperatures higher than indicated
between 7 a.m. and 6 p.m. (daily).

Frequency, number of hours
in h

150.2
Room temperatures following a
five-day fair weather period in
summer
Weather data from test reference
year (TRY region 8)

— Fresh air
— Option 2a (g = 0.12)
– – Option 2b (g = 0.20)
- - - Option 2c (g = 0.35)
· · · · Option 2d (g = 0.60)

Room temperatures are indicated
as perceived temperatures (from
DIN 1946, Part 2), including building component and surface temperatures.

Frequency in h

151.1
Window superstructures for self-
contained light transmission

▨	Glass
▨	ITO electrode
☐	WO₂ layer
▥	Ion conductor
▨	Back electrode
▥	Catalyser
→	Gas

Electrochromatic pane   Gasochromatic pane

151.2
Transmission behaviour
in gasochromatic panes

— Two panes
— One pane coated
— Tinted
Solar transmission
0,82
0,74
0,14

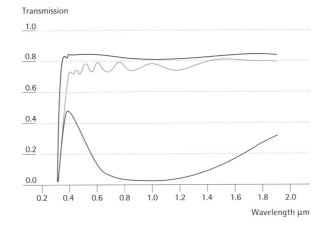

Transmission

1.0

0.8

0.6

0.4

0.2

0.0

0.2 0.4 0.6 0.8 1.0 1.2 1.4 1.6 1.8 2.0

Wavelength μm

152.1
Normal hemispheric transmission
Thermotropic layer between
2 x 4 mm glass

— 8mm glass without TTL
— 21°C
— 25°C
— 30°C
— 35°C
— 40°C
— 60°C

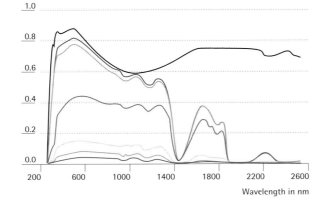

Normal hemispheric
transmission

1.0

0.8

0.6

0.4

0.2

0.0

200   600   1000   1400   1800   2200   2600

Wavelength in nm

152.2
Integral transmission
in thermotropic layers

— Visual, glass with TTL
-- Visual, glass without TTL
— Solar, glass with TTL
-- Solar, glass without TTL

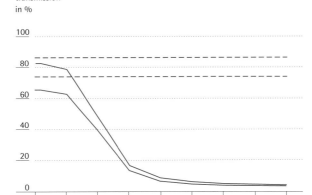

Normal hemispheric
transmission
in %

100

80

60

40

20

0

20   25   30   35   40   45   50   55   60

Temperature in °C

oxygen-containing gas, for example air, is sufficient. Since these processes are reversible, they do not require external electricity, which drastically reduces the number of coatings. All that is needed is one tungsten oxide layer with a thin catalyser coating. This method has two main benefits: a more economical manufacturing process as compared to electrochromatic panes and the option of evacuating heat resulting from light absorption via the gas flow. Finally, higher transmission values make this method clearly preferable to electrochromatic systems *(Figure 151.2)*.

In addition to these developments, the Fraunhofer Institute is currently studying panes with thermotropic layers: panes with self-regulating protection against overheating. In principle, this is a translucent blend of several materials (mostly polymer plastics) with differing refractive indices between the panes. Within a specific temperature range, which can be defined, a segregation of components occurs which strongly disperses the incident light in the layer and thus creates a diffuse reflection of the radiated light. During this process, the thermotropic layer clouds to white. Since the process is reversible, the layer quickly becomes translucent again when the temperature falls.

In *Figure 152*, solar and visible transmissions are indicated in relation to wavelength or temperature for the entire spectrum. By defining the switch temperature and the installation location on the façade, this type of layer can be used to regulate the heat flow in a building.

Figure 152.2 contrasts the transmission of natural light and solar heat through clear glass and through panes with thermotropic layers. The thermotropic panes become increasingly opaque when temperatures rise above 25° C, and visual comfort is compromised. However, the same could be said of blinds and louvres.

9.3 Daylight Incidence and Glare Protection

Figure 153 shows characteristic data for the newest pane combinations. The ideal pane combination of the future is the one shown in the upper left of the diagram, which also illustrates how poor the standard double insulating glazing of earlier years was, or rather is, since it is still being used in many homes.

The ideal scenario would be a combination of a U-value around 0.5 W/m²K with a variable g-value, without the use of shading. These developments, however, do not mean that there is no need at all for cooling to achieve ideal room conditions (a g-value of approx. 0.12 still produces room temperatures of approx. 32° C in high summer; see *Figure 150.2*).

The placement of daylight openings

The more horizontal the placement of a daylight opening in a building, the greater the amount of daylight carried into the room (for same-sized openings). It would be best to let the necessary amount of daylight into a building mostly through horizontal panes and to use vertical panes only for visual contact with the outside. This is, however, only possible in single-storey buildings. Attempts are being made to use technical means to re-direct the zenith light fraction of daylight into the building even from horizontal light openings. Although such high-tech systems have been developed and even celebrated, we should be critical in our assessment of whether these systems deliver what they promise.

Light-transporting systems

Heliostats and lightpipe systems transport sunlight into buildings across greater distances and can be used to create very bright zones in specific areas. This allows occupants to perceive whether or not the sun is shining on the outside. Such systems are well suited for lighting large stairwells and for special effects in closed halls. They are not useful for lighting with diffuse natural light in large areas *(Figure 154.1)*.

153
Typical glazing ratings for state-of-the-art pane combinations

✳ Honeycomb structures
✶ Aerogel granular
+ Capillaries
☼ 3-fold 2 x sel. Crypton
▲ 3-fold 2 x sel. Xenon
○ 2-fold 1 x sel. (Ag)
■ 2-fold 1 x sel. (SnO₂)
⌂ 2-fold
▼ 3-fold

Future potential of switching windows

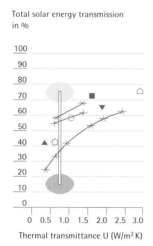

Total solar energy transmission in %

Thermal transmittance U (W/m² K)

154.1
Light defraction with heliostats

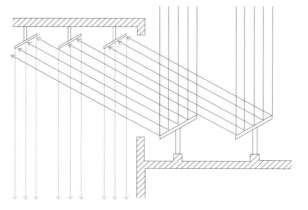

Shading with prisms

Prismatic light systems are usually designed to serve as shading systems as well. Direct sunlight is defracted and only the light above the top zenith angle is directed into the interior *(Figure 154.2)*. Prisms in skylights and angled glazing can thus be very effective, while prismatic shading and light defraction systems in vertical windows capture only a relatively small section of the sky. The effort necessary to redirect light and the resulting reduction of burning hours of artificial lighting systems are often disproportionate. To effectively use daylight, additional light defraction elements and reflectors on ceilings are necessary. Rooms equipped with redirecting prisms have a high-tech look but often require careful maintenance (without even taking the use of grey energy into consideration).

154.2
Shading with prisms

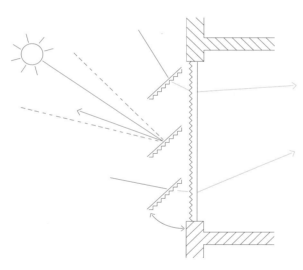

154.3
Shading with mirror grid reflectors

Mirror grid systems

Mirror grid systems are effectively optimized north "sheds" whose side sections are parabolically warped and mirror coated. As a result, sunlight is deflected and the northern light is directed into the building. These sheds can be of such small dimensions that they can be installed in the air cavity of a double-glazed system in the manner of closed prisms, making them virtually maintenance free *(Figure 154.3)*. In large hall systems, shading elements of this type can be used cost effectively. Bright reflections must be tolerated, but may be incorporated as a design element.

Refracting louvre systems and deviating struts

Refracting systems are usually designed as rigid systems that refract daylight from an upper window area into greater room depths *(Figure 154.4)*.

From a lighting technology perspective, it is unimportant whether these systems are installed on the outside, on the inside or between panes. What is important is to capture as much sky as possible. Optimally, the design of the louvres is different for east/west façades than for south façades. Rigid systems are always compromise solutions because an azimuth angle of less than 20° on a south façade in winter is often lower than it is on an east façade in summer. Louvre systems such as the one designed by Helmut Köster (Oka-Solar) reflect incident solar radiation in summer and refract the radiation to the ceiling in winter *(Figure 154.5)*. Light-refracting louvre systems fascinate mainly by their high-tech appearance combined with a light-tech operation, while being, in fact, low-tech systems.

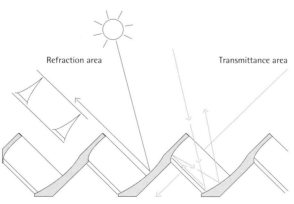

Refraction area   Transmittance area

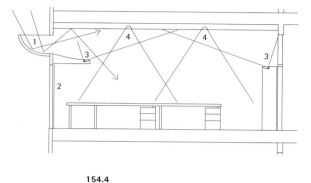

154.5
Functional principle of
Oka-Solar shading louvres

1 Shading and daylight refraction
   with OKA-Solar
2 Glare protection screen
3 Supplementary daylight lighting
4 Night lighting, indirect
5 Night lighting, direct

154.4
Deflection principle with
deviating strut

1 Daylight refraction
   with anidolic mirror
2 Sun and glare protection,
   internal or external
3 Supplementary daylight lighting
4 Night lighting

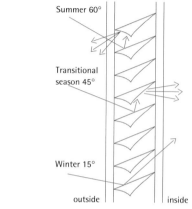

Summer 60°

Transitional
season 45°

Winter 15°

outside   inside

to 154.5
Functional principle of newly
developed light-deflecting louvres
(Helmut Köster)

10°

20°

30°

40°

50°

60°

70°

80°

Holographic systems

Holographic systems operate on three-dimensional grids which direct light to an output area depending on the wavelength. Holograms can also be used for light refraction and for shading. The first stage of the development of holograms is completed; further developments will surely follow.

Rigid systems and mobile systems

All rigid systems are compromise solutions because they cannot react with the same degree of efficiency to different azimuth angles over the course of a day or year. For large spaces, rigid systems make sense, but small spaces and rooms designed to be occupied by only a few individuals should be equipped with mobile systems, that is to say, systems that can be individually adjusted.

All shading elements such as louvres, awnings and blinds of all kinds always have the disadvantage that, while they reduce incident sun radiation, they also limit the daylight that enters a room. Treating the upper and lower sides of louvres differently is a simple technical approach to maintain extremely good g-values while achieving diffuse radiation.

9.4   Natural Ventilation

Generally speaking, all buildings should be naturally ventilated. Yet there are some exceptions, such as special requirements for production in clean-room conditions. There may also be safety reasons for not opening the outer skin. Usually, however, people prefer direct contact with their environment rather than being closed in. The logical solution, then, is natural ventilation through façade designs employing large window elements that can be opened: top-hung windows, sliding windows, etc.

Natural ventilation also creates a positive effect in the transitional seasons when a surplus of incident heat can be ventilated simply by using thermals to prevent overheating. As architecture has moved from single-leaf to double-leaf buildings and further to buildings under glass, natural ventilation has been a constant challenge. The future is likely to bring even greater urban density: this means we will have to take a second look at skyscrapers. Thus, the problems inherent in the double-leaf façade will be revisited.

Double-leaf façade: A must for skyscrapers?

The use of double-leaf façades is currently in fashion and is usually justified by an apparent early return on the initial high investment. This is generally, in simple terms, a misconception. Double-leaf façades cost per square metre anywhere from 1,500 to 3,000 DM and thus much more than well-insulated and finished single-leaf façades, while the energy savings often amount to only approximately 2 % to 4 % of the extra investment. Hence, in the case of double-leaf façades, it is worth considering whether they should be marketed solely on the basis of energy savings or whether other essential aspects argue for their use. These may be factors like sound protection or the reduction of wind pressures on skyscraper façades. A double-leaf façade should never jeopardize the budget for a building, as it did in the case of a prominent office building in Basel where the second-skin façade added to an existing multi-storey building cost nearly twice as much as the buildings services installed in each square metre of usable space. The main factors with regard to single- or double-leaf façades are discussed in the following sections, exemplified in a small bank tower *(Figure 155)*.

Meteorological conditions

To begin with, the issue of single- versus double-leaf is not so much a question of design or construction, but one of use. The meteorological conditions at the site are key to determining the kind of wind forces that will act on the body of the object. These natural conditions also indicate the distribution of temperatures and wind velocities over the course of a year. Special attention must be given to outside temperatures above 20° and to air velocities exceeding 8 m/sec *(Figure 156)*.

The ground plan in *Figure 155* indicates predicted wind pressure coefficients for a westerly wind direction. These pressure coefficients can be measured precisely in a wind tunnel experiment or determined empirically from the typical conditions of air movement near cylindrical buildings. The wind pressure coefficient represents wind pressure in relation to dynamic pressure in undisturbed flow. The wind pressure coefficient $c_p = + 1.0$ corresponds to full dynamic pressure; a coefficient $c_p = - 0.5$ corresponds to the suction often occurring on the leeward side and near the roof. *Figure 155* shows that in the air movement around a cylindrical skyscraper, one can expect much more pronounced negative pressure peaks — almost double the wind pressure, creating an impetus for floor cross-ventilation.

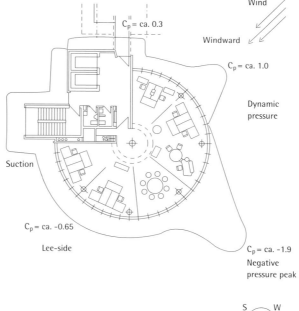

155
Schmidtbank skyscraper in Hof
Model photo and wind pressure values on façade
Architects:
BFK-Bertsch-Friedrich-Kalcher, Stuttgart

Wind

Windward

$C_p^{II} = $ ca. 0.3

$C_p = $ ca. 1.0

Dynamic pressure

Suction

$C_p = $ ca. -0.65

Lee-side

$C_p = $ ca. -1.9
Negative pressure peak

S W
E N

Reduction of wind pressures

The pressures inside a double-leaf façade are essentially defined by the relation of flow resistance for the ventilation louvres and flow resistance for façade cross-ventilation. The latter is influenced by the distance between the double-leaf façade and the constructional components inside the façade.

Ventilation slits in the outer glass skin can have cross-ventilation resistances c_V of approximately 0.65 (the flow resistance z being approx. 2.4). For horizontal cross-ventilation between two glass skins (inner and outer glazing), the flow resistance z is nearly 0.2. This is a result of wall friction and losses due to constructional components as well as redirected flow within the perimeter façades. A distance of 60 cm between outer glass skin and inner façade results in the pressure curve shown in *Figure 155*, depending on the louvre dimensions, oncoming wind flow and orientation.

Evaluating natural ventilation

Figure 157.1 presents four different façade options, of which two are double-leaf façades and one is a single-leaf façade. The arrows indicate the influence of

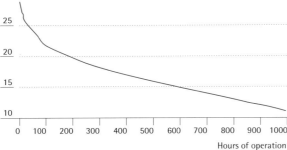

Outside air temperature
in °C

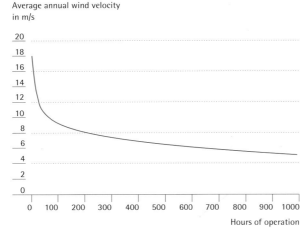

Average annual wind velocity
in m/s

156
Wind statistics and average distribution of outside temperatures and wind directions in Hof during hours of operation

157.1
Façade options

A   Double-leaf perimeter façade
B   Box window
C   Top-hinged sash window
D   Slot window

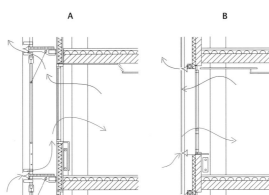

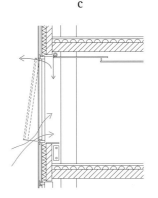

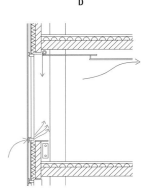

window ventilation due to thermals, natural cross-ventilation for winds from a westerly direction and natural building cross-ventilation when stairwell doors are open *(Figures 157.2 to 157.4)*.

The study thus demonstrates a range of options for façade design. The first option shown is a perimeter double-leaf façade. The second double-leaf façade option features vertical glass struts, making it basically a box window solution. The two single-leaf façades show, first, a design with top-hinged sash windows and, second, one with ventilated slot windows.

The slot window has a narrow fresh-air vent above the parapet or below the ceiling. Such openings can also be designed around the whole perimeter of the window. The slot can be created with a special supporting element, a gap slider or a so-called louvre window with mechanical controls. A comparison of window ventilation on days with low winds (presumed outside air temperature of 18°C) shows that the single-leaf façade with top-hinged sash windows provides the most active air change rates. Here, the high intensity may warrant either a fresh-air surge or simply a slight opening of the pivot-hung window.

The two double-leaf façades also promote sufficient air flow, which can, again, be influenced by the inward-opening pivot-hung windows. The lowest air change rate is associated with the ventilated slot window (approx. 2.5 ac/h^{-1}). This fact indicates clearly the limitations of slot or joint ventilation.

Cross-ventilation is presented as an example of wind impact (presumed average wind velocity 4 m/sec and 10 m/sec, west wind). The perimeter double-leaf façade shows clear evidence of intense outside air flow between the two glass skins; the air change rates in the offices range from 8 to approx. 40 ac/h. These air change rates for inner, opened windows can be limited by controllable tilt positions; i.e the users adjust the level of ventilation. For the double-leaf bow window solution, we can see similarly high air change rates, in like manner near the negative pressure peaks of the façades. In contrast, the wind-protected side exhibits low air change rates, so that we must define this option as marginal natural ventilation.

For the single-leaf façade with top-hinged sash windows, six windows were assumed open at regular distances. Even for average wind velocities, the air change rates are extremely high on the windward side. This solution requires a good mechanism for the openable element, which is rare. With high wind velocities, one can observe extremely strong cross-ventilation, possibly accompanied by noise, and therefore restricting the natural ventilation from the windows.

The solution of slot windows and exhaust air ventilation produces moderate air change rates, at times

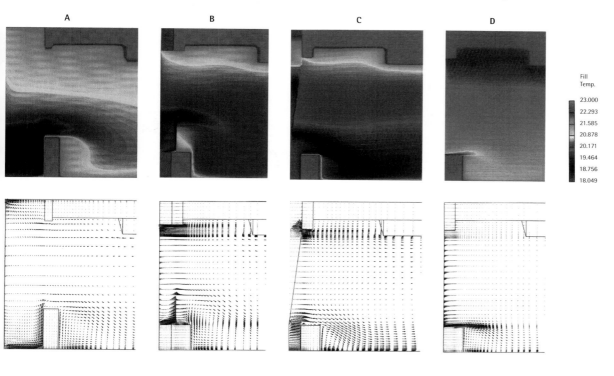

Fill
Temp.

23.000
22.293
21.585
20.878
20.171
19.464
18.756
18.049

157.2
Window ventilation and thermals on days with very moderate winds and outside temperatures of 18°C

even too low. On still days or during low winds, slot windows should be used together with smaller openable window elements for cross-ventilation to compensate for the shortcomings of the system.

As in all tall buildings, natural ventilation in a building with doors open to the stairwells can have a great impact on the overall operation of the building. As in figures illustrating cross-ventilation with oncoming winds from the west, this section once again indicates expected air change rates, the difference being in the presumed outside temperatures *(Figure 157.4:* first value $T_0 = 15°C$ / second value $T_0 = -18°C$).

For the perimeter double-leaf façade, there are excellent air change rates when outside temperatures are moderate; however, these rates rise considerably as temperatures fall, meaning that the air change would

then need to be limited by some means. In the box window solution, the analogous air change rates are approximately 50% of those in the first option, an air change which remains more or less moderate even when outside temperatures are extremely low. In the case of partially opened top-hinged sash windows and the same presumed thermal conditions, the air change rates achieved are similar to those in the double-leaf perimeter façade. In the case of joint or gap ventilation, thermals have only a limited effect (transition season, $T_0 = 15°C$), and demonstrably better effects when outside temperatures are correspondingly low.

Door-opening forces in individual office rooms are another important factor to consider. For normal operation, door-opening forces should not exceed

157.3

Natural cross-ventilation for west wind

Approximate local degrees of flow for average wind (4 m/sec) and strong wind (10 m/sec) with 6 tilted windows at regular intervals or ventilated slot windows (96 m slot, option D)

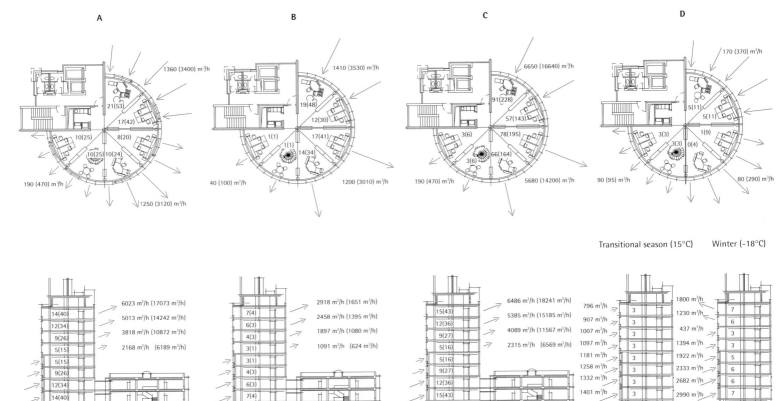

Transitional season (15°C)   Winter (-18°C)

157.4

Natural cross-ventilation with doors opened to stairwell

Approximate air change rate in transitional season (15°C) and in winter (-18°C)

Transitional season:
6 windows are tilted open on each floor

Winter:
1 window is fully opened on each floor

approximately 25 N (or 2.5 kg). Door-opening forces of up to 40 N are acceptable only for a few days or hours per year. *Table 6* indicates forces acting upon interior doors (approx. 2 m² door surface) opening in one direction. In the perimeter double-leaf façades, door-opening forces exceed 25 N only nine hours per year, which is an acceptable range.

In double-leaf façades with box windows and in single-leaf façades with tilt windows, similar door-opening forces are manifest; on upper floors, door-opening forces greater than 25 N can be expected for 40 %

of operation time and forces above 40 N for 30 % of the time. These façades are either poorly designed or need better pressure compensation near doors, which would introduce new problems such as the risk of fire spreading, reduced soundproofing, etc. The single-leaf façade with slot windows has somewhat better values, but here, too, above average door-opening forces occur frequently. This type of façade is therefore assessed in the same manner as the previous two options.

Table 6

Frequencies of excessive door-opening forces when office doors are open for oncoming wind and different façade options

Double-leaf Façade Options

Perimeter Façade

Wind direction	Frequency (h/a)	Δp > 25 Pa (h/a)	v_{max} (m/s)	Δp > 40 Pa (h/a)	v_{max} (m/s)
N	180	0	14	0	18
NNE	189	0	14	0	18
ENE	121	0	14	0	18
E	77	0	14	0	18
ESE	133	0	14	0	18
SSE	199	0	77	0	98
S	219	0	77	0	98
SSW	330	0	77	0	98
WSW	508	8	14	0	18
W	265	1	14	0	18
WNW	114	0	14	0	18
NNW	135	0	14	0	18
$\Sigma_{absolute}$	2470	9		0	
$\Sigma_{relative}$	100 %	0 %		0 %	

Box Window

Wind direction	Frequency (h/a)	Δp > 25 Pa (h/a)	v_{max} (m/s)	Δp > 40 Pa (h/a)	v_{max} (m/s)
N	180	82	4	45	
NNE	189	118	4	86	
ENE	121	54	4	41	
E	77	33	4	25	
ESE	133	66	4	46	
SSE	199	0	20	0	2
S	219	0	20	0	2
SSW	330	0	20	0	2
WSW	508	380	4	318	
W	265	173	4	131	
WNW	114	33	4	20	
NNW	135	53	4	31	
$\Sigma_{absolute}$	2470	992		743	
$\Sigma_{relative}$	100 %	40 %		30 %	

Single-leaf Façade Option

Top-hinged Sash Window

Wind direction	Frequency (h/a)	Δp > 25 Pa (h/a)	v_{max} (m/s)	Δp > 40 Pa (h/a)	v_{max} (m/s)
N	180	82	4	45	5
NNE	189	118	4	86	5
ENE	121	54	4	41	5
E	77	33	4	25	5
ESE	133	66	4	46	5
SSE	199	0	20	0	26
S	219	0	20	0	26
SSW	330	0	20	0	26
WSW	508	380	4	318	5
W	265	173	4	131	5
WNW	114	33	4	20	5
NNW	135	53	4	31	5
$\Sigma_{absolute}$	2470	992		743	
$\Sigma_{relative}$	100 %	40 %		30 %	

Slot Window

Wind direction	Frequency (h/a)	Δp > 25 Pa (h/a)	v_{max} (m/s)	Δp > 40 Pa (h/a)	v_{max} (m/s)
N	180	13	7	4	
NNE	189	30	7	5	
ENE	121	15	7	9	
E	77	10	7	4	
ESE	133	16	7	9	
SSE	199	0	35	0	4
S	219	0	35	0	4
SSW	330	0	35	0	4
WSW	508	144	7	109	
W	265	66	7	33	
WNW	114	7	7	1	
NNW	135	5	7	1	
$\Sigma_{absolute}$	2470	306		175	
$\Sigma_{relative}$	100 %	12 %		7 %	

Building climatology

In addition to natural air movement and wind pressures, insulation in summer and the related climate conditions in offices in summer are important factors. The four façade options are structured as follows; related technical data appears in *Figure 158*.

– Double-leaf façade, perimeter
Outer skin single glazing (clear glass)
Ventilation slit 5 cm top and bottom
Integrated louvre shading (high reflecting)
Inner façade insulating glazing (position 2)

– Double-leaf façade with box windows
Outer skin single glazing (clear glass)
Ventilation slit 2 cm top and bottom
Integrated screen-fabric
Inner façade insulating glazing (position 2)

– Single-leaf façade with neutral sun protection glazing
Sun protection insulated glazing (51/39)
Interior shading/glare protection (Z = 0.7)
Single-leaf façade with exterior sun protection
Insulating glazing (position 2)
Exterior louvre sun protection (high reflecting)

The graphs indicate the total solar energy transmission and light transmission factors for each façade, as well as a detailed representation of secondary heat emission and radiation transmission. Depending on façade orientation, the diffuse and direct radiation on the façade varies greatly for each structure *(Figure 159)*, calling for a flexible handling of shading measures. *Figures 160.1 to 160.5* contain further comparisons; due to the total solar energy transmission values, the radiation input in summer is especially significant.

As expected, the cooling loads are lowest in the perimeter double-leaf façade with external shading, although the exterior shading in combination with a single-leaf façade also produces comparably good values. The radiation input in summer for the window box solution is somewhat higher due to the lower total reflection value (higher secondary heat transmission, higher radiation transmission). The highest heat yield occurs in the single-leaf façade with reflective glazing and interior shading *(Figure 160.1)*.

158
Technical parameters for each façade option

Light transmission in %

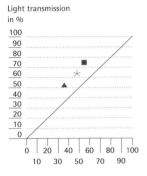

Total solar energy transmission in %

☆ Double-leaf façade
☆ Box window
▲ Infrastop neutral
■ Insulating glazing Pos. 2

%

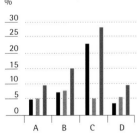

A Double-leaf façade
  Integrated shading
B Box window
  Integrated screen
C Glass with sun protection
  Glare protection
D Insulating glazing
  External sun protection

■ Secondary heat transfer
▦ Radiation transmission
■ Total

External and internal cooling loads *(Figure 160.2)* call for moderate to high effort to maintain temperatures in the offices in summer, depending on the type of façade. The façade design and above all the shading component make the "double-leaf façade, perimeter" option with quasi-external shading and the single-leaf façade with external shading the most energy-efficient solutions; less efficiency is provided by the box window solution and by the neutral sun protection glazing with interior shading *(Figure 160.3)*.
Diurnal room temperatures were studied for each option on the basis that a mechanical ventilation system with secondary cooling (air change approx. 2–5 ac/h) would transport fresh intake air at approximately 16° C into the rooms in summer, compensating for at least part of the cooling load *(Figure 160.4)*.
The air and building component temperatures as well as the resulting room temperatures are graphed on a daily basis for the month of July. All temperatures should be interpreted as mean temperatures within office areas. The window temperature is the temperature measured at the inner window pane, deviating only slightly from the air temperature, especially at night, and rising during the day due to sun exposure. The average floor and ceiling temperatures are nearly identical to the mean air temperature during the day. When the thermal masses heat up overnight, the air temperature is naturally lower. In the case of the single-leaf façade with neutral shading and night cooling, air temperatures in the room are no longer low-

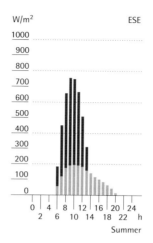

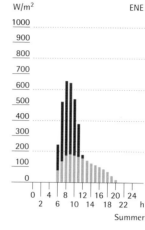

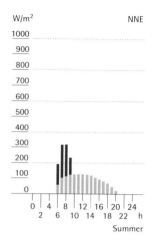

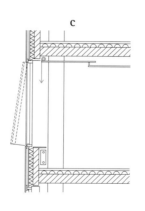

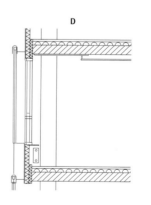

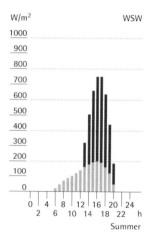

159
Incident radiation over the course of a day on a sunny day in July for different façade orientations

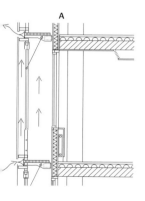

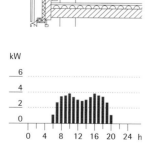

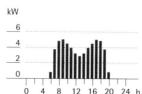

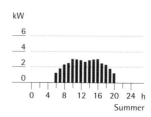

160
Shading options

A   Double-leaf perimeter façade, integrated shading
B   Box window, integrated shading
C   Neutral sun-protection glazing, internal glare protection
D   Insulating glass, external shading

160.1
Incident radiation in summer

160.2
Internal and external cooling loads

160.3
Load compensation

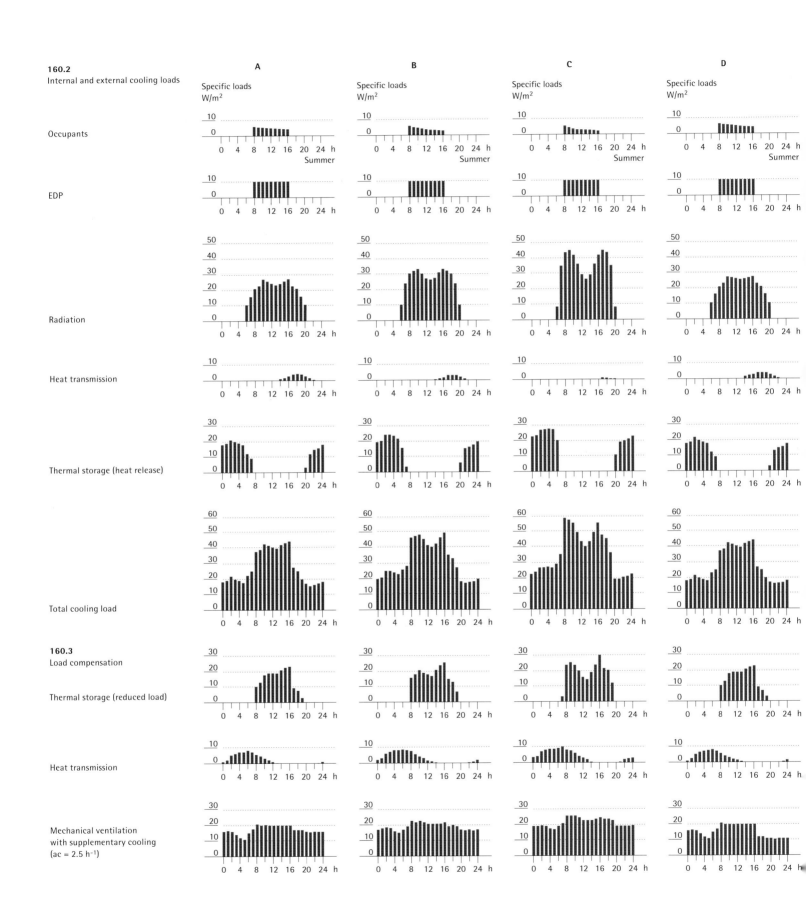

ered to 22°C; in other words, the whole structure is unable – even with optimal thermal storage – to maintain sufficient temperatures. In the perimeter double-leaf façade and in the single-leaf façade with external shading, an air temperature of 22°C can be achieved by about 2 a.m., showing a greater cooling potential.

As the comparison of façades shows, the double-leaf façade with quasi-external shading has by far the best values, with the single-leaf façade with external shading a close second. Clearly the worst solution is the single-leaf façade with neutral sun protection glazing and interior shading; equally poor is the choice of a double-leaf façade with box windows and awning.

Conditions improve considerably in a typical year with low outside temperatures and no good weather periods. For the perimeter double-leaf façade and the single-leaf façade with external shading, room temperatures peak just above 27°C, and room tempera-

tures of 26°C are exceeded only a few hours per year. The room temperatures in box window solutions are still acceptable, while the temperatures resulting for single-leaf façades with neutral sun protection glazing are clearly too high.

These comparisons confirm that the double-leaf façade, especially the perimeter type with quasi-external shading, makes the most sense and is often preferable to all other solutions. The criteria included in the assessment indicate that double-leaf façades are usually best suited to being regulated for the most part manually, with only partial automated systems. Whenever double-leaf façades can be constructed, especially in skyscrapers or to protect against noise emissions, in a cost-efficient manner, their advantages are absolutely convincing and they are thus the obvious choice. Yet, and this cannot be emphasized

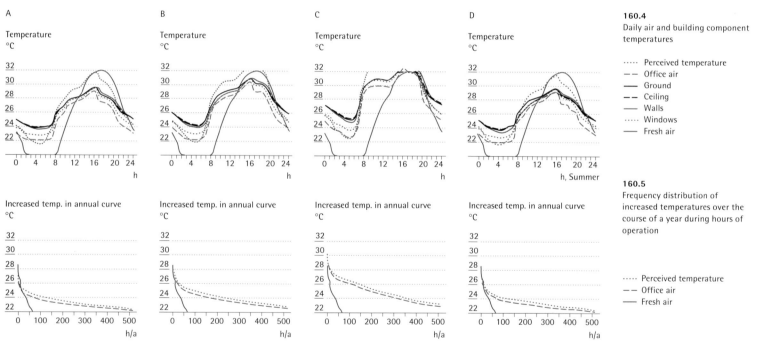

160.4
Daily air and building component temperatures

.... Perceived temperature
– – Office air
——— Ground
– – Ceiling
——— Walls
.... Windows
——— Fresh air

160.5
Frequency distribution of increased temperatures over the course of a year during hours of operation

.... Perceived temperature
– – Office air
——— Fresh air

enough: the second skin must not drastically increase the total investment costs and more specifically the costs for the façade. The topic of double-leaf façades is not only relevant to skyscrapers, as the following example of a competition design illustrates:

Midfield Building, Zurich Airport
(Architects: Theo Hotz, Zurich / von Gerkan Marg + Partner, Hamburg)

Busy airports are not suited to natural ventilation because of the poor air quality in the immediate environment. The project shown in *Figure 161* required a design that would keep energy consumption to a minimum during constant operation; this type of terminal building is in operation around the clock, seven days a week.

The overall concept developed for the Midfield Building creates a harmony between the environmental conditions and the requirements for use. The concept is founded in an integrative method of observation, and the construction was conceived accordingly. The building's main façades lie to the north and south, with its narrow façades facing east and west *(Figure 162.1)*. It offers a variety of options in the sense of being an ecologically correct building: the main areas of interest are the façades; the thermal

161
Midfield terminal,
Zurich Airport
Competition design,
Architect: T. Hotz

masses and air spaces function as thermal buffer zones *(Figure 162.2)*.

Another significant issue is the requirement for thermal, hygienic and visual comfort. With this in mind, an integrated façade concept was developed which approximates the performance of a polyvalent wall, that is, the requirements for the interior spaces utilize natural resources whenever possible. For thermal, hygienic and visual comfort, the spaces inside the terminal should have the following attributes:

- Comfortable room temperatures in winter and summer (20° C – 27° C)
- Comfortable relative humidity (30 – 65 % rH)
- Comfortable temperatures in surrounding surfaces (surface temperatures of 19° C in winter, 30° C in summer).
- Maximum daylight incidence (daylight quotient clearly above 20 %)
- Unobstructed visual contact from the inside out and vice versa

Furthermore, hygienic interior air conditions are ensured by ventilating all occupied rooms from floor to ceiling whenever possible to exhaust noxious materials and odours with minimal air volumes by using thermal air currents.

To fully harness the annual sun and light volumes, a façade was developed that is able to exhaust the incident heat energy in summer through reflection and rear ventilation while absorbing the heat energy in winter by using solar heating for the cavity between inner and outer glazing.

The façades to the south and west are double-leaf façades with single external safety glazing and internal insulating glazing with blinds between the two panes. The technical data are as follows:

- Total solar energy transmission with shading: approx. 0.07
- Total solar energy transmission without shading: approx. 0.45
- Thermal transmittance: total 0.95 W/m²K

Depending on the season, requirements for use and solar conditions, façades exposed to too much sun radiation are regulated and rear ventilated to minimize the necessity for mechanical cooling or heating. The façades to the north are triple-leaf, their glazing structure being the same as described above. Instead of partially translucent blinds with absorption and reflection surfaces, these façades will be equipped with a partially translucent Agero film for total solar transmission of approximately 0.25 when the film is in place and 0.45 when the film is not used. The light transmission factors for the complete pane combination without shading are in the range of 0.45 and are mainly the result of the insulating glazing capabilities used in the installation.

162.1
Floor plan, level 2

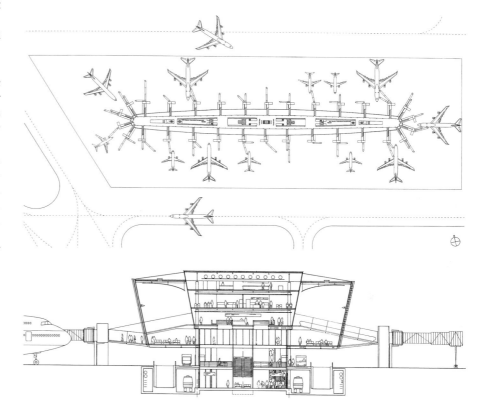

162.2
Cross-section

To improve the variable thermal transmittance, it has been suggested that the blinds on the east, west and south façades be lowered, and the Agero film be activated overnight on the north façade in winter. This makes it possible to split the space between inner and outer façade into two air cavities, to dampen the internal circulation and to reduce heat loss. The operating conditions are shown in *Figure 163.1*.

To reduce energy requirements, the buildings are predominantly naturally cooled in summer and overnight during good weather periods in spring and fall (from about 1:30 p.m. to 5:30 a.m.) Filtered fresh air is drawn into the building, flowing through it from floor to ceiling because of thermal air movement. Skylights evacuate air due to the negative pressure created by oncoming winds and also transfer heat out of the building, unloading the thermal masses.

The extremely large skylights virtually bathe the building in daylight, requiring few lighting hours late in the evening and at night. The visual demands (contact with the outside) and lighting demands (daylight) are thus fully compatible *(Figure 163.2)*.

The great room heights and a supplementary water cooling system results in a temperature range of approximately 20° C to 30° C in the terminals, while a temperature increase from 20° C to 23° C can be expected during the day in the waiting areas (rooms with approx. 3 m height). Similar temperature variations occur in the mezzanine storey in the different terminal areas. The use of earth heat with bore hole technology and adiabatic cooling systems round out the concept. The total volume of rainwater is collected from the roof and used for adiabatic desorptive cooling as well as in the sanitary areas where appropriate, substituting for the use of potable water in these areas.

163.1
Functional principle of double-leaf façade

Summer - sunny day	Summer – overcast day	Winter - sunny day	Winter – overcast day	Winter - night
g-value approx. 0.07 U-value = 0.95 W/m²K	g-value approx. 0.45 U-value = 1.0 W/m²K	g-value approx. 0.40 U-value = 0.95 W/m²K	g-value approx. 0.45 U-value = 0,95 W/m²K	g-value = 0.85 W/m²K

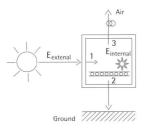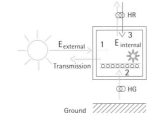

Building envelope options

Summer scenario

1 Reduced incident radiation through polyvalent second skin façade with integrated sun protection
2 Thermoactive cooling by transporting the direct 'remaining' radiation to floors and ceilings respectively
3 Transporting the external and internal 'remaining' heat by means of cooled hygiene ventilation (air conditioning)

Winter scenario

1 Heat gain (HR) through passive solar energy use
2 Heat management by means of polyvalent second skin façade with high insulating glazing combination
3 Thermoactive component heating through earth (thermal) heat pumped from the soil
  HR (heat recovery) from exhaust air for the purpose of heating the hygienic intake air

163.2
Room milieu

9.5 Buildings under Glass

The history of buildings under glass began nearly two hundred years ago with simple glass enclosures and exorbitant heating requirements. Today, we are able to manufacture glass with low heat-loss attributes; nevertheless, the glass house is still far from being a low-energy house. Comfort comes into play: the savings from reduced heating requirements may easily be outweighed by an increased need for cooling. The glass building has therefore little to recommend it as a structure used for mainly sedentary activities. A detailed study is necessary in each case to establish the potential advantages in energy and in material consumption. Glass-covered atria, winter gardens and buildings under glass are good solutions whenever the specific use goes hand in hand with low requirements for room climate, especially when glass-clad buildings are naturally ventilated in warm weather.

When heating, ventilation and glazing types are synchronized, interior atria can drastically reduce heating requirements. Especially in combination with the growing urban density predicted for the future, buildings with glass halls, glass arcades and winter gardens are once again being considered, more so than they were even ten years ago. *Figure 164* shows the schematic development of a building envelope based on a traditional comb structure (and on the headquarters of the Landeszentralbank Hessen in Frankfurt). The illustrations show that the surface volume ratio (A/V ratio) is improved by creating a glass-covered arcade. The next step introduces winter gardens instead of open courtyards, leading ultimately to a glass envelope around the entire building. The diagrams of heat consumption and cooling loads indicate that heat requirements fall as each step is introduced and are finally cut nearly in half.

The cooling load, by contrast, rises, but to a lesser degree. The increase in the load is approximately one-third of the original value (63 % to 100 %). The individual options and their main technical data are as follows:

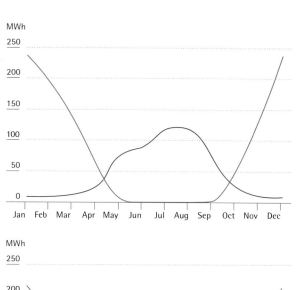

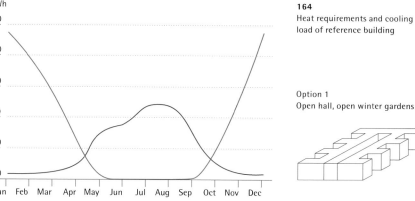

164
Heat requirements and cooling load of reference building

Option 1
Open hall, open winter gardens

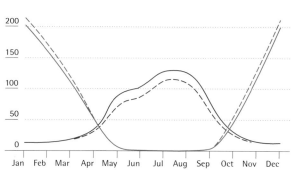

Option 2
Glazed hall, open winter gardens

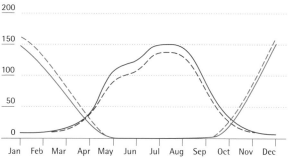

Option 3
Glazed hall and winter gardens

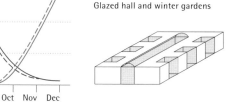

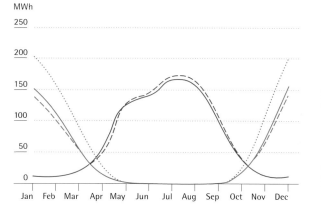

Option 4
Fully glazed building

Option	1	2.1	2.2	3.1	3.2	4.1	4.2	4.3
U - value:								
– Hall		6.0	1.6	6.0	1.6	1.6	6.0	6.0
– Rooms	1.6	1.6	3.0	1.6	3.0	3.0	1.6	3.0
Heat requirement kWh/m²a	51.2	43.5	46.7	30.5	34.3	28.5	25.9	40.3
Cooling load kWh/m²a	27.3	30.5	25.9	37.4	32.7	41.7	43.3	42.2

Table 7.1
Building envelope parameters

SG — Single glazing
IG — Insulating glazing
TIG — Thermal insulating glazing

*) additionally with 3 heating options each for central courtyard and for winter gardens

Options 3.1.1 and 3.2.1
$T_{min} - 3°$ C
Options 3.1.2 and 3.2.2
T_{min} 7° C
Options 3.1.3 and 3.2.3
T_{min} 18° C

Type	Option	External Façade/Glass Envelope			Internal Façade facing courtyard/Winter garden		
		Glass	Thermal transmittance U in W/m²K	Total solar energy transmission	Type of Glass	U-value in W/m²K	Total solar energy transmission
No glass envelope	1.1	TIG	1.5	62 %	–	–	–
Glass roof over central courtyard	2.1	SG	6.0	97 %	TIG	1.6	62 %
	2.2	TIG	1.6	62 %	IG	3.0	77 %
Glass roof cover over central courtyard and lateral winter garden	3.1 *)	SG	6.0	87 %	TIG	1.5	62 %
	3.2 *)	TIG	1.6	62 %	IG	3.0	77 %
Full glass envelope	4.1	TIG	1.6	62 %	IG	3.0	77 %
	4.2	SG	6.0	87 %	TIG	1.0	62 %
	4.3	SG	6.0	87 %	IG	3.0	77 %

Table 7.2
Building Climatological Approach

Sliding up min. ventilation heat

Takes total floor area of building into consideration (20 700 m²)

			Winter	Summer
Shading:	Winter garden areas facing outward with external shading	z = 0.18 (shading diminution factor)		
	Rooms facing central courtyard with interior sun protection	z = 0.50 (shading diminution factor)		
Percentage of window surface to total surface	Exterior	40 %		
	Windows facing courtyard and winter garden windows	75 %		
Interior loads:	Occupants:	12 m²/person		
	Mach./appliances	12 W/m²		
	Lighting	15 W/m²		
Room temperatures:	Basic load (outside of operating period)		18° C	18° C
	Min. heating temp. (during operating period)		21° C	20° C
	Summer temperatures (cooling)	for outside air temperatures up to 24° C	24° C	24° C
		for outside air temperatures up to 32° C	to 27° C	27° C

The heating of the inner courtyard and the winter gardens was varied for the computed example *(Figure 165)*. Furthermore, the inner and outer U-values of the glass cladding were varied to provide an overview. The cooling loads in all options represent the heat gain that has to be evacuated unless the building can be constantly ventilated or unless outside air can flow into the occupied areas by natural means. *Table 7.1* lists the technical parameters as well as temperature variations, again based on inner load conditions.

Figure 166 is a diagram of annual energy requirements for lighting a reference building: they rise the greater the glass envelope. Atria are often incorporated into urban and architectural solutions to create more attractive space for use. Whether or not the ultimate goals of environmental protection and resource conservation are truly achieved can be determined only by taking a close look at material and energy consumption.

In conclusion, here are some successful recent examples. *Figure 167.1* shows a small semi-circular atrium, several storeys high, for a multi-use building on Avenue Montaigne, Paris. Designed by Epstein, Glaiman + Vidal, the building features a cost-efficient, light filigree glass-clad structure with four-point fastenings for the glass panes. The glass construction for this project, completed in 1993, was designed and planned by the renowned office of RFR (Peter Rice, Martin Francis, Ian Ritchie), Paris. *Figure 167.2* is a close-up of one of the H-shaped four-point fastenings showing the constructional details. In this area, especially, an astonishing variety of solutions has been developed by architects who have committed themselves to light-tech.

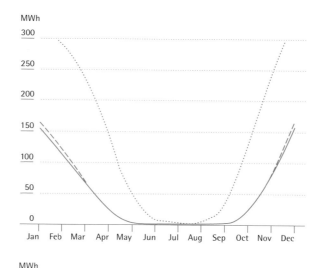

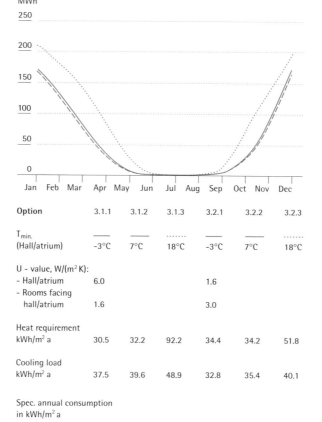

Option	3.1.1	3.1.2	3.1.3	3.2.1	3.2.2	3.2.3
$T_{min.}$ (Hall/atrium)	-3°C	7°C	18°C	-3°C	7°C	18°C
U - value, W/(m²K):						
- Hall/atrium	6.0			1.6		
- Rooms facing hall/atrium	1.6			3.0		
Heat requirement kWh/m² a	30.5	32.2	92.2	34.4	34.2	51.8
Cooling load kWh/m² a	37.5	39.6	48.9	32.8	35.4	40.1

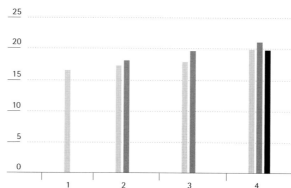

165
Heat requirements and specific cooling load of reference building
Options for heating of inner courtyard and winter gardens. Thermal building simulation according to test reference year

Options 3.1

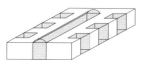

Options 3.2

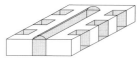

166
Annual energy for lighting in reference building
Building with increased cladding and glazing options

■ Sub-variant 1
■ Sub-variant 2
■ Sub-variant 3

Figure 168 shows a competition design (first prize) by the architectural office HPP Hentrich-Petschnigg & Partner KG (R.Thoma/Duk-Kyn Ryang). The building has a ring-shaped structure and an integrated glass atrium where conference, lecture and training rooms are designed as suspended cable cars. *Figures 169.1* to *169.6* provide a final overview of the topics relevant in an energy-efficient planning of large glass-covered spaces.

167.1
Avenue Montaigne
A 24-metre-high glass curtain wall completes the half-circle atrium; the curtain wall is braced with radial cables to the ceiling.
By carefully optimizing the supporting framework, an elegant and cost-efficient structure was achieved.

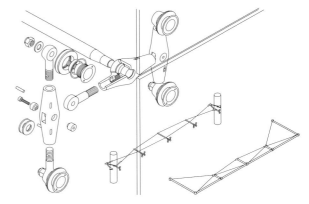

167.2
La Villette
First application of point fasteners with ball bearing in glass.
The "La Villette system" of the glass curtain with cable braces for wind resistance became the prototype for new glass construction.

Design for a corporate
headquarters
Architects: HPP-
Hentrich Petschnigg & Partner KG

Highly reflecting translucent
Agero foil, screen, light grey
Vertiso louvres, sun and glare
protection

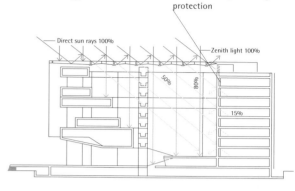

Offices facing courtyard,
daylight quotients in %
on overcast day

— Office 1st floor
- - Office 5th floor
···· Office 9th floor

169.1
Temperature layers
in the atrium

In summer, roughly 10 % of the
glass surfaces are opened to create
natural ventilation and heat evac-
uation. To maintain comfortable
room conditions, floor cooling has
been suggested (using recirculated
water from the cooling system).
When the atrium is open to the
wind, the air change rate is close
to 6 ac/h (outside air velocity:
approx. 2.5 m/sec). The open
spaces in the lobbies and on the
suspended floors are partially
cooled or heated.

In winter, the floor cooling is
switched to heating, and recirculated water (approx. 23°C) flows
through the pipes in the floor, creating a surface temperature of
approximately 20°C in the occupied areas. In addition, the vertical
and horizontal glass surfaces are
equipped with integrated façade
heating (MSH profiles, System or
similar), derived from radiation to
such a degree that the interior
surface temperature of the clear
insulating glazing reaches 16°C.
This creates a thermal circulation
with an air velocity of 0.2 m/sec
maximum.

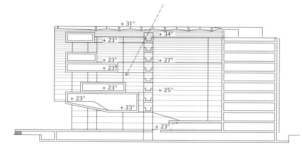

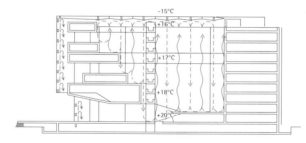

169.2
Daylight, natural lighting

Since there are no shading components other than the glazing itself
and the construction, light penetrates freely into the atrium, which
creates good lighting in all adjacent areas. Losses due to the exterior insulating glazing (ESG
Isoglass) reduces daylight incidence
by only 20 %.

The offices are naturally lit; the
lighting system merely supple-
ments the daylight. Following
estimates of the daylight quotient curves for the offices adjacent to the atrium and for those
located on the perimeter, all
offices are equally lit by natural
light (see separate illustrations).
The supplementary lighting system will be designed, directly and
indirectly, to allow each user the
freedom to compose a lighting
system to individual needs, using
two-component lamps.
A corresponding lighting system
is used to achieve a specific performance level of approximately
7 to 8 W/m².

169.3
Natural ventilation

The atrium is a naturally ventilated space with high light incidence and correspondingly high
passive heat gain.
On still days, the atrium is ther-
mally ventilated by opening windows in the lower area and simultaneously opening skylights in the
roof.

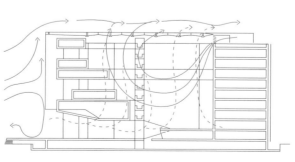

- - - Without wind /
thermal ventilation
—— With wind /
thermals and suction forces

169.4
Glass roof cooling with rainwater
The typical temperature variations and the frequency of specific temperatures in the atrium prove that sprinkling the atrium roof and thus cooling the glass surfaces surrounding the inner courtyard leads to more comfortable temperatures.

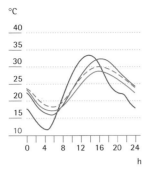

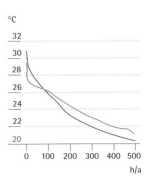

Temperature in courtyard, sprinkling of glass roof (50 % wetting), summer

- – – Perceived temperature
- ——— Air temperature, outside
- ——— Glass roof
- ——— Fresh air

Temperatures in average year, frequencies of increased temperature between 9 a.m. and 7 p.m.

- ——— Perceived temperature, sprinkling (50 % wetting)
- ——— Fresh air

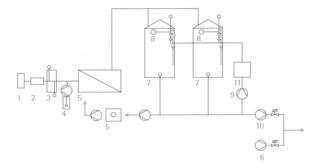

Developed view of glass area with nozzle projection

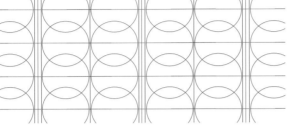

Diagram of sprinkling installation, structural diagram of water treatment

1 Reversible flow filter
2 Pipe disconnector
3 Activated carbon filter
4 Dosage
5 Reverse osmosis plant
6 Rinse installation, include. rinse pump
7 6-piece permeate container
8 Pipe water pump (cleansing)
9 Circulation pump
10 Permeate pump (cooling)
11 UV-disinfection

169.5
Rainwater treatment: diagram
The process water for rainwater treatment is used for watering the gardens and for sprinkling the roof surfaces.

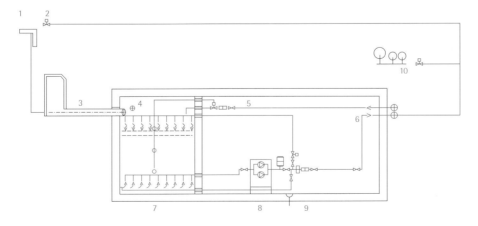

1 Roof
2 Roof irrigation
3 Rainwater
4 Overflow
5 Backfeed potable water or well water
6 Grey water for landscaped gardens and roof gardens
7 Collecting basin
8 Filter
9 Booster installation
10 Garden irrigation

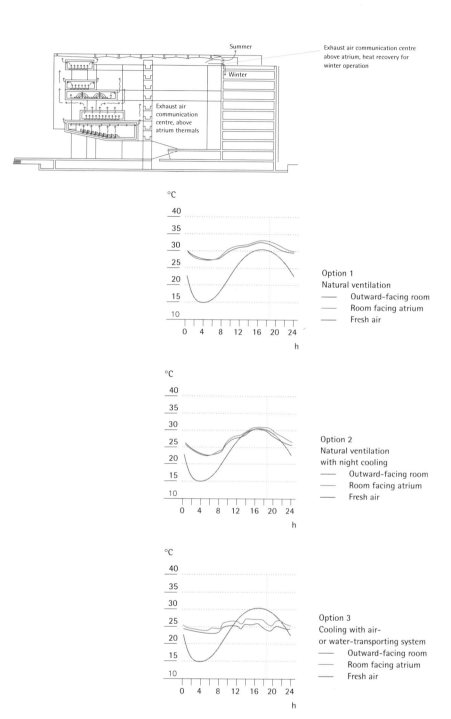

Option 1
Natural ventilation
—— Outward-facing room
—— Room facing atrium
—— Fresh air

Option 2
Natural ventilation
with night cooling
—— Outward-facing room
—— Room facing atrium
—— Fresh air

Option 3
Cooling with air-
or water-transporting system
—— Outward-facing room
—— Room facing atrium
—— Fresh air

169.6
Thermal, hygienic and visual comfort

The rooms facing the inner atrium are equipped with a translucent interior glare protection, while the rooms on the perimeter are fitted with adjustable shading in combination with individually controllable glare protection. This ensures visual comfort: visual contact to the outside is maintained at all times as well as visual contact into the atrium space. Each user can adjust the illumination according to personal preference.

The combined measures minimize the total solar energy transmission to approximately 10 %. This reduces the cooling loads owing to an outside heat incidence of only 20 W/m².

Thermal comfort that is conducive to high performance levels should provide a maximum room temperature of approximately 27°C in summer. Various options were studied for the design to determine which room temperatures could be achieved with minimal technical effort.

A comparison of three typical temperature curves for the rooms facing the atrium and those on the perimeter shows that with natural ventilation (Option 1), room temperatures of 35°C occur. In Option 2, natural ventilation was supplemented with targeted night cooling with fresh air, resulting in maximum temperatures of 31–32°C. Additional cooling with air or water would result in room temperatures for thermal comfort (Option 3).

Combination offices require minimal ventilation for multiple-use zones to maintain hygienic air conditions (ventilation of pollutants and odours), a standard which also applies to the offices adjacent to the inner atrium. An air change rate of roughly 2.5 ac/h was therefore established as appropriate for these areas, in addition to cooling or dehumidification in summer. To avoid creating different room standards, the same approach has been suggested for the offices on the perimeter.

The rooms on the perimeter can be heated either with convector units or with plate radiators. Minimal heating for the offices adjacent to the atrium is achieved with convectors. This solution guarantees good control in combination with cold air intake. Another characteristic of thermal comfort is the position and temperature of the surrounding. For the offices on the perimeter, window panes with thermal transmittance coefficients of approx. 1.2 W/m² K are suggested. This would result in inner surface temperatures above 17°C for outside temperatures of 12°C. The window components to the hall can consist of single-pane glass (sliding elements), since the atrium has a temperature of at least 16°C to 18°C through solar heat gain and minimal supplementary heating.

10   Clever Construction: Ecological Assessment and Planning

10.1   Motives for Ecological Planning

Contribution by
Prof. Peter Steiger and
Roland Stulz,
Dr. H. Gugerli,
Intep AG, Zurich

In Chapter 1 we established the urgent need for action to protect resources and to reduce emissions. According to UN climate conferences, environmental damage must first be stabilized and then reduced by at least 50% to 80% to halt the rise in the temperature of the atmosphere. Considering the unstable economies and the projected population growth of the Third World, industrialized countries must determine to lower their own emissions to one-sixteenth or 6% of their current use. The effort required to achieve this goal will be enormous; we will need more than rhetoric about "links between energy and economy" or the "burden and sensitivity of the relevant ecosystems" (Code of the Association of Architects and Engineers, HOAI 1991). We must establish basic principles and practical methods of achieving ecological management. To do this, we must improve our skills in ecological assessment and planning.

The construction sector is responsible for a high percentage of total material use and thus for a large degree of pollutant emissions. In high-rise construction alone, for example, nearly 20 million tonnes of material are used in Switzerland; this corresponds to a fully loaded cargo train stretching from Madrid to Moscow. The material used in all the German-speaking countries of Europe would, continuing with the same analogy, correspond to a train as long as the earth's circumference. In some regions, construction waste constitutes 60% of total waste. Serious problems arise not only from the sheer volume but due to non-separable toxic substances. We only need to add the amount of energy consumed in building operation to achieve an overall impression of the potential influence of planners and builders in the field of construction.

The better solution wins. Yet neither eloquence nor legislation will initiate the quantum leap necessary for better planning. For the construction industry, these are difficult times; solutions that are labour intensive or costly have little chance of success, however ecologically correct they may be. Good architecture and integrated planning are employed only when they offer the very best solution.

The best solution will:
- Be no more expensive than conventionally planned buildings
- Use ecologically sound materials, taking into account the complete life cycle of the building
- Be in tune with the environment (ventilation, daylight, solar energy, rainwater, plants)
- Provide natural comfort in all seasons
- Reduce operating costs
- Offer unique architectural solutions
- Create positive feelings in the occupants

Only architecture geared to ecology can deliver such optimal solutions. Ecological planning means conceiving a building as part of nature. The planner must design the building for specific climate conditions and must build a structure that can respond to seasonal changes, using such approaches as the polyvalent wall. In a building of this kind, occupants are made aware of specific weather conditions outside the building. The leap from viewing climate as a nuisance, against which buildings should protect us, to climate as a potential for intelligent use, will create not only ecologically planned buildings but improved quality of life as well.

Building: A Social Process

Building planning and construction are social processes in several respects. First, the costs of resources and material are directly related to the environmental issues at the heart of this book. Even a rough analysis reveals that much of the building material used in the industrialized nations has little to do with protection against cold, wind and weather, and more with satisfying high levels of comfort. By contrast, much of the rest of the world has yet to fulfil the basic requirements for shelter. One could challenge the industrialized nations with this goal: surpass basic requirements for shelter only if it can be achieved without burdening the environment. This "demand" may seem utopian because no powerful lobby is forcing us to undertake the necessary effort and because the global village is largely unfathomable to the individual. Nevertheless, this demand is clearly justified and, as experience with ecological building has shown, achievable with intelligent planning.

Second – an issue more closely related to modern building practice – current decision-making and selection procedures are dominated by experts. The work of experts in many fields is labour intensive (and expensive); this tends to generate unquestioning support for standard solutions "which need no further discussion and leave no questions unanswered". This kind of conservative thinking is harmful and does not permit an atmosphere open to innovation. The lack of communication among experts must also be addressed. We need integrated planning procedures with project-specific goals achieved with ecologically sound solutions. Architecture must leave its pseudo high-tech image behind and turn towards intelligent concepts that include natural solutions (low-tech and high-tech).

To apply ecological concepts tested in special projects on a wider basis and to further improve them, everyone active in building has to become involved: the manufacturers of construction and building materials, the contractors handling these materials, and, most importantly, the clients working with architects and planners. Manufacturers are not interested in innovation when existing products continue to be in demand. There is still a great need for educating these participants in the act of building, with special emphasis on persuading clients and architects to think about buildings in terms of total life cycles.

Calculating Costs Correctly

Cost optimization is often identified with saving time in labour and work processes and in maintenance. The apparently rational argument is that less time means fewer wage hours and therefore lower building and maintenance costs. When time is the deciding factor for choices in materials and procedures, the constructional approach must operate independent of weather conditions, allowing construction to continue into the winter months, for example. It must also limit any waiting periods between stages, thereby controlling external maintenance and upkeep. This type of constructional approach may appear advantageous at first; however, to speed up the processes, more chemicals are used, such as additives in glazes, stains, base paints, pre-treatment mediums and joining as well as insulating materials – burdening the environment over the entire life cycle of the building from construction to demolition. This enormous and toxic burden could be avoided altogether without compromising comfort given a little more time and effort. Moreover, the cost argument doesn't work either. Buildings constructed by simple means and with basic materials tend to last longer than those pieced together from a multiplicity of heterogeneous building materials. In composite constructions, the weakest link in the chain determines the life cycle of the whole *(Figure 170)*. The consequent expenses for renovation and upkeep will far exceed any savings in the initial construction phase. On the other hand, a building constructed with few and simple materials will easily amortize the initial costs given careful operation and maintenance. Hence, it is far better to invest less in elaborate material and more in correct work.

Ecological Know-How as a Tool

The preamble to the Code of the Swiss Association of Architects and Engineers (SIA) calls for responsible action with regard to the environment. The equivalent German document includes the obligation to consider energy efficiency (rational energy consumption and the use of renewable energies) and related biological and ecological concerns. The will to build ecologically exists, but the tools to translate theory into practice are lacking. Furthermore, the problems posed by ecological building are so complex that no single expert can provide good solutions in all areas. There are no simple recipes that can be applied to all projects. Nevertheless, progress in recent years has given us the know-how. This chapter highlights two tools from this fund of knowledge available to us: the SIA paper D 0123 *High-Rise Construction from an Ecological Perspective* and the handbook entitled *Environmental Management of High-Rise Projects,* published by the Swiss Office for Federal Buildings and the Union Bank of Switzerland.

Figures 171 and *172* show contrasting images of modern building: the 425-metre Petronas Towers in Kuala Lumpur, Malaysia, and the local manufacture of concrete bricks in Peru – both projects realized with the help of western know-how. Global environmental problems demand that ecological know-how and expertise become standard in architectural planning

170

Life cycle costs

In composite construction, the weakest links in the chain (often the joints) require periodic upgrading. This creates not only ecological but also material expenses which, seen over the entire life cycle, raise the cost of the building. The rationalization of work processes for construction is thus advantageous only in the shortterm.

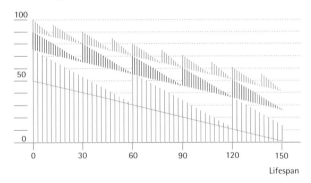

% of building works

Lifespan

Life cycles:
|||| Building services
|||| Façade
||| Interior fit-out
||| Structure

worldwide. In fact, it is evident that ecology has become an essential principle of the modern building culture.

In Germany, Professor Niklaus Kohler at the Institute for Industrial Building Production, Karlsruhe, and Dr Thomas Lützendorf, Head of Building Climatology and Building Ecology at the Bauhaus University in Weimar, have studied this topic for many years. Dr Kohler has developed a life cycle model that can be used to determine the ecological balance (ECOINVENT database).

10.2 Ecological Assessment of Building Construction: Methods

There is no standard method for assessing the ecological characteristics of construction. Although statements relating to the ecological quality of building materials have commonly been included in product brochures, this information is of no use for systematic comparisons because it relates always to one specific product or material. Criteria for assessing structures and methods using composite materials are generally unavailable. For example, a recyclable building material in a structure is only truly recyclable (i.e. truly ecological) if the structure as a whole is suited to separate recovery. The parameters and assessment variables now given for ecological criteria are largely available only from the manufacturer, resulting in disparities from one product to another.

A uniform method of assessing building construction is the answer to this hitherto impractical and vague treatment of the environmental effects of building materials. The evaluation method for "eco-inventories" developed at the University of Leiden provides the first real basis for such a method. It has been used at various centres (SIA/ETH Zurich, TU Karlsruhe, TU Weimar, TU Eindhoven) to compare the environmental effects of different processes in construction. This is a first step towards an international standard in assessing pollution factors in construction. Professor Peter Suter, Chair of Energy Technology at the ETH (Zurich), has been working on a similar document; the first data are now available.

171
Petronas Towers,
Kuala Lumpur, an example of the
skyscraper cult

172
Local manufacture of concrete
bricks

Document D 0123

A Ground-Breaking Document: The SIA D 0123

In September 1995, the Swiss Association of Architects and Engineers issued the documentation D 0123 "High-Rise Construction from an Ecological Perspective". This publication documents and evaluates the ecological characteristics of roughly 60 standard types of high-rise construction. The evaluation includes quantifiable pollutant emissions during construction as well as during other phases such as processing on site, emissions during use, resource use for maintenance, renovation, expansion and, finally, recovery and disposal.

The D 0123 document was designed as an expandable tool. It contains detailed descriptions of evaluation methods and criteria, which enable experts to address specific questions or to assess other construction projects according to the same standards and to optimize the planning phase for new projects. Data on building materials are included for the same reason. The supplementary SIA document 380/1 entitled "Energy in High-Rise Construction" has received wide attention as well. What is even more important is that the handbook is being applied in Switzerland (e.g., the Federal Building Office) as well as in other German-speaking areas of Europe (e.g., the World Fair in Hannover) and elsewhere. Chances are good, therefore, that theoretical knowledge will soon be followed by the practice of ecologically optimized building.

Greenhouse Effect and Acidification: Variables for a Quantitative Index

The method developed in D 0123 is based on two variables: the greenhouse effect and acidification. Together, they represent the overall environmental stress created by manufacturing processes in construction. These criteria, selected from a larger number of environmental factors, are well suited as variables for several reasons. The predominant factor is that calculating the negative environmental impact of gases such as carbon dioxide (CO_2 eq.) or sulphur dioxide (SO_2 eq.) allows for objective, quantifiable comparisons with the current state of research and legislation. Second, both phenomena, especially the greenhouse effect, have become the focus of international talks on the environment; both have been targeted for stabilization and reduction according to the climate convention signed by 50 countries.

Table 8

Greenhouse Effect	Emission		weighted as
Several gases contribute to the greenhouse effect; most are by-products of manufacturing processes. These gases are converted into carbon dioxide (kg CO_2 eq.) by calculating with equivalence factors. The greater the kg CO_2 eq. content in a building material, the greater its contribution to the greenhouse effect.	CO_2	carbon dioxide	1
	CH_4	methane	24.5
	N_2O	nitrous oxide	320
	R134a	FKW	1300
	R22	FCKW	1700
	H 1301	halon	5600

Acidification	Emission		weighted as
Different elements in this list of gases bond with water in the atmosphere. Rain becomes more acid as a result of pollution and causes regional damage in plants, animals and buildings. These gases are converted into sulphur dioxide with the help of equivalence factors (kg SO_2 eq.). The greater the kg SO_2 eq. content in a building material, the greater its contribution to acidification.	NO_x	nitrogen oxide as NO_2	0.70
	HCl	hydrochloric acid	0.88
	SO_x	sulphur dioxide as SO_2	1
	HF	hydrogen fluoride	1.6
	NH_3	ammonia gas	1.88

Grey Energy:
The Link between Known Variables
The main variables in the quantitative index are weighted in the total assessment. In addition, the primary energy content is indicated for each construction. The so-called grey energy consumed during production bridges the gap between the two main variables. The primary energy content (PEC) can be determined from the energy carriers (oil, gas, wood, electricity), always including the maximum heating value in the calculation and differentiating between renewable and non-renewable energy sources.

Technical Data
In addition to the environmental effects and the energy required for production, technical data are listed for each construction. These data are for different areas of the construction and are necessary for comparisons between different types of construction. The thermal properties of a construction are of prime importance; they are listed in the index by static thermal transmittance (U-value) and dynamic parameters (phase shift, amplitude distortion). Allowances are made for transmission losses through the exterior skin being not fully represented by the U-value alone, owing to the fact that heat streams flow at different speeds from the inside to the outside and vice versa, depending on construction, exterior wall materials and sun position. Changing external and internal air conditions can be properly documented only over time with dynamic U-values. The dynamic U-value combines the thermal conditions of internal and external air with the insulating and storage properties of all building surface layers. Other technical data include condensation/drying properties, airborne soundproofing and footfall or impact soundproofing. Generally, the index provides a detailed and inclusive image for each construction; it pertains to the technical qualities and options for application within the totality of a building.

Qualitative Profile
of Practical Building Properties
A description of any construction would be incomplete and abstract if the quantitative inquiry of production processes and technical data were seen in isolation without considering subsequent phases in the life cycle and other practical properties. These include processing on site, emissions during operation and energy consumption for maintenance, renovation and restoration as well as recovery and disposal. This is a qualitative rather than a scientifically quantifiable profile; it has deliberately been given equal weight in the D 0123 documentation and has been integrated into the total assessment. Weighting the practical aspects of building is important for two reasons: first, to deliver a practical handbook that helps the industry to shift from theory (ecological balance) to practice (ecological buildings); second, because the true testing ground for any new ecological construction is its practical application on the building site. Is it possible, for example, to replace one building approach with another of comparatively shorter utilization or does this turn out to be impossible for practical reasons? Are individual building materials easily separable for recycling or is recovery impractical?

10.3   An Evaluation Grid

The evaluations for each of the 60 assessed constructions are clearly and concisely presented double pages. The well-structured grid provides a quick overview of the main characteristics of each construction *(Figure 174)*.

For the first edition of the handbook some 60 examples of contemporary residential high-rises were studied, all of which met the technical and legal requirements in sound, heating and building services. These examples represent only a sample of the variations used in the German-speaking areas in Europe today; they are nevertheless a good selection for initial orientation. To increase the selection and to establish relationships to current building practices, standard cross-sections of three ecologically and aesthetically advanced residential buildings were used as the basis, to prevent extreme differences between variations from distorting the comparison. The following construction variants were studied:

    4   Foundations/basement floors
    4   Heated floors versus unheated
    6   Ceilings / floors
    9   Flat roofs
    9   Steep roofs
    5   Exterior walls below ground
    14   Exterior walls above ground
    8   Interior walls
    6   Dividing walls

As is evident in this list, exterior walls and roofs were evaluated more than any other component. This is not surprising as these two components have the greatest influence on the total ecological balance of a building *(Figure 175)*. On the one hand, they form roughly 35 % of the built mass in the pilot project and, as exposed components, they are the decisive factors for reducing transmission losses and for creating balanced heat management in the operating of buildings. The following basic conclusions can be derived from the results. The top factor for determining environmental impact is building mass. The greater the mass

Qualitative Total Assessment
Versus Simplified "Eco-Cipher"

To determine the qualitative parameters for the profile, a criteria grid was developed for objective assessment and a high degree of comparability. In theory, this profile can readily be converted into a scale with ordinal numbers and, together with the quantified index, could be condensed into an "eco-cipher". Such over-simplification was deliberately avoided, even though it might have had more impact in the short term and might have made it easier to communicate the results. On the contrary, the total assessment is less driven by a faith in numbers, providing instead a descriptive commentary. The language-based presentation delivers, even at first glance, a broad evaluation of the ecological properties and distinguishing characteristics of a construction. The assessment also includes remarks on further improving how a construction could be handled.

173
Total assessment
Document D 0123 divides the total assessment of a construction into two categories:

1. Index: pollutant emissions associated with the manufacturing process (according to the evaluation method developed by the Centre for Environmental Science at the University of Leiden)

2. Profile: the practical assessment of a building (work necessary on building site, effort required for operation and maintenance, suitability for recovery etc.)

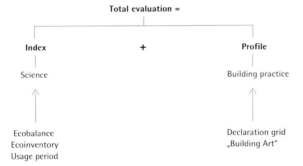

Total evaluation =

Index   +   Profile

Science   Building practice

Ecobalance   Declaration grid
Ecoinventory   „Building Art"
Usage period

Brick, double wall with rock wool, plastered on the inside

E4.41

a b   c d   e f   g

Technical data

U-value	[W/m²K]	**0.24**
Phase displacement	[h]	15/16
Amplitude distortion	[.]	50/26
Condensate / desiccation	[g/m²a]	300/5000
Dead sounding R'ᵥ	[dB]	**59**

Rock wool 60 kg/m³, λ = 0.035 W/mK.

Total assessment

Medium greenhouse effect.
Some acidification.
Given good technical design,
long lifespan of surfaces.
Great potential for damage if details
are poorly designed.
Great potential for damage if execution
is shoddy.
Some effort required for disposal.

Authors' note

Dead sounding characteristics sufficient
for use as multi-purpose building.

174.1
Assessment grid
(from SIA D 0123)
The building specifications are
listed to the right of the sectional
drawing. The column headed Total
Assessment contains author com-
ments, summarizing the index and
profile assessments. Additional
notes on specific characteristics or
special requirements for processing are indicated in the top right
corner.

Index

		Construction			Spec. build. material data Manufacture		Lifespan (materials)	Environmental effects Construction + renovation		Notes on disposal and recovery	
	ECA No.	Thickn. (cm)	Mass (kg/m²)	Building material No.	CO₂eq. (gCO₂/kg)	SO₂eq. (gSO₂/kg)	(a)	CO₂eq. (gCO₂/m²s)	SO₂eq. (gSO₂/m²a)	Waste categories	Waste categories Non recyclable
a Brick	E4	15.0	148.0	1.04	225	0.81	80	417	1.50	Recyclable	Inert material waste
b Diluted mortar	E4		59.0	2.07	167	0.51	80	123	0.38	Recyclable	Inert material waste
c Low-alloy steel	E4		0.5	4.04	2949	13.65	80	18	0.09	– –	Inert material waste
d Rock wool	E4	12.0	7.2	9.02	1042	4.22	80	94	0.38	– –	Inert material waste
e Brick	E4	15.0	133.0	1.04	225	0.81	80	375	1.34	Recyclable	Inert material waste
f Diluted mortar	E4		62.7	2.07	167	0.51	80	131	0.40	Recyclable	Inert material waste
g Single-layer - (gypsum) plaster	M4	1.0	10.0	2.04	106	0.91	40	26	0.23	Recyclable	Inert material waste
h											
i											
Total			420					1184	4.31		

174.2
Index
The index is structured from left to
right as follows:

The first set of columns list the
building materials marked with a
literal in the sectional drawing.
The Construction columns include:
– ECC No.: numbers from the catalogue of element cost classification. These are used to establish
links to the standardized cost
calculation system (CRB) in
Switzerland

– Thickness
– Specific weight (mass)
– Building material number: this
number refers to the building
material appendix to the documentation, which indicates the
environmental emission CO₂
equivalent and the SO₂ equivalent
as well as the primary energy
content of the building material.

Specific Building Material Data:
environmental effects from a manufacturing process, indexed to one
kilogram of material

Utility Period gives a rough estimate of the longevity of each material. When long-lived materials have
to be demolished in a building section to replace short-lived materials, this is indicated in the profile
section.

The calculations essential for a
quantified assessment of the environmental impact of a building are
listed in the two columns headed
Effects in Manufacture and
Renewal. They are based on the
mass of each material per kilogram

and the environmental emissions
during the manufacture of the
material. This total effect is then
"spread" over the entire utility
period. The figure represents the
annual environmental effect of a
building.

The last two columns contain basic
notes on disposal. Whether the
materials indicated as theoretical-
ly recyclable are in fact recoverable in practice is established in
the profile section that follows.

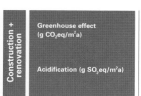

Greenhouse effect
(g CO₂eq/m²a)

Acidification (g SO₂eq/m²a)

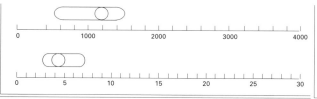

| 0 | 1000 | 2000 | 3000 | 4000 |

| 0 | 5 | 10 | 15 | 20 | 25 | 30 |

Primary energy content

Non-renewable	995 (MJ/m²)
Renewable	27 (MJ/m²)

11 Comparative constructions

174.3
Index diagram
The index section is completed by
a graphic representation of the
results. A grey bar indicates the
environmental impact of comparable constructions (e.g. other
external wall options). The smaller
black circle marks the position of
the assessed construction, indicating how this construction com-
pares with others. The diagram
also visualizes the parameters as
computed values. Finally, the percentage of renewable and non-
renewable energy required for
manufacture as indexed to total
energy use is indicated.

Construction + renovation

174.4

Profile section

The profile follows the life cycle of a building component. First, this section profiles qualitative and practical aspects. Second, it features ecologically and toxicologically relevant data from the SIA document D 093 "Declaration Grid for Ecological Characteristics of Building Materials" to provide tips on work hygiene during processing and room air quality during utilization.

For the processing phase, emission levels from D 093 are indicated and an assessment of the construction is given.

Emissions: When materials are processed on a building site, hazardous emissions may occur. These are indicated here according to document D 093. In addition, recommendations are made (e.g. with regard to respirable fibres or options for solvent-free priming coats). For the assessed constructions, the overall results were favourable in this area.

Building process: This section attempts to estimate the effort required for technical aids, work and time. The following criteria were evaluated:
– Complexity: few or many working cycles
– Technical aids: construction with greater mass and heavy single components requires more technical aids (cranes, formwork, concrete mixer, transportation, etc.)

	Profile	Commentary	Evaluation favourable — unfavourable	Notes
Construction	Emissions (source: D093)	No relevant elements.	■□□□□	Traces of respirable fibres in rock wool.
	Building process	Many work cycles. Extensive effort for transport on construction site. Great effort for caps and covering on site. Great effort in case of water intake at construction site. Execution-dependant chemical process materials commonly used in mortar for fair-faced brickwork. Long construktion time including drying times. Re-purchase of rock wool by manufacturer.	□■■■□	
Usage	Ecological/ toxicological components (source: D 093)	No relevant elements.	■■□□□	
	Maintenance/ Repair	Gap filling composition must be renewed every 10 years. Simple repairs.	□■■■□	
	Replacement and renovation	Low damage potential near hook-ups, penetration points, base (socle) and roof edge. Exterior shell difficult to separate from supporting framework in case of replacement.	□■■■■	Do not use adhesive for rock wool panel.
Disposal	Recyclable	Difficult to seperate. Rock wool and steel not reusable because of pollution with construction rubbish. Great percentage by mass of reusable materials. Recovery requires extensive effort.	□■■■□	
	Non recyclable	Only inert waste. Great effort for recovery.	■■■■□	
	Notes			

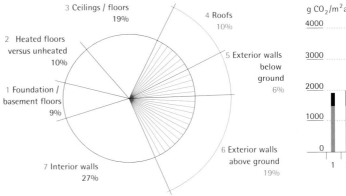

3 Ceilings / floors 19%
4 Roofs 10%
2 Heated floors versus unheated 10%
5 Exterior walls below ground 6%
1 Foundation / basement floors 9%
6 Exterior walls above ground 19%
7 Interior walls 27%

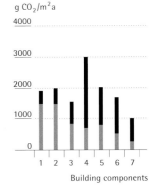

$g\ CO_2/m^2a$
4000
3000
2000
1000
0
1 2 3 4 5 6 7
Building components

175

Optimization potential

The illustrations show the optimization potential (■) with regard to the greenhouse effect in a typical residential building. The potential is especially great in exterior walls and floor and ceiling constructions, which together constitute roughly 35% of the total surface of a building.

of a building, the greater the stress on the environment. This becomes very apparent in comparisons of the greenhouse effect for different exterior wall structures *(Figure 176)*. Monolithic block structures are the least advantageous. As soon as the mass is reduced and insulation is handled separately, environmental impact is reduced as well. Material is the other main factor in the ecological balance of a building, especially as regards manufacturing processes. To reduce the greenhouse effect, steam-hardened sand-lime brick is preferable, for example, to brick that requires higher temperatures to manufacture. Natural building materials are best. The results of comparisons in the individual building component categories are documented in detail in the publication "erfa info 5/95" (Source: Swiss Federal Office for Public Buildings).

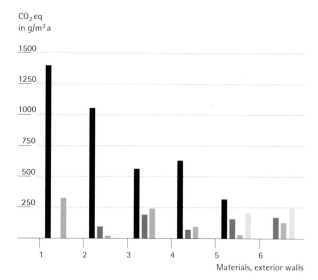

CO_2 eq in g/m^{2}a

Materials, exterior walls

176

The greenhouse effect in different exterior walls

A comparison of the greenhouse effect for different exterior wall structures demonstrates the options for ecological optimization of different construction types. The values listed indicate the greenhouse effect in raw material extraction and the manufacture of the individual constructions, indexed to the total utilization period. The monolithic brickwork structure exhibits by far the highest emission levels. This is the direct result of great mass and high energy consumption required in the manufacturing process (brick firing). The mass and thus the CO_2 emissions are considerably reduced when insulation is dealt with separately, as in this diagram with a structure consisting of double-wall brick with glass wool as the insulating material. Other steps for ecological improvement range from the exchange of the entire material or even of a single framework. In the sample calcula-

tion, these steps are indicated for a double-wall sand-lime brick construction and for a sand-lime brick construction with one-sided sheathing. For exterior wall constructions, the following general ecological attributes can be formulated:

1. The mass contributes to a great degree to ecological stress. Monolithic blocks are therefore not recommended.
2. Insulation is not a big factor ecologically. Separate solutions are therefore very positive (e.g. glass or rock wool).
3. The choice of materials can be very important. Wood is especially good from an ecological point of view. Options for optimization are also found by replacing parts of a construction (e.g. wood sheathing).

■ Solid building materials
■ Insulating materials
■ Facing and revetment
▫ Derived timber products

1 Monolithic plastered brick walls
2 Brick, double-wall with rock wool, plastered on the inside
3 Brick with external EPS insulation, plastered
4 Sand-lime fair-faced brickwork, double wall with rock wool
5 Sand-lime brick with external glass insulation, sheathing
6 Wood posts with external glass wool insulation, sheating

10.4 Economic Optimization

The inquiries for the preparation of the handbook proved that environmental impact is determined first by the volume of the built mass and second by the type of material. To encourage planners to make ecological choices, there must be an efficient tool for calculating the different options, indicating not only environmental impact, but cost as well. The method developed in the SIA documentation D 0123 in Hamm (Germany/North Rhine Westphalia) is such a tool. A newly developed database enables planners to try out construction options for each building component on a CAD (ArchiCAD) model of the building. The calculation presents cost factors in addition to environmental values. The percentage costs of newly used components on the total building structure are automatically calculated. This tool can be combined with economic and ecological optimization procedures. The database is still more or less limited to shell construction. On this basis, three options for expanding a school building were investigated in a pilot study *(Table 9)*. The first option consisted of the existing plans, while the other two options aimed for ecological optimization. The study was limited to investigating alternatives in exterior wall construction. For all three options there are further optimization potentials. The pilot results show that the experts' longstanding experience is borne out in the cost calculations: ecology and economy are far from being mutually exclusive; on the contrary, they combine to form a better whole.

The ecological evaluation of selected constructions will soon be a standard element in modern building planning and will, at the same time, become a sales argument for planners and integrated planning teams *(Figure 177)*. By order of the Swiss Federal Office for Building and the Federal Office for Energy, a relevant DP-tool was to be developed as part of research on how to optimize total energy consumption, environmental factors and building costs. This will prove to be a convincing decision-making instrument for clients as well. Here, finally, is an independent instrument for research in building ecology.

Table 9
Example of Optimization
Procedure

		Option A Double wall masonry with fair-faced bricks; internal fair-faced brickwork	Option B Double wall masonry with sand-lime brick; internal fair-faced brickwork	Option C Rear-ventilated façade and wood sheathing; internal sand-lime fair-faced brickwork
Effect on the environment	CO_2 eq.	100%	76%	54%
	SO_2 eq.	100%	82%	75%
Primary energy	renewable	100%	119%	140%
	non-renewable	100%	81%	54%
Costs		100%	99%	98%
Amortization		100%	99%	97%
Weight		100%	91%	85%

Construction   Component   Element

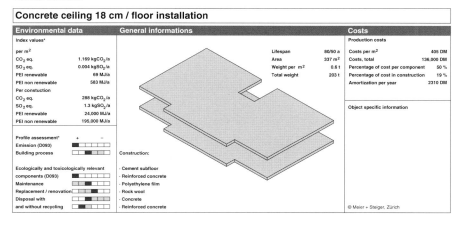

Data sheet

177
"Ecological" building component calculation (excerpt)
By combining a building model (ArchiCAD) and a database (Filemaker), one can isolate different building components and compute them separately. This method is demonstrated for the ceiling structure of a residential building.

10.5 Ecology and Economy in the Life Cycle

It would indeed be a mistake to assume that building exclusively with ecological materials will result in the most ecological building. The environmental impact of a building is linked to its total life cycle, from the manufacture of the materials to operation and renovation, to demolition and disposal of the materials. Buildings must be planned with regard to the full life cycle, and all emissions and costs must be considered. In a pilot study, the environmental stresses created during the shell construction of a multi-family home were calculated according to the method published in the handbook *High-Rise Construction from an Ecological Perspective*. Furthermore, the environmental stresses arising from expansion work and from building services were established. Finally, renovation and repair work projected over a period of 80 years were also evaluated. These total environmental stress factors (calculated with the main variables of greenhouse effect and acidification) were then indexed to the energy consumed for heating, warm water and electricity as the main operating costs. For the calculation of the energy required for operation, SIA 380/1 ("Energy in the High-Rise Building") was approved in Switzerland. The result of the study demonstrated that the CO_2 eq. effects from operating the building for 80 years had an approximate four-fold environmental impact by comparison to the entire building process, while the environmental effect with regard to acidification was approximately the same for operation and for construction. This preliminary result based on a pilot project gives some idea of the leeway that exists for different approaches and of the need for action. However, in connection with this estimate of environmental impact during construction in comparison to the impact during operation one should remember that while emissions during operation are proportionately smaller in low-energy houses, the material effort and thus the environmental stress during construction are conversely higher. The bottom line is that ecological optimization is profitable both in the construction and in the operation of buildings.

Intelligent Concepts for Ecological Operation

The greatest potential for reducing the impact of a building on the environment exists during the operation phase. Ecological planning should focus on this phase of the life cycle, especially with regard to improved heat management. We need intelligent concepts for active and passive solar energy use, for utilizing internal heat losses and for replacing artificial cooling services. These measures alone can cut consumption in half. The same applies to electricity, where consumption can also be halved by installing energy-efficient appliances and improving the use and application of photovoltaics.

These ecological principles of operation have one thing in common: the building is no longer seen as a finite operating unit, a machine supplied with energy from the outside, functioning regardless of seasonal changes. Instead, the design for a new building should treat it as part of the environment and climate – tapped into as sources for heat, light and comfort. Practice has demonstrated that this way of thinking creates buildings that can be operated with greatly reduced energy demands. The advance into a new dimension of energy efficiency is all the more welcome because energy consumption cannot be reduced to less than $30W/m^2$ heated surface by improving the building skin alone. Further reduction is possible only with considerable material effort. Comfort limits are reached as well, because heat losses must be minimized with the help of air exchange rates to achieve the highest savings level. The result is a hermetically closed skin that is ventilated and exhausted with a ventilation system where the lost heat is recaptured by technical means; this cannot be the ultimate solution.

The future lies not in the building as a well-insulated energy machine, but as an entity that links inside and outside. Using the properties of environmental energies can create a down-to-earth, natural and sensual environment for living and working. The rays of the sun can bring warmth directly into rooms or indirectly through heat storage. Experiments show that well-designed buildings can be heated exclusively by the sun on clear days, even with temperatures far below zero, provided the building mass is used as thermal storage. While the greater mass increases the impact on the environment in the construction phase, this is compensated for by the reduction during operation *(Figure 178)*.

10.6 Ecology as Part of the Planning Process

The client's greatest influence is at the beginning of the planning process, when he has the freedom to formulate the strategic goals for a new project. Realizing these goals is a task for planners. The Suglio headquarters of the Union Bank of Switzerland in Lugano-Manno is a good example of how ecology can be concretely integrated into the planning process. In this planning process, the primary ecological goal was clearly defined from the start: to create a model energy building in Lugano. The experience gained in this planning process became the basis for a handbook entitled "Environment Management in High-Rise Projects", compiled in co-operation with the Federal Office for Building. Published in 1996, the handbook describes the different ways in which clients and planning teams can contribute to all project phases, from strategic planning to occupancy. Fundamental questions are formulated for each project phase and concrete planning steps are enumerated. The handbook is thus a kind of checklist for planning processes.

Strategic Planning

Before the first planning steps are undertaken for any specific building project, one should ascertain whether the goals could be achieved by other means. Space problems don't always require architectural measures. And new construction isn't necessarily the best solution. Once the strategic plan has been established, the ecologically correct solution is more or less clear. Goals have been set for environmentally sustainable building; for new building projects, a rough layout will have been drafted. These parameters form the basis for the subsequent planning phases. Site selection is especially important in this phase with regard to the future impact of the building on the environment. In office buildings, the largest percentage of the total energy consumption arises from indirect factors such as the commuting distance of employees. Access by public transport and parking policies are thus central issues in ecological building planning.

Environmental Management Brochure

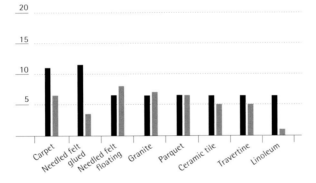

Annual costs of floor coverings
in DM /m^2 a

178
Annual costs of floor coverings
The environmental impact of a building over the course of its life cycle is largely influenced by choices in construction. A comparison of variables for initial investment and subsequent costs for different floor coverings illustrates this relationship. The effort required for cleaning leads to very different ecological and economic costs.

■ Upkeep
■ Investment

Preliminary Study:

Project Performance Specification

The project performance specification is created during this phase. This important tool contains the goals and specifications for all relevant project sectors. It is the basis for the competition programme and ensures that the concrete ecological demands defined in it are met in competition entries. The following description illustrates the importance of the project performance specification in the case of the planning process for the Union Bank of Switzerland headquarters. Above all, the planning process for the Suglio building confirms how important the commitment of client and ecological project management is. The client and the project management must insist on finding truly innovative solutions. All participants must understand from the very beginning that new solutions are being sought, for ecological planning is always innovative: the goals cannot be met without innovation and foregoing conventional high-energy solutions.

Preliminary Project

During the preliminary project phase, the basic operating systems (ventilation, energy supply, building services, building components) are determined. This allows for an initial quantification of the environmental impact of the planned building. As a prerequisite for the function of the ecological concepts, the selected systems for building service (e.g. natural ventilation, use of daylight) must be efficiently supported in the building design (e.g. storage mass, façade). This in turn calls for communication and integrated co-operation between different specialists, that is to say, efficient and well-structured communication channels, regular conferences and above all the willingness of all participants to think and work in a team. Moderation is especially important in these group-dynamic processes, which require a high level of expert knowledge coupled with interpersonal skills (*see* Chapter 2).

Building Project

The building project includes detailed planning up to pre-construction building application. At the same time, the fine-tuning of the planning is the last opportunity for ecological decisions. To ensure that decisions are possible in each phase, planning must be flexible, especially with regard to spatial or technical options that leave room for future changes (*see* Chapter 7). It is therefore sensible to plan for new elements in a test phase, simulating real conditions as much as possible. For the Suglio project, a pilot and a demo room were constructed at the same time as the shell. These rooms were used to test the ventilation concepts and the function of the façade in particular, so important for ventilation. The main building was erected parallel to this testing phase, in part with possibilities for expansion, e.g. cooling ceilings in offices at exposed positions in the building.

Request for Tenders

Submission conditions are formulated and samples taken during this phase. The ecological requirements are entered into the requests for tenders and into the contracts, the performance specification once again forms the basis for this. It begins with general requirements such as product declaration and goes all the way to binding guarantee parameters in the performance ratings of the suppliers. The openly declared quality assurance plans and the control linked to QA are especially important.

Execution

Quality assurance and communication are also part of executing the project in accordance with submission conditions for the most important tasks. This is achieved by controlling the agreed-upon ecological requirements for all supplies as well as the executed tasks. Final corrections and improvements can be made during the finishing of the interior. Practical approaches are preferable here to theoretical planning, enabling optimization of detail. Part of clean finishing work is the ecological organization of the construction site, for which specific instructions should be given to the site management. This can help promote the careful handling of valuable resources. Furthermore, good construction site organization is cost efficient. An example of this is the savings in disposal costs through strict recovery of construction waste in accordance with the multi-dumping concept (MMK, or Multi-Müll-Konzept) of the Swiss Builders Association.

Initiation

Ecologically planned buildings aren't machines – they are part of their surroundings. Initiation is more than a matter of pushing a button; instead, it must be carefully optimized. In larger buildings, careful timing of the occupancy is important. In fact, it may be necessary to plan occupancy in phases. Information for the occupants plays an important role because they will carry out the concepts in an "ecosystem building". Finally, the motivation and competence of the building services support staff is extremely important. It must receive full support, especially in the beginning, to quickly adjust for any possible shortcomings.

Example: Planning Process for Suglio

In 1988 the Union Bank of Switzerland decided to apply the theories on energy-efficient building to a concrete project in order to gain practical experience for future UBS buildings. The background for this unusual commitment was the decision to put energy first and the fundamental willingness of the UBS to participate in projects with a futuristic outlook. And last, but not least, this project *(Figure 179)* was to provide a counter-argument to the image of banks as energy gobblers.

Project Phase 1: Detailed Goals Formulated in an Energy Performance Specification

From a climate perspective, Lugano-Manno was an especially challenging site for a model energy building. The first planning phase was therefore dedicated to defining the specific parameters and concrete goals for the project. In contrast to standard planning procedures, architectural designs were not sought at this stage due to the unique space and user requirements; instead, the focus was on developing different energy options. A detailed energy performance specification was the result of the analyses and simulation calculations, containing binding criteria for the subsequent planning. This innovative approach turned out to be elaborate; it was executed by the relevant UBS departments, together with the planning association Enerconom/Intep and the architectural office Quaglia & Berger. In addition to quantitative defaults, the per-

179
Suglio, the Union Bank of Switzerland administrative building in Lugano-Manno, was planned and built according to the principles of integrated planning. The building opened in 1997. Architect: Prof. D. Schnebli, Professor F. Ruchat, Zürich

formance specification also established basic principles for planning and quality assurance.

Project Phase 2:
Drafting Architectural Studies

The preamble of the performance specification states that the challenge of the Suglio project "can only be solved with integrated planning". This emphasis on comprehensive, team-oriented planning characterizes the entire project. For the preparation of the five different architectural project studies, this meant in practice that the architects received intensive support from a team versed in the various specialized areas. The team consisted of UBS specialists and external expert consultants for energy technology, building services, building simulation and ecology. The task of the team was first and foremost to provide detailed input about the demands defined in the performance specification and to assist the architects in the interpretation of specific questions which arose as a result of developing the project studies. The initial step was a seminar on new energy technology and ecology for all participating architects, with follow-up workshops and one-to-one consultations. It was considered of primary importance to create an enriching dialogue for co-operation and to prevent the architects from feeling that they were in any way restricted in their creative work. The five very different designs, some of which are shown in *Figure 180*, and the evaluation of the participating teams of architects are proof that this novel approach to planning can produce excellent results. From the architects' point of view, the approach had the advantage that it allowed for a response to the concrete wishes of the client and energy experts during the development of the architectural concept. The project study phase was thus more in the nature of a commission than a competition.

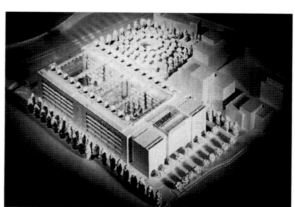

180
Models of four competition projects
Different architectural paths can lead to the same goal: ambitious energy-consumption specifications were achieved by all five project studies with negligible differences. On average, these projects, which were all analyzed with state-of-the-art simulation methods, featured an energy consumption of roughly 28 % lower than the SIA standards 380/1 and 380/4. The photographs of the four featured studies bear witness to the architectural variety despite the defaults set in the specifications. More detailed and ambitious standards set by the client are therefore no impediment to creative architecture.

Project Phase 3:
Team Planning of Details

In response to the submitted designs, a jury composed of architects, clients and internal and external experts formed the architectural group Schnebli/Ammann/Ruchat for further design work: the comb-like structure facing south with an open inner courtyard is in keeping with the natural conditions of the site and fulfils the urban requirements. The model furthermore uses daylight wherever possible owing to its uniformly shallow building depth, while operating with natural ventilation and allowing for the use of passive solar energy through its large window surfaces. The detailed planning of the large project was handed to a team of planners from the Tessin region and from other areas in Switzerland. Although the defaults defined in the performance specification formed part of the work contracts, they were not intended to be rigid. On the contrary, constructive criticism and additional ideas and suggestions for modification were invited to further improve the planning. It was therefore vital to create a creative working atmosphere open to innovation and particularly encouraging to team thinking. Equally vital, however, was the provision of a precise organization with clear rules and hierarchies to minimize the risk of endless discussions and to ensure goal- and deadline-oriented decisions. The project management had the task of accommodating and ensuring all of these different requirements, which included not only the important function of team moderation but also the integration of a staff position for quality assurance. The QA staff was composed of the client, the user representatives and the key players responsible for the performance specifications.

Project Phase 4: Construction of the Main Building and of Pilot and Demo Rooms

In 1990 a detailed schedule for completion of the building by 1997 was developed as part of the overall project management. This schedule was successfully achieved. Due to the ecological approach to construction in combination with the organized recovery of the former industrial buildings, any delay in the execution phase could be averted. More time was invested, however, in the intensive preliminary study phase, which became an important prerequisite for the smooth execution of this large project unique in its goals and demands. The intense communication between all participating planners and contractors was very important as were the detailed structures and decision-making procedures. First of all, a mailbox was created where all relevant documents and data were constantly accessible in updated versions. Regularly scheduled meetings further contributed to personal contact and informal exchange of experience among the participants.

As part of the detail planning, the decision was made to test the selected solutions on a 1:1 scale. For this purpose a pilot and demonstration room was erected on site at the same time as the shell of the building was constructed. The cube-shaped P&D room contained two office rooms whose proportions and orientation simulated the future office areas in the main building. Because the internal thermal loads (i.e., the thermal load created by machines and occupants) played an essential role for the correct functioning of the natural ventilation, the P&D room was used as a workplace over a period of 18 months by an UBS team of six to seven persons. This proved to be advantageous for improving details in the interior design, because aside from readings it also made available the subjective impressions and experiences of the test users, which could then be integrated into the planning that was under way. The P&D room turned out to be unequivocally positive as a planning tool; it provided a kind of insurance, which was profitable in several aspects.

Project Phase 5:
Occupancy, Analysis and Optimization

The Suglio building was opened to occupants in phases beginning in June of 1997. As a result of experience gathered in the P&D room, large areas of the building were only opened in the fall of the same year to avoid having to make detail adjustments during the warmest season. Training the future users of the building will undoubtedly be important since behaviour plays a decisive role in an ecologically heated, cooled and ventilated building. It is essential, for example, that ventilation is intense and in bursts in winter to prevent excessive cooling of walls and ceilings. In summer, users should wear clothing appropriate for the predominant temperatures. To facilitate this, users will have access to information about correct behaviour directly on their PCs. As far as the building planners are concerned, Suglio is far from finished upon completion of construction. During the first two years of operation, the architects and expert engineers are responsible for final analyses and optimization. Above all, at the end of this period, proof must be given that the demands defined in the performance specifications have been met.

10.7 Perspectives of Ecological Planning

Ecological building has undoubtedly made some important advances. The argument that architects and planners still lack the means to integrate ecology in the realization of mega-projects, and that this is why ecology and biology are still delegated to the sidelines in building, may have been true even five years ago, but not today. Ecological planning no longer depends on the experience of environmentally oriented planners; there are now a growing number of instruments for realizing truly optimized solutions and limiting the trial and error phase. Many of the projects documented in this volume illustrate this development. In addition to copious documentation, planners can today assess dynamic processes in computer simulations.

We need concrete facts to argue ideas and solutions, not only with clients but with those colleagues in the field who participate in a planning process. Nevertheless, planning ecological buildings requires not only expert know-how and intelligence, but intuition and feeling. Sustainable architecture must lead to buildings that provide not only more comfort but also more natural comfort.

The Next Step: Considering the Whole of a Building
The handbook "High-Rise Construction from an Ecological Perspective" has achieved the first step towards viewing building construction from specific building materials to the structure as an integrated whole. With a view to future requirements, several construction options for a standard building were therefore assessed for the shell of the building. The next investigation would logically be construction techniques to the building as a whole. This would enable the maximum optimization of total energy consumption, environmental stress and building costs, which in turn would probably quickly become a standard in building planning. The path to this goal is strewn with obstacles in knowledge and research. We need more knowledge beyond shell construction – know-how relating to completion and building ser-

data for many new materials are still unavailable, especially for synthetics, for several metals and for surface treatments. More information is needed about windows in residential construction, and about different façades in industrial construction. Methodological gaps relating to the building process, utilization periods and application for renovation must still be filled. To fulfil these tasks, we must see a continued and co-operative effort among experts, universities, manufacturers and the public. Most importantly, it is crucial for all members of the building industry to be open to new solutions and to participate in a renaissance of the art of building.

Part 3   Measures for Expansion and Renovation

Part 1 analysed the challenges of ecology and information technology on architecture. Part 2 introduced strategies for sustainable building that draw on the knowledge of master builders as well as modern building technology. These issues mark the path of architecture as it enters the information society and are at the same time a basic condition for architecture's longevity in the sense of human survival.

While previous chapters focused mainly on the ecological side of building (low-tech/light-tech), Part 3 will present concrete measures for technical expansion and renovation, that is to say, high-tech systems. These include:

- Information and communication systems
- Building automation and process optimization
- Ventilation, heating and cooling systems
- Lighting systems
- Other prerequisites for the integration of modern system technologies.

In the past, shoes could stink.
In the present, shoes can blink.
In the future, shoes will think.

This humorous poem by N. A. Gershenfeld of the Massachusetts Institute of Technology captures the essence of the material in Parts 1 and 2: multimedia research is in pursuit of total mobility with the help of a new, intelligent generation of communications technology. In a time characterized by an explosion of information, people's expectations of their surroundings are higher. "Our shoes should receive individualized information from the office carpet and relay this information to us before we've even had time to take off our coats".

MIT researchers are not only fascinated by the idea of "computer shoes" operated exclusively by body and motion energy, absorbing data from floor coverings and transferring this information to the skin, glasses or wristwatch of the wearer. They are currently devel-

oping, for example, electronic business cards which could be stored in miniature portable computers – accessible at all times and at any location. The basic idea is that humans and technology should communicate informally – and as discreetly as possible – wherever they come in contact.

Whether these futuristic visions are the ultimate solutions seems doubtful to telecommunications experts and trend researchers. One problem has already become evident: it is less important to receive information in general than to receive specific information which is of use. Already software is being developed that can separate important calls, e-mail and faxes from less important items of communication and then transfer the bits of information that the recipient actually wishes to receive to mobile devices.

The mobile and data transmission industry is striving to create a world in which each citizen can produce, trade, learn and converse, regardless of where he or she is located. In such a world, economic and political borders will collapse because tyrants will no longer be able to restrict access to knowledge. Expanding communications technology might also create a new type of nomadic existence where isolated teleworkers and autistic Internet surfers dominate: that is, multimedia is a source of hope, but also of equally justified concerns.

By the year 2000 the number of mobile phone users in Germany is expected to grow from the current 4 million to 12.7 million. Being mobile has become a status symbol. The household budget for mobile communication is growing and, with the expanding market, the individual user will expect to pay less for the same service. To keep the market healthy and expand the global market economy, it will be necessary for PCs and mobile phones to merge. The Internet can then develop into a global mega data pool to which anyone can have access, even while travelling. There are, however, clear disparities between prognosis and reality: in 1995, an estimated 800,000 people in the United States used the Internet to transmit data, while

user potential is 38 million – this means that the actual rate of participation is a mere 2%. The reasons for this restraint are more or less the same in all industrialized countries:
- Data connections are currently roughly ten times as expensive as standard long-distance cable connections.
- Stationary modems cost only a quarter of the price of the mobile version
- The transmission rate is sometimes too slow
- Incompatibilities of hardware and/or software between users and servers and between users
- Insufficient network density

The primary goal of futuristic research is to maintain human mobility into old age through the use of electronic devices. Researchers have zeroed in on residential buildings as the most interesting locations for mobile communication. Life expectancies continue to grow, especially in the industrialized countries. *Figure 181* illustrates some of the mobile communication tools and their hardware. To maintain the mobility of the elderly, their physical data would be constantly monitored and the findings transmitted online to the family doctor or hospital. The condition of the eyes, respiration, circulation, weight and body shape are the main areas that are monitored. The physician's computer would then assess the results on a regular basis. The doctor can give instructions for behaviour to the patient via a monitor and two-way speakers (Shades of Orwell's *1984!*).

Ideally, not only the inhabitants but the building itself would have a dedicated computer. The virtual house and the virtual human being in the computer would be stand-ins for their real counterparts, whose conditions would be continuously communicated to the computer via cable and wireless devices. The home computer in connection with other servers then takes on the role of family doctor, repairman and butler, intervening whenever and wherever problems arise in the day-to-day operation of the building or in the health of the user.

The experts at MIT are working towards removing technology from our field of vision and making such devices more autonomous. These researchers are well aware of the confusing array of technology at the present time and of the common experience of information overload. The solution lies, in their view, in creating a better technology that will be unobtrusively and intelligently integrated into its surroundings. Here, wireless communication will play a key role.

Professor Gershenfeld believes that technology is still too conspicuous and that communication between devices must be improved. To solve these problems, new devices are being developed that could be worn on a shirt collar or in the frame of a pair of glasses.

181
The bathroom of the future

1 Breast exam
  (sensor or infrared)
2 Full body scanning
  (biophysical exam)
3 General exam and bone test
  (video or laser)
4 Weight scale
5 Eye exam
  – Retina
  – Eye pressure
6 Hearing sensor
7 Consultation (monitor)
8 Sound scan and analysis of breath
9 Language unit
  – Patient identification
  – Consultation
10 "Health arm rest"
  – Blood pressure measurment
  – Pulse and trembling
  – Body temperature
11 Temperature sensor
12 – Urine analysis
  – Biogas analysis (sensors)

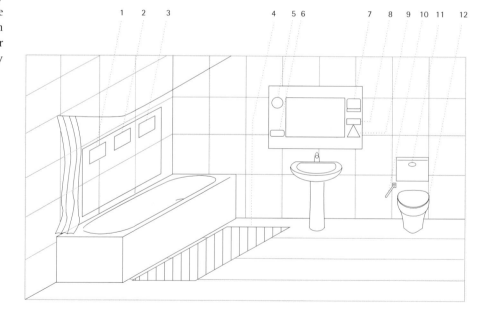

Efforts are also under way to develop a "personal-area network", which would utilize interactions between the human body and electrical tension fields for communication purposes. Instead of transmitting radio signals, the body itself is being reconfigured as a data network. Commonly used gestures could be given digital meanings. For example, shaking hands is an indication of a certain level of intimacy (mutual greeting or introduction). This gesture may usefully be linked to the transfer of certain personal data. Telecommunication may also provide an elegant solution for our persistent traffic problems: news or message mobility instead of traffic mobility.

A systematic analysis of all activities in the areas of living – working, education, consumption and leisure – shows that the physical movement of people and goods is ultimately for the purpose of linking information sources and destinations and of transporting the news itself (apartment to office, where information is both received and conveyed; or, apartment to supermarket, where information is absorbed and goods are acquired). Letters, newspapers, books and electronic data carriers are being transported because of the information they contain, not because of the material content. Reducing physical traffic by tele-work from home, by establishing satellite offices, by shopping via a monitor or screen (teleshopping) and by telephone and video conferencing for meetings can lead to a substitution potential of 8 to 15 %, given certain parameters (for example, in reference to the traffic predicted for the year 2025).

The most dramatic impact can be expected in the area of shopping traffic (possible reduction of 15 to 28 %). Teleconferencing and office communication will eliminate a percentage of business-related traffic as well: airlines are estimating up to 20 % reduction in passengers. But telecommunication together with navigation systems can also optimize transportation – the estimated reduction for personal traffic lies between 3.5 % and 7 %, and in goods traffic at between 5 % and 25 % depending on the circumstances.

Mobile news and communications can clearly reduce traffic volume. Since teleworkers not only save by not travelling a distance to work, but also save the time required for the trip to and from work, they could use this additional time for more leisure, which might in turn increase leisure traffic. Here we have to consider that leisure traffic is already a large percentage of personal traffic and is a rising trend. Telecommunication supports the type of urban development desirable for the future (mixed-use developments) but at the same time encourages urban sprawl, which would in turn create more traffic flow.

In conclusion, we can say that the use of telecommunications is not so much trend-setting as it is trend-enhancing: a desirable trend (less traffic, for example) or even trend reversal is unlikely to occur simply by expanding the technical infrastructure for communication mobility. This change can only be achieved by cost realities (direct and indirect costs incurred from personal traffic) and – in the area of spatial organization – by adjusting urban development to the capaci-

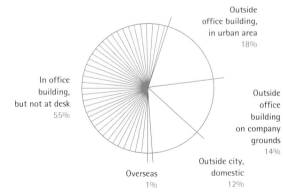

In office
building,
but not at desk
55%

Outside
office building,
in urban area
18%

Outside
office
building
on company
grounds
14%

Outside city,
domestic
12%

Overseas
1%

182
Mobile workers
In the United States some
48 million workers and employees
are on the road in the course of
their work.

11 Intelligently Operated Buildings: High-Tech Systems

11.1 Information and Communication Systems

ty of the existing infrastructure. The mobile office must become a reality, as is evident in *Figure 182:* even when working within a company (office building, factory, etc.) many people are already involved in mobile communication. Mobility and information are by common consent an absolute requirement for the work and economy of the future.

Another broad field for reducing consumption, pollution and cost is satellite-supported corporate training. Market analysis and research have shown that the effort required for employee training (travel to and from training location, training time etc.) could be reduced by up to 70%. This area is especially important for global economic systems; to some degree, it is the area that makes the global economy possible and viable.

Computer-integrated buildings- erroneously called "intelligent buildings" – are buildings that are able to accommodate all technologies required for data processing, communication and automation. *Figure 183* is a structural overview of the systems used in these buildings, differentiating systems for data processing and communication from systems for automation and process optimization.

Basic Principles

Communication is a one-sided or reciprocal exchange of information between individuals, between people and technical systems and among technical systems. *Figure 184* illustrates the reciprocal relationships. Information can be transferred by sound, image, text or data. Information of any kind is rarely transferred physically or directly processed by a computer. All types of information are coded and translated into a

183
System structure of a computer-integrated building (CIB)

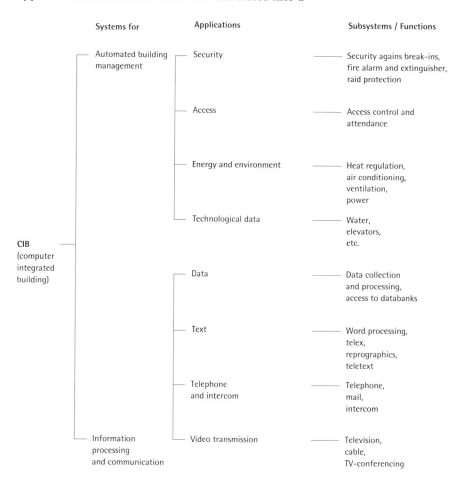

Systems for	Applications	Subsystems / Functions
Automated building management	Security	Security agains break-ins, fire alarm and extinguisher, raid protection
	Access	Access control and attendance
	Energy and environment	Heat regulation, air conditioning, ventilation, power
	Technological data	Water, elevators, etc.
CIB (computer integrated building)	Data	Data collection and processing, access to databanks
	Text	Word processing, telex, reprographics, teletext
	Telephone and intercom	Telephone, mail, intercom
Information processing and communication	Video transmission	Television, cable, TV-conferencing

binary sequence; one bit (or binary digit) is the smallest unit, coded either as one or as zero. *Figure 185* illustrates the principle with a sample binary code for all potential states of a traffic light.

Communication systems translate information into binary sequences. The installations necessary for this translation must be able to transmit the bit sequences at sufficient speed. Destination devices unscramble the bit sequences arriving via the network into their original format. The following operations can be executed with the help of binary data:

- Communicating
- Sending
- Receiving
- Storing
- Searching
- Calculating/computing
- Filtering

Transmission time is the decisive parameter in the transfer of bit sequences. It is indicated in bits per second; transmission speeds vary greatly from one service or information type to another. *Table 10* provides an overview of today's standard rates:

The data-processing systems or computers are the devices that execute processes according to specific rules (software programs). A series of processes results in an executed act (such as calculating, sorting, assigning, creating, deleting, comparing or storing).

Computers can be used in two basic set-ups. Central data-processing systems consist of a mainframe computer, the host, and many terminals where data are entered and retrieved. The advantage of these systems is the coordination of the processes; the disadvantages are higher costs and less flexibility as a result of the limited application options.

Decentralized systems are based on a number of linked personal computers (PCs). The advantages of PCs – cost, performance and flexibility – make them widely popular. The main disadvantage in PC systems is the fact that the combined and linked knowledge in a company can be lost. To eliminate this and other disadvantages, local networks are developed that provide common access to files, printers and software via a server, as illustrated in *Figure 186*.

184
Types of information

185
Binary encoding of traffic light settings

Service	Type of information	Standard transmission rate
Telephone service	sound/language	64 kbps
Voice Mail	sound/language	64 kbps
Radio (stereo)	sound/music/language	768 kbps
Telemetry	data	< 300 bps
Data transfer	data	up to 64 kbps
Telex	text	50 bps
Teletext (broadcast videotex)	text	2.4 kbps
E-mail	text/data	2.4 kbps
Videotext	text	2.4 kbps
(Tele)fax group III	text/image (graphics b/w)	2.4 – 14.4 kbps
(Tele)fax group IV	text/image (graphics b/w)	64 kbps
Static image transfer	image	64 kbps
Video display telephone in ISDN	image/text	128 kbps
Television	image (motion))	140.000 kbps
Video conference	image (motion)	140.000 kbps

Table 10
Typical transmission rates

Networks located within one building are called LANs, or local area networks. Networks configured in large urban centres are often called MANs, or metropolitan area networks, while networks dedicated to long-distance service are abbreviated as WANs, or wide area networks. A company's communication technology is determined by existing and projected demands and by the volume of traffic.

In communication technology, comfort and economic viability are of paramount importance. Developments in communication technology are focused mainly on technical ease, available networks and available standards (including market acceptance). In the area of data transmission, three types of systems are differentiated:

– Office and telecommunication systems
– Technical information systems
– Administrative information systems

Office and Telecommunication Systems

Systems for data transmission and communication are defined by the terminals and the use at the workstation. *Figure 187* illustrates typical areas of application. The workstation is organized to accommodate changing needs with simple means, quickly and flexibly without disrupting the operation. The terminals for language, text, data and image transmission are linked to a central system such as a central information processing system, a decentralized computer or a server (Internet link) via LANs. The hardware link requires uniform sockets and cables as well as network structures conforming to approved norms. In the interface area of workstation-dedicated terminals (stand-alone terminals), the current standard calls

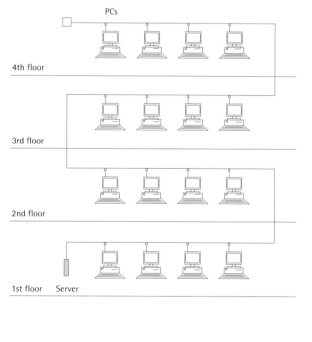

186
Local area network (LAN)

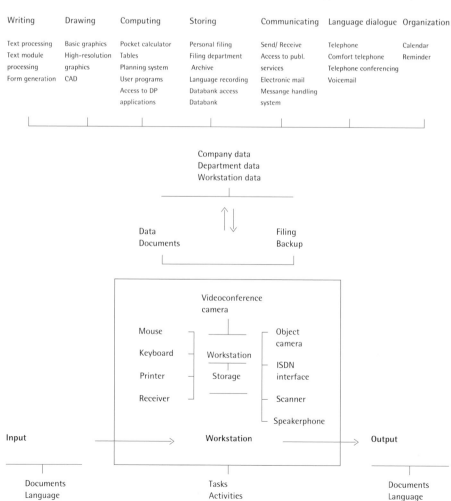

187
Applications at the workplace

Writing	Drawing	Computing	Storing	Communicating	Language dialogue	Organization
Text processing	Basic graphics	Pocket calculator	Personal filing	Send/ Receive	Telephone	Calendar
Text module	High-resolution	Tables	Filing department	Access to publ.	Comfort telephone	Reminder
processing	graphics	Planning system	Archive	services	Telephone conferencing	
Form generation	CAD	User programs	Language recording	Electronic mail	Voicemail	
		Access to DP	Databank access	Messange handling		
		applications	Databank	system		

Company data
Department data
Workstation data

Data   Filing
Documents   Backup

Videoconference
camera

Mouse   Object
                                            camera
Keyboard   Workstation
                                            ISDN
Printer   Storage   interface

Receiver   Scanner

                                            Speakerphone

Input   Workstation   Output

Documents   Tasks   Documents
Language   Activities   Language

for the use of twisted pair copper cables with 155 Mbps transmission speed and fibre-optic cables *(Figure 188)*. Logical network structures are built within routers depending on communication requirements and the necessary bandwidth.

Point-to-point application with high bandwidths (2-155 Mbps) per network user will be achieved in the future with the help of virtual LANs (ATM based) and switching components with routing functions. *Figure 189* shows the different cabling structures. Corporate networks (CN) are created by integrating language, animation and data transfer in one company network. They provide national and international telecommunication for all types of information transfer with access options to all public and private networks. Companies with decentralized structures are usually accessible to their clients at local rates or through the nearest local network at commensurate cost savings.

188
Cabling structure (from EN 50173)
The cabling layout in the building
is differentiated for the primary,
secondary and tertiary net.

1 Primary network
   External cabling between:
   Local distributors (LD)
   Building distributors (BD)
   Local distributor and
   building distributor

2 Secondary network
   Internal cabling between:
   Floor distributors (FD)
   Building distributor and
   floor distributor

3 Tertiary network
   Floor cabling between:
   Floor distributor and
   connector box (CB)

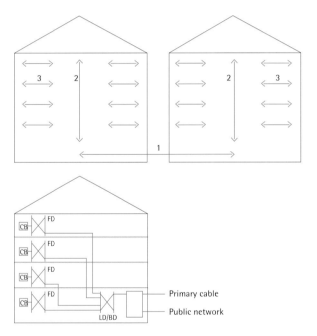

Ring

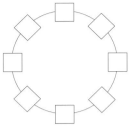

189
Logical cabling structures in data-
processing networks

Star

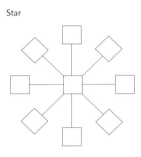

Tree

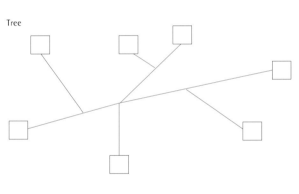

Bus

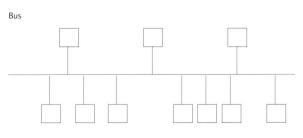

Mesh

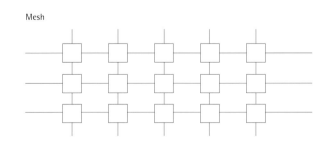

Technical Information Systems

Technical information systems support decisions in the operation of a building. Tasks include notification, routing, automation, comparison and optimization. The combined functional effect of different and independent systems is vitally important for optimal information transfer. After all, well-considered decisions are only possible when the right information is in the right place at the right time.

Technical information systems are often stand-alone, or independent; this and the differences between manufacturers make integration difficult. Open communication is currently reserved for danger messages and alarm systems in buildings. Technical information systems increasingly use bus networks for information transfer between a central system, an operation and display system and the sensors. In contrast to systems for technical building automation, message and alarm generators can only route information to the central system. The information exchange is currently possible only via a central system and a superordinate routing system; *Figure 190* illustrates this type of structure. Other technical information systems such as search and signal installations as well as television and antenna installations are increasingly integrated into or being replaced by telephone systems.

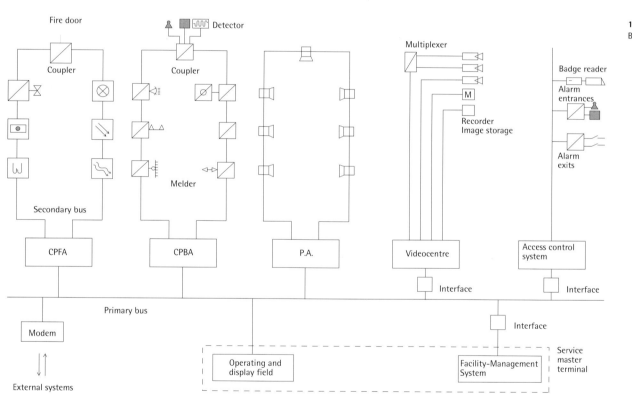

190
Bus installation for alarm system

Administrative Information Systems

Administrative information systems convey data about all aspects of a building, including changes over time. Information is available on personnel and time sheets, accounting and data acquisition, as well as information about the running and administration of parking areas.

Since these systems are for the management of a particular building, they have a uniform information structure. Technical information systems with open communication further integrate facility management systems (linked through internal LANs).

Internet

The Internet is the largest computer network imaginable. Currently it consists of some 10 million networked computers (Internet servers) linked by data lines to which a total of 40 million individual PC users can connect via modem. Servers are operated by corporations, universities, government offices and private individuals. The server makes data available to which any user has access through the Internet (database, text, tables, graphics, images, audio and video clips etc.). Software packages are available for downloading as free or shareware. The totality of the computers linked by this network represents what we've come to call the information highway.

11.2 Systems for Building Management and Process Optimization

To achieve ever-changing goals, humankind has created technology to alleviate the burden of physical work and to free up time and energy. Automation has even made it possible to let machines do a certain amount of intellectual work. The pinnacle of technical development would be a world in which humans set the goals and machines do the work to achieve the goals.

An automation system processes information by independently following a program and making decisions at branches in the program. While today's information systems are still characterized by deterministic behaviour, future systems will move in the direction of auto-didacticism and artificial intelligence (AI).

Building automation systems include:
– Measuring, control and regulation systems
– Central building management systems

These two areas have become inseparable owing to technical developments (DDC, or direct digital control, and SPC, or storage programmable control) and for reasons of communication, compatibility and (inter-)operability.

Figure 191 is a schematic of a building automation system showing the principal levels, components and special tasks. Communication among the components on the higher or "more intelligent" levels occurs via buses per data telegram. The prerequisite of bus communication is a common protocol that functions as a mother tongue or default language in homogenous systems (systems where all components are from the same manufacturer). All tasks, even the most complex automation processes, are based on four principal physical functions:
– AI   (analogue input for measurement)
– AO   (analogue output for positions)
– DI   (digital input for measurement, counting)
– DO   (digital output for switching)

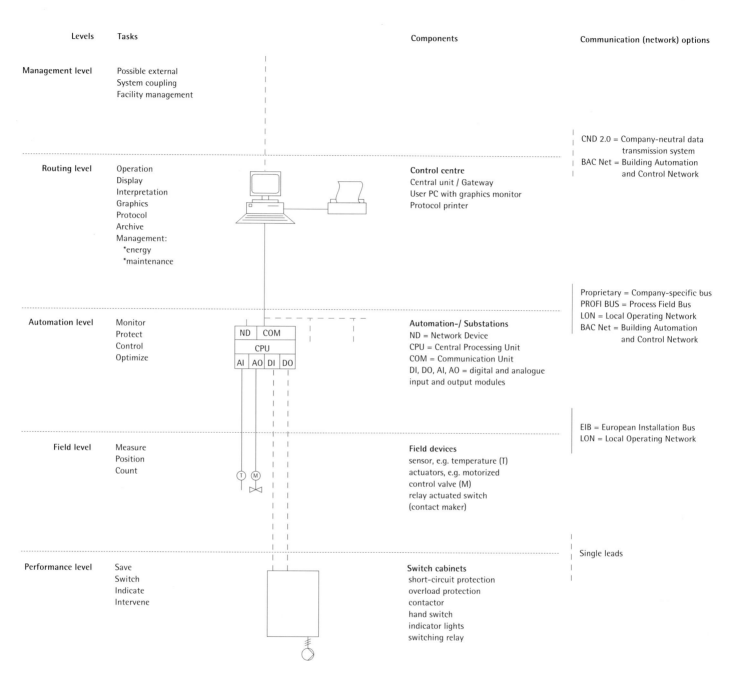

Levels	Tasks		Components	Communication (network) options
Management level	Possible external System coupling Facility management			
				CND 2.0 = Company-neutral data transmission system BAC Net = Building Automation and Control Network
Routing level	Operation Display Interpretation Graphics Protocol Archive Management: *energy *maintenance		Control centre Central unit / Gateway User PC with graphics monitor Protocol printer	
				Proprietary = Company-specific bus PROFI BUS = Process Field Bus LON = Local Operating Network BAC Net = Building Automation and Control Network
Automation level	Monitor Protect Control Optimize		Automation-/ Substations ND = Network Device CPU = Central Processing Unit COM = Communication Unit DI, DO, AI, AO = digital and analogue input and output modules	
				EIB = European Installation Bus LON = Local Operating Network
Field level	Measure Position Count		Field devices sensor, e.g. temperature (T) actuators, e.g. motorized control valve (M) relay actuated switch (contact maker)	
				Single leads
Performance level	Save Switch Indicate Intervene		Switch cabinets short-circuit protection overload protection contactor hand switch indicator lights switching relay	

191
Building automation system

Regulation Systems

Regulation is essential in the meeting of goals or in preventing a failure to meet them, even when unpredictable events occur. Long before the advent of technology, nature applied this principle to all living creatures through such functions as body temperature, blood pressure and heart beat regulation and the regulation of breathing according to the CO_2 content in the blood.

When we abstract the processes, separating information from the carriers, we can clearly see the functional commonalities applicable in an interdisciplinary fashion (cybernetics). Regulation is characterized by closed cycles in a negative feedback system. Control, on the other hand, is characterized by open cycles, represented by control chains.

The advantage of regulation versus control is that the former can react to glitches without having to compute them. Its disadvantage is that it can be unstable; that is, once it has lost its equilibrium, it oscillates constantly, an effect that is impossible to control.

Figure 192 illustrates the analogies between machine and human temperature regulation. In a futuristic scenario, heating and air-conditioning will be regulated by direct and wireless communication with the human body. Human regulation would achieve customized comfort as it would respond not only to physical but also to psychological factors. (The human temperature regulator, the hypothalamus, is located in the diencephalon; temperature receptors and actuators are located in the skin and internal organs; nerves transmit the regulating signals.)

"Fuzzy logic" closely resembles human perception and expression; "fuzzy control" is an innovative regulation and control principle along the same lines. It was developed to process complex sequences or sequences that require high levels of mathematical computing. For standard feedback control systems in the areas of heating, cooling or air-conditioning and refrigeration systems, this is rarely necessary. In the case of a mass-produced machine such as a boiler or a furnace, this new type of regulation system can compete with established temperature-dependent flow control if:

– The influence of external temperature is minimized through good insulation.
– The damping behaviour and the differential between external and room temperature are too great owing to massive construction.
– External temperature sensors cannot be optimally placed.

192
Technical and human temperature regulation
Goose-flesh and reduced circulation of surface blood vessels to increase insulation reduce heat loss.

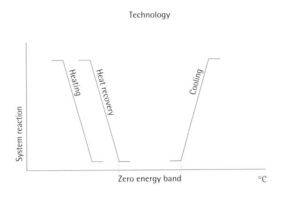

Technology

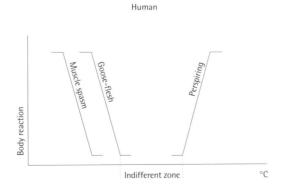

Human

Self-regulating Behaviour

Passive building components, frequently used to reduce energy consumption, often exhibit inherent self-regulating behaviours:
- Water-conducting cooling ceilings
- Low-temperature heating systems
- Thermal storage masses (to harness solar energy)
- Permanent shading installations

Cooling ceilings function on the principle of a temperature difference between the room air temperature and the mean surface temperature of the cooling surface. Since the average temperature differences of approximately 5 to 10 K are relatively small, a room air temperature change of as little as 1 K has a fairly strong impact on cooling performance.

In low-temperature heating systems, self-regulating behaviour is noticeably less owing to greater differences between room temperature and heating surfaces; in high-temperature heating systems, self-regulation is barely existent. Since rooms with cooling ceilings become cool too quickly when the heat load is insufficient or, conversely, since rooms with low-temperature heating systems heat up too much and cooling loads are insufficient due to a lack of heat loss, they must be equipped with an independent regulation in addition to self-regulation.

Thermal storage masses act as heat buffers during periods of short-term temperature loads (e.g., sun incidence). When the temperature rises in high-thermal storage rooms over the course of a day, the thermal storage mass counteracts and lowers the rise in temperature. Conversely, when the room temperature falls overnight, the thermal storage mass acts as a heat source and minimizes temperature loss. Massive storage rooms exhibit damping behaviour in the rise and fall of temperatures – in other words, they are self-regulating.

Permanent shading systems (e.g. on south façades), are also self-regulating in that they shade the façade when the sun is high in the summer, thus protecting it while allowing sun to fall into the rooms in winter when the angle of the sun is more moderate. The disadvantage by comparison to adjustable shading systems is the reduced amount of daylight penetration. Deciduous trees, planted in front of glass façades as shading elements, are self-regulating in the sense that they shed their leaves in winter, allowing for passive solar energy use when it is needed.

Process Optimization

There is today an absolute need to optimize all processes connected with energy consumption. The principal optimization goals are:
- Increased environmental sustainability
- Decreased energy consumption
- Improved room quality
- Improved operation safety
- Reduced operation and maintenance effort
- Reduced cost

Today's standard optimization strategy strives to achieve these goals in as cost-effective and rational a manner as possible. This may mean that some potential options are ignored – unless the approach is creative, integrating and innovative. Nature has handled the interplay of mutation and selection for millions of years with a flexible and self-correcting evolution strategy. It either adjusts to changes or selects.

Model experiments or simulation calculations enable us to apply the evolution strategy to technical optimization in a time-lapse method; depending on the complexity, applicable results are often achieved after only a few dozen optimization steps, or mutations.

The table below lists the goals for process optimization and the possibilities for their realization offered through building automation systems:

Optimization Goals	Realization Possibilities
– Valve design	· No oversizing
	· Optimal valve authority
– Load-independent damping	· Unilateral valve characteristic for heat exchanger
	· Load-independent KR adaptation
– Part load regulation	· Large control ratio
	· Additional part load valve
– Measuring accuracy	· Low work tolerance
	· High range resolution
	· Low long-time drift
– Easing the regulation	· Additional flow regulation
	· Additional utility or stand-by regulation
	· Compensation for disturbance variables
	· Cascade regulation
– Control algorithms	· PI-/PID – instead of P- characteristic
	· Fuzzy control
– De-coupling	· Absolute instead of relative humidity control

Energy Savings

Optimization Goals	Realization Possibilities
– Prevent latent consumption	· Well-sealed valves
	· Neutral zone or delay in heating and cooling sequence
	· Switch-off through window contact
– Zero energy band	· Boundary value regulation
	· Utilizing tolerances
– Use-independent switching	· Presence switching
	· Time switching
	· Sliding switching
– Load-dependent switching	· Event/AC-DC dependent switching
	· Sequential switching
	· Interval/cyclical switching
– Utilization/efficiency ratio	· frequency / variable air volume regulation
	· Washer instead of dewpoint regulation
	· Regulation of outside air portion
	· switching on-off heating / cooling modules
	· Summer-night ventilation for cooling
– Heat recovery/ Environmental supply	· Room temperature increase in summer
	· Enthalpy / psychometric-regulation
	· Heat Reclaim-Bypass control in VAV
	· Shading/utilization control
	· Brightness-dependent lighting control
	· Sun collector control

Optimization Goals	Realization Possibilities
Energy reference costs	
– Electrical demand charges	· Maximum load limit
	· Load shedding of kitchen consumers
	· Delayed activation of thermal storage masses
– Low-tariff electricity	· Ice storage
Operational Reliability	
– Modular redundancy	· Interference switchover
	· Cyclic switchover of sequence
– Blockage protection	· Cyclic pump circulation
– Anti-cooling/freezing	· Restart operation
	· Stoppage control frost coil-pumps
	· MI start-up control
	· Anti-wind-up
– Emergency service	· Notification priorities (alarm, interference and maintenance priorities)
	· Hand-switch/manual regulator
– Monitoring	· Boundary value monitoring
	· Elapsed time indicator
	· Watch-dog
User friendly systems	· Graphic user interface / WYSIWYG (What you see is what you get)
	· Ergonomic software, automatic functions
	· Self-adapting
	· Self-optimizing
	· Self-learning functions

The services originally developed for large building projects, such as regulating and control systems as well as central coordinating systems, are now being applied to residential building as well. New terms such as Smart Home, Homesystems, and Integrated or Intelligent Home all describe homes where components such as lamps, switches, radiator valves and ventilators and sub-systems like kitchen appliances or alarm systems are linked not only physically (e.g. with also by information technology and are equipped with local and central machine intelligence. The synergy of these systems vastly increases the utility of conventional building services based on isolated components and devices. The additional utility factors created by system integration include co-ordinating sub-processes for optimization, visualizing information and procedures, streamlining and simplifying multi-tasking and generally moving towards lower operating costs, reduced environmental pollution, improved safety and comfort, as well as unimpeded productivity. Home systems are functionally and structurally similar to process automation systems, especially building control systems. For residential buildings, technical implementation must be adapted from that designed for large high-rise buildings and modified to the smaller scale, installation and operation appropriate for homes.

An internal network for data transmission, specifically, a house-fieldbus system, is the technical basis for the Smart Home technology. This system is responsible for integrating the local and central network nodes of the system. Potential transmission media for Home systems include existing electrical wiring, twisted pair wire, coaxial cables such as feeders to TV antennae, high-frequency lines associated with cordless phones, infrared as in remote controls or even ultrasound. Sensory (sensors, detectors etc.) and motor technology (motors, actuators etc.) are linked via a special sensor-actor bus to ensure that the technical services in the home react appropriately to environmental resources and external conditions. A con-

trol switchboard similar to the one designed by architect Christoph Ingenhoven (Ingenhoven, Overdiek, Kahlen + Partner, Düsseldorf; *Figure 193*) could be installed to monitor the condition and energy consumption of the house.

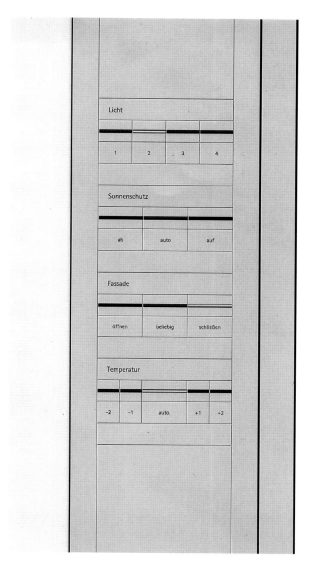

193
Control board
(Design: Ingenhoven, Overdiek,
Kahlen + Partner, Düsseldorf)

11.3 Systems for Ventilation, Heating and Cooling

Building services have already been discussed in the preceding chapters in the context of several specific projects. Systems for ventilation, heating and cooling as well as for water supply, etc., amount to such an extensive topic that it is impossible to discuss each one in detail in this volume alone. What follows are tables of room and finishing standards for different building types. "Low", „medium" or "high" standard in these tables indicates what actions are possible according to the available investment.

Generally speaking, we can assume that building services will develop further, although surely not in leaps and bounds as in recent years. The following *Tables 11* to *13* (prepared by Wilfried Müller[†], an engineer at HL-Technik AG) provide an overview of different types of buildings and functions:

– Residential
– Commercial
– Offices
– Residential and services
– Boardinghouse

Table 11 lists the room and finishing standards for residential building types and one can see for which type of home these standards are typically applied. *Tables 12* and *13* contain analogous lists for office buildings. Naturally, these tables represent only a sampling and not all possible scenarios, especially as they are based on current levels of technology. They are, nevertheless, indicators of future developments.

Table 11
Room and finishing standards for residential buildings
The different standards are equally applied to all residential building types such as single and two family home (duplex), row house, terrace, multi-family home (fourplex), apartment block. The high quality standard is not normally applied to buildings with mixed apartment and commercial use.

		Low standard	Average standard	High standard
Room standards	Room temperature t_R	20 – 38°C	20 – 38°C	20 – 26°C
	Room humidity φ	10 – 80%	10 – 80%	30 – 60%
	Guaranteed air change AC	0 – 10 ac/h	0 – 10 ac/h	0.5 – 1.0 ac/h
Fit-out standards	Heating energy supply	District heat or single cauldron	District heat or single cauldron and possibly heat pump	District heat or single cauldron and possibly heat pump
	Cooling energy supply	./.	./.	free cooling + mechanical cooling + mechanical ventilation
	Solar utilization	passive	passive and possibly photovoltaics	passive + active
	Rainwater utilization	possibly for watering garden	for watering garden	separating system grey water
	Electr. energy supply	mains through EVUS	mains through EVUS	mains + photovoltaics
	Communication systems	telephone (digital)	telephone (ISDN-capability)	telephone (ISDN-capability) plug in each room
	Sanitary	cold water + stationary warm water heater	central warm water supply	central warm water supply Sauna (Pool)

Table 13
Applying equipment standards to office buildings

Office building	Low standard	Medium standard	High standard
Mixed residential and retail	x	x	x
Office building / headquarters	x	x	x
Office building / satellite office	x		
Office – high-rise		x	x
Apartment and office building	x	x	
Shops and services			
Boardinghouse	x	x	

Table 12
Room and finishing standards for office buildings

		Low standard	Medium standard	High standard
Room standards	Room temperature t_m	20 – 38°C	20 – 38°C	20 – 26°C
	Room humidity φ	10 – 80%	40 – 60%	40 – 60%
	Guaranteed air change AC	0-10 ac/h depending on climate conditions	2 – 2.5 ac/h mech.	2.5 – 3.4 ac/h mech.
	Luminance e	350 – 600 Lux (user fit-out possible)	350 – 500 Lux	350 – 500 Lux
	Surrounding light density L_S	150 cd/m² (user fit-out possible)	150 cd/m²	150 cd/m²
Fit-out standards	Heating	Static heating conventional energy supply (district heat, boiler)	Static heating conventional or alternative system (e.g., heat pump)	Static heating conventional or alternative energy system (CHP) (e.g., heat pump – CHP – combined heat and power coupling)
	Natural ventilation	openable windows	openable windows	openable windows with window contact (monitoring and switch-off function for heating – ventilation – cooling)
	Supplementary ventilation Mechanical	. /.	top/top or bottom/top	up to air-conditioning standard
	Static cooling Building component cooling	. /.	possibly suppl. up to 40 kW/m²	up to 80 kW/m²
	Sanitary installations	Service water cold	water economizing setting service water cold/warm	water economizing setting service water cold/warm
	ELT installation Mains current	Balustrade duct, possibly surface installation visible cable lines	Hollow floors/ installation below floor	Hollow floor – double floor highly flexible
	ELT installation Weak current	space for surface installation visible cable lines	Space for duct system or hollow floor	Bus-system technology
	Degree of automation (energy management)	min. (thermostat valves)	Central energy management Room regulation	Comprehensive energy management system in combination with bus-system technology
	Fire protection	according to legal regulation	according to legal regulation + possibly smoke alarm etc.	according to legal regulation and specific requirements including automatic fire extinguisher
Retrofit	Alternative heating systems	not provided, but possible	not provided, basic constr. fit-out in place	central supply provided, heat pump or CHP, power heat coupling, possibly earth coils, aquifer storage, photovoltaics
	Alternative cooling systems	not provided, but possible	not provided, basic constr. fit-out in place	central supply provided, heat pump or CHP, power heat coupling, possibly earth coils, aquifer storage, photovoltaics
	alternative electr. supply systems	not provided, but possible	not provided, basic constr. fit-out in place	central supply provided, heat pump or CHP, power heat coupling, possibly earth coils, aquifer storage, photovoltaics
	Rainwater	not provided, but possible	not provided, possible constr. fit-out in separating system	Grey water system Super efficient autom façade
	Expanded passive measures	acc. to heat protection regulation (HPR) expansion possible (e.g. improved insulating values) windows/Lv-ratio 1:1 possibly night cooling	according to HPR expansion with automatic shading night cooling	(polyvalent wall, transparent insulating materials TIM) storage concepts (night power, ice storage)
	Heating requirement	55 – 80 kWh/m²a	35 – 60 kWh/m²a	25 – 50 kWh/m²a
	Daylight systems	. /.	Daylight – supplementary lighting (automatic timed light switch-off)	Daylight refraction system automatic supplementary lighting to daylight automatic on/off switch when room is occupied /unoccupied

11.4 Interior Lighting

194.1 – 3
Light-tech/low-tech residential
building: light construction and
flooded with natural light,
demonstrating an excellent
utilization of natural resources
Architect: B. Meyerspeer

Artificial lighting is essentially a means of complementing daylight. It is increasingly necessary to provide additional interior light appropriate to the milieu. Still, the issue is primarily one of daylit rooms, as in the residential project illustrated in *Figures 194.1* to *194.3*. Designed by architect Bernd Meyerspeer, Munich, this project aimed to create a bright living area. As the images show, conditions were close to ideal in all respects: the building is surrounded by green, the living areas are enclosed by light constructions, large, elevated windows to the north allow large amounts of zenith light into the rooms and low-positioned windows to the south open so that the whole living area can be opened to the outside. The concept ideally complements a "living environment for the future". Lighting is mainly from below, reflected from large wood surfaces, making it possible to use high-efficiency lamps.

Light Sources

Energy crises and greater environmental awareness have promoted the development of lamps. Between 1950 and the present, the efficiency of fluorescent lamps has more than doubled. The greater light efficiency is at present achieved with a spectrum that yields poor colour quality. When we compare the spectrum of daylight with those of artificial light sources, we can see that the colour rendition decreases as the system performance increases. For lighting systems used mainly in work areas, the following status quo exists:

Light sources with continuous spectrum:

Type of lamp	Efficiency (lumen/W)
– Incandescent lamp	approx. 14 lumen/W
– Halogen HV	approx. 16 lumen/W
– Halogen NV	approx. 22 lumen/W

Light sources with excellent colour rendition qualities, class 1a/colour rendition from DIN R_a 90 to 100%:

– Fluorescent lamp Lumilux de Luxe	approx. 64 lumen/W
– Compact fluorescent lamp	approx. 48 lumen/W
– Halogen metal-vapour lamp (HIT-D)	approx. 61 lumen/W

Light sources with good colour rendition qualities, from DIN RA = 80 to 90%:

– Fluorescent lamp Lumilux+	approx. 88 lumen/W
– Compact fluorescent lamp Lumilux L	approx. 77 lumen/W
– FH-fluorescent lamp	>100 lumen/W
– Halogen metal-vapour lamp (HIT-NDL)	approx. 67 lumen/W

In sum: while "high-tech lighting" is more energy-efficient, the efficiency is purchased at the cost of light spectrum quality. Since medical studies prove that light intensity as well as the composition of the spectrum have great influence on humans, artificial lighting should have the best possible continuous spectrum with good colour rendition qualities. This is especially important in the workplace, where people may spend many hours each year working under artificial light.

Types of Lighting

Lighting concepts for offices of the future must maximize daylight use. The goal is to prevent situations where high daylight incidence on sunny days cannot be utilized because shades and blinds need to be lowered, which in turn means that artificial light needs to be switched on. There are already some solutions for shading units with high daylight factors, and they are becoming more popular.

Good-quality lighting for the future can generally be kept to a basic luminance of 300 lux by using spot lighting in work areas to round out the concept. The surrounding light densities on walls, ceiling and floor near a workstation should function in comfortable relation to the light density at the workstation itself. These requirements should be met by light-density reduction near windows. Here, too, intensive R & D has been carried out in recent years to develop new concepts; an optimal solution may be in sight in the form of polyvalent wall structures.

Modern electronics makes it possible to regulate many types of lamps according to natural light conditions and other needs (dimming/switching), which is advantageous in all respects. Lighting supplementary to daylight should always be indirect; it is created with lamps whose colour temperature is at least 4,000 Kelvin. *Figure 195* illustrates such a concept where Oka-Solar louvres are used to combine shading and daylight defraction. Daylight is supplemented by lighting systems located along the top of the walls. Workstations can be lit more brightly with downlights or with special floor or desk lamps. Desk lamps are usually the light systems first used when daylight

195
Light principle:
Willi-Brandt house, Berlin
1 Shading and light defraction with OKA-Solar
2 Glare protection screen
3 Supplementary daylight lighting
4 Night lighting, indirect factor
5 Night lighting, direct factor

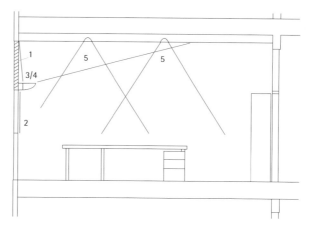

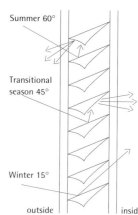

begins to wane. It is especially important to use warm colours in these lamps.

Lighting systems to supplement daylight and systems for night lighting can be installed with systems using direct / indirect luminaires and lighting means that localized lighting can achieve a comfortable room ambience while reducing electrical energy requirements. *Figure 196* illustrates such an example in a computer simulation for an office building (software Luxor – HL-Technik AG, Lichtplanung).

11.5   Integrated Acoustic Systems

Architects, designers and the building industry in general strive to develop products that meet the demands for cost-efficient room requirements and innovative solutions.

In addition, the most innovative concepts tend to meet the demand for light tech, such as the concept currently offered by floor and ceiling manufacturer Wilhelmi *(Figure 197)*. This solution optimizes lighting and acoustic room requirements with minimal material effort. With a system solution of this kind, suspended ceilings are no longer necessary when the other installations are put in place in a hollow or double floor.

The Solitär components (acoustic/reflecting elements) make it possible to create acoustic islands where necessary. The same applies to lighting technology. The advantage of this type of concept is that the acoustic components can double as lighting units, leading to more material savings. These flexible installations are

196
Milieu lighting with reflector lamp
Computer simulation with Luxor,
Nürnberger Insurance competition

197
Acoustic and lighting element
"Solitär", Wilhelmi Works

moveable and can be repositioned when rooms are rearranged. The illustration shows how little material effort is required to achieve the projected goals.
Lighting systems of this kind, suspended from the ceiling, can help reduce floor heights (less material consumed in construction) and above all expose storage masses (concrete ceiling etc.), improving cooling effects.

11.6 Installation Rooms and Zones

Installation rooms and zones for building services depend on the degree of fit-out. There are no fixed rules, only basic requirements for flexibility, reversibility and conversion for completely different uses, as well as demands that arise from the necessary interior works.

In the past, primary technical installations in suspended ceiling areas were only partially installed in floors (usually electrical installations in ceiling cavities of approx. 40 to 60 cm). Recent developments are more and more geared to installations in floors.

For many years, the tendency has clearly been to introduce cooling energy into rooms not only on the basis of circulated air systems, but to reduce the air volumes that require cooling or heating, and to ensure air hygiene. For energy efficiency and resource conservation, water has been used for several years for cooling; hence the logical reversal with regard to installation zones in each storey from top to bottom.

The standard space required today to install heating and cooling systems as well as a flexible electrical system for both power and communications will probably remain the same. It may become necessary, however, to increase the flexibility of the installations by making them more accessible and by facilitating additional installations. This applies equally to the floor area and to the vertical risers.

Especially in residential construction where electrical lines are still installed with and without empty conduit systems, there may be a greater need for true shaft areas. The future may even bring options for installing a bus system to link all automated systems in the floor area.

The reduction of connected services (heating and cooling performance, electricity) will likely remain unchanged owing to the typical floor height – better access will undoubtedly become a greater issue.

12 Mobile Real Estate: New Uses for Existing Buildings

Observers of current and future trends predict that the nature of work will change so drastically, and the scope expand so greatly, that we will soon be faced with completely new structures. In the past, information-processing organizations gathered and stored data at a single location. In an era of economic globalization and often rapid political and technological change, this localization is less and less practical. In fact, at the start of a new project it is strategically more important to form a partnership among several groups of specialists who may be geographically dis-

persed and to dissolve the partnership as soon as the project is completed.

We are on the threshold of an era that will be defined by temporary, combined and virtual organizations. The dynamic organizational structures developing in response to these changes require environments that are suited to data processing rather than large, permanent, central structures. Evidence of the break-up of large structures and even of decentralization are apparent everywhere.

Companies and organizations are leaving the inner cities because of high rents and logistical problems; city buildings will have to be retrofit or assigned to completely new uses. At the same time, many large industrial enterprises are leaving their old industrial sites in search of better conditions; often, existing buildings are revitalized and retrofit to meet these needs.

From Brewery to Mill to Multi-Purpose Object

Revitalized objects, especially old industrial buildings, retain a special character. This is evident in Mühle Tiefenbrunnen, built in 1889 as a brewery and sold in 1913, after which it was used as a mill – reassigned to a new use. After the mill closed, the complex was once again renovated and revitalized, becoming a lively environment for residential, commercial and cultural use. The central segment of the original brewery machinery and its vertical transportation was preserved as a museum. *Figure 198* provides an overview of the project.

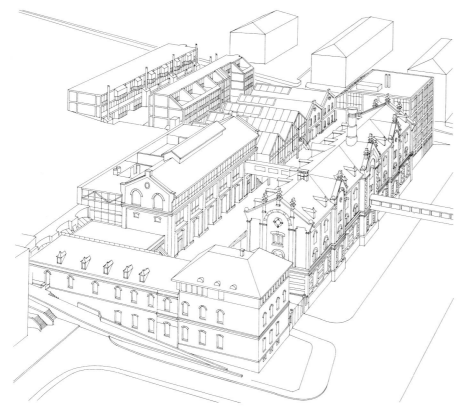

198
The factory building
Mühle Tiefenbrunnen, Zurich
Architect: Pierre Zoelly, Zollikon

From Industrial Hall to Theatre

The former VIII mechanical workshop of the Friedrich Krupp Works in Essen was built between 1898 and 1902 and formed, together with the hall complex opposite, the gateway into "Kruppstadt". The exterior measurements are 105 metres by 50 metres. The structure is defined by the steel construction of the middle hall, which was reinforced with several bridges, each with a load-bearing capacity of up to 40 tonnes. The three-aisle hall is divided into two aisles with balconies and a central aisle with a height of 28 metres to the ridge of the roof. In keeping with its symbolic importance, the brickwork façade was structurally articulated.

When production ended in the 1980s, the hall was classified for preservation. Beginning in mid-1995, the hall was converted to a musical theatre designed by Kohl + Kohl Architects, Essen.

The theatre as "transformation machine" serves as a container for three-dimensional, technical, virtual and real worlds. The hall is divided into orchestra and balcony sections, with 1,000 seats in the orchestra and 550 in the balcony. The steel supports, loading bridge and glazed roof give the hall its strong character. The lobby was left unchanged and is separated from the main theatre by a metal-clad wall. This wall, positioned within the room volume, marks the transition from the preserved historical industry hall to the theatre enclosure.

The design is based on two premises: first, the structural system of the original steel construction was to be preserved; second, the theatre components were to be recoverable. These structural, conservation and economic considerations led to the application of two building approaches. The orchestra and balcony levels are constructed independently as a cantilevered gallery. The three new levels in the five-storey rear building combine as a steel construction with the existing steel building into a structural and architectural system. To stay within the permissible load for the existing structure, all new walls are light constructions.

For the façade, there were two prerequisites: to maintain the visual appearance of the single-glazed steel windows and to provide natural ventilation for the office areas. A second façade was added behind the original façade; to create fresh air flow in front of the new façade, louvred glass leaves were installed at the base of the original glazing and grating was installed near the roof.

199.1
Concert Hall, Essen
Architects: Kohl + Kohl,
Historic condition of site

199.2
The new concert hall

199.3
Archival image of machine hall

The new façade replicates both the proportions and sectioning of the multi-storey original façade. It is structurally independent and can be removed to return the building to its original condition. In the lobby areas, the historic design of single glazing is preserved. Along the west side, some windows that had been bricked in were reopened, and a new façade was created to restore the overall appearance of the building *(Figure 199).*

199.4
Condition of machine hall prior to renovation

199.5
The new theatre

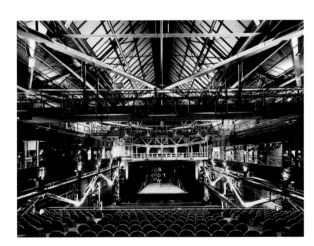

From Office Tower to Hotel

The Deutsche Genossenschaftsbank tower, planned and designed by Diedrich Praeckel of Speer + Partner, was completed in 1978. The building is shown in *Figures 200.1* is *200.3* and is representative of many such objects from the seventies.

Owing to phenomenal growth in the early eighties, the banking institution was forced to move to a larger building. From 1986 onward, the building was mostly used for subsidiaries and banking-like institutions; it was finally sold in 1989 to a Swedish investment group. Currently, there are plans to turn the building into a hotel; *Figure 201* shows the plan for a typical floor.

Renovating an office tower into a hotel requires considerable changes to the building services, especially the sanitary installations. Creating a restaurant and kitchen on the top floor is no problem in this case, because a small facility already existed. Conference and meeting rooms and a small ballroom can be accommodated in the bottom three-storey section of the complex (originally open-concept offices, later on used as a computing centre).

The site is suited to a hotel renovation for several reasons. It is located close to the banking quarter, and the Intercontinental Hotel is next door; both buildings face the Main River. Also, the corner-tower structure means that the entire building is column-free, offering views in all directions. The absence of

200.1
DG Bank, Frankfurt, site plan
Arch.: A. Speer + Partner
1   Access lane
2   Canopy
3   Lobby
4   Teller
5   Teller area
6   Office
7   Telephone switchboard
8   Teleprinter
9   Entry
10 Exit
11 Elevator

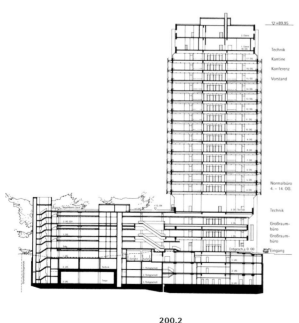

200.2
Section

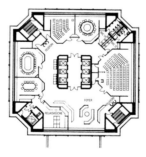

200.3
Conference floor

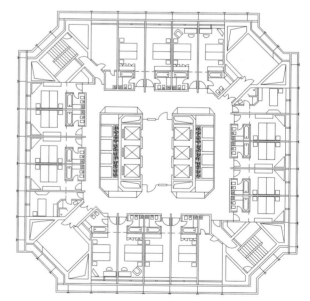

201
Potential use as hotel

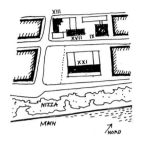

STÄDTEBAULICHE
SITUATION 1971

STÄDTEBAULICHES
GUTACHTEN
1. PREIS SPEERPLAN 1971
↓
BEAUFTRAGUNG + PLANUNG
SPEERPLAN + NHS
1972-1975
↓
AUSFÜHRUNG
1974-1978

STÄDTEBAULICHE
SITUATION 1979

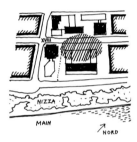

columns and the unusual floor height of 3.98 metres pose few limitations to changing the technical installations. In addition, wraparound balconies create additional escape routes. Several sketches from the initial stage of the project illustrate these changes and document the main elements that make renovation possible *(Figure 202)*. In light of the changes brought about by global markets and the information age, renovation and especially retrofitting will be essential in future planning.

The building market is increasingly controlled by project developers and large-scale investors; private owners tend to invest more in the "development of production", and less in the built structure. At the same time, the uncertain future of the real estate market forces basic questions: what, for whom, to what purpose, and at what cost? A new strategy is evolving to avoid the risks of low occupancy by ensuring flexibility to accommodate shifting needs: everything must be changeable.

12.1 Basic Construction: User Fit-out

Buildings of the future must be adaptable to the needs and values of tomorrow. "Optimizing user values" means creating values for users in consideration of future requirements, targeting investment to this end. At any rate, securing utility and thus profitability must be the main goal for each investor, who is therefore intent on creating buildings with the highest utility value – and the longest possible life cycle. The true market value of the object is determined by the quality of the built environment in the eyes of the tenant, by how the building interacts with its surroundings and the building's inherent integrity. The greater the utility value, the greater the attraction of the building for future users.

Utility values of buildings of the future are also increasingly determined by ecological demands – nature is integrated into the building. Another important factor contributing to value is the infrastructure, that is, the user fit-outs and technical options for change and assigning new uses, in other words, the overall adaptability. A well-planned building must be able to react to changes in society and in the marketplace. This is the source from which the demand for architectural flexibility springs.

The Product Life-Cycle Concept
A breakdown of the lifespan of a building includes the following phases:
– Shell cycle, lasting over 50 years
– Building envelope, lasting over 30 years
– Technical fit-out (general), lasting over 10 years
– Fit-out of information and communication tools, lasting over 5 years

202
Design sketches

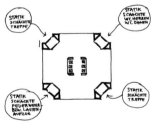

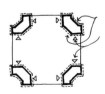

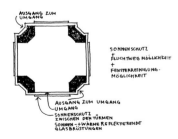

Basic fit-out includes:
– Heating
– Water supply and disposal
– Electrical supply and disposal

All other fit-outs are in the broadest sense user fit-outs:
– Heating systems (in part)
– Sanitary installations and fire extinguishing systems (in part)
– Ventilation systems
– Refrigeration systems
– Air-conditioning systems
– User-specific electrical work
– Information and communication systems

Of these, the latter are a product of future work and organization structures, and as such are subject to change.

The Galleria project (New Space), Zurich, is a prime example of a building concept generated by a project developer, in this instance, Spaltenstein Immobilien AG. *Figure 203* illustrates the concept, which emphasizes ecological requirements. The basic and user fit-out resulted in the floor height and stack design illustrated in *Figures 205.1* and *205.2*. The floor height is 3.75 metres; 30-centimetre high hollow floors and suspended ceiling structures approximately 30 centimetres deep, combined with vertical supply options at 18-metre intervals, deliver the flexibility required to meet all future user needs. Cooling energy, treated supply air, heating energy, electricity and information systems can be supplied to each user from below or above or in combination – anything is possible in this building design.

This high level of flexibility has proven valuable in this project. The Schweizerische Volksbank became lessor and co-investor; the bank set up, among other things, workstations for stock exchange and trading – workplaces with extraordinarily high heat loads and correspondingly high cooling requirements. Several

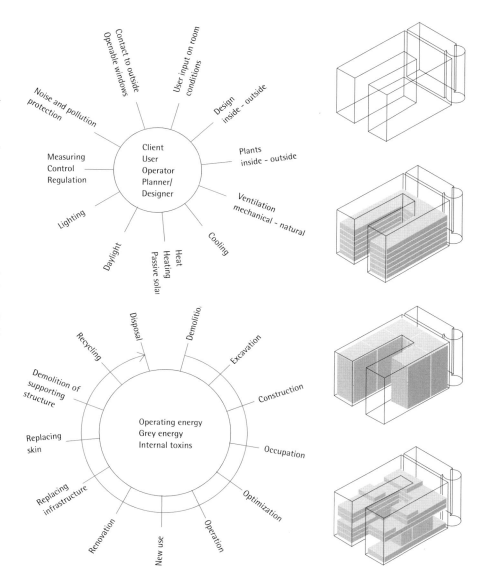

203
The house within the house, concept by Spaltenstein Immobilien AG
The basic structure is fully defined and designed. The finishing of the flexible floor plans is left to each user.

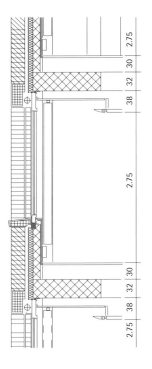

years of operation have been trouble-free with regard to upgrading, retrofitting or reassigning to new uses. Adaptable buildings enjoy a long lifespan – these are certainly not "disposable objects". The buildings are extremely ecological in that the main body of the building lasts for many decades.

205.2
Detail section of façade

205.1
Section of office areas

204
Galleria – New Space
Architects cooperative:
D. Gerber & X. Nauer,
Burckhardt + Partner AG,
B. E. Honegger and W. Glaus, Zurich

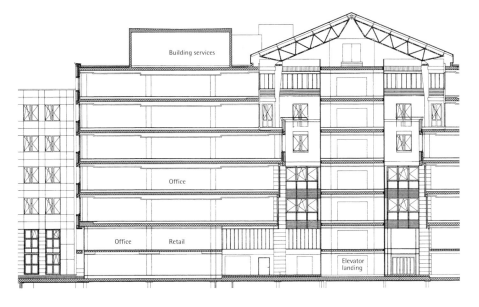

Building services

Office

Office | Retail

Elevator landing

12.2 Changeable Building Structures

We must save costs
We must conserve resources
We must save energy
We must, we must ... but how?

In the history of architecture, there have been many attempts to build houses that meet these demands by using prefabricated systems, structural systems and panel-and-board elements. Panel construction used in the former East Germany and in other former Eastern Bloc countries created a barren architectural landscape; the same can be said of modern satellite cities. The immobility characteristic of architecture in the past was not the main factor inhibiting architects from creating designs for flexible buildings structures with high aesthetic values; rather, they were hampered by the technical and economic reality of the time, which made structural flexibility virtually impossible. The duplex in cellular construction shown in *Figure 206* is a good illustration of the problem, taken from the T 2687 research report issued by the laboratory on wood technology at the Fachhochschule Hildesheim/Holzminden (Professor of Engineering M. H. Kessel) and by Otto Bauckmeier GmbH & Co. KG, Hameln. Is this to be the ultimate answer? A completely different world and architectural language unfolds with the Skydeck project *(Figure 207)*. Richard Horden consciously abandoned all tenets of the construction industry for this prefabricated residential architecture; instead, he found inspiration in car, boat and aircraft construction (imagine the boat or yacht as a floating residential unit, powered by a renewable energy source: wind).

In the Skydeck design, individual modules are outfit-

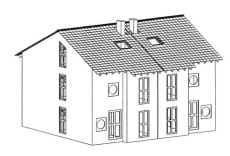

206
View of duplex in cellular construction: German Gemütlichkeit?

In the Skydeck design, individual modules are outfitted with elegant and attractive details, just as in cars or yachts. The basic module can have different openings and walls, which can be adapted at a later point. Depending on price category, different product qualities are available, choices in colours, surfaces, accessories and components. An "intelligent" control and regulation system reacts to local and temporal conditions, minimizes energy consumption and provides information on running costs (costs for water, electricity and heating; operating conditions and maintenance intervals are also indicated). Extensions to the Skydeck system can be ordered, delivered and installed at any time *(Figure 208)*, especially during periods when users can be spared from experiencing any expansion or renovation work. The advantages of such system solutions are that most of the work is done in safe factory conditions, improving the quality of the finished product. Grey energy consumption can be controlled and reduced. Waste and excess material are recycled immediately in the factory. Made-to-measure manufacture tends to prolong the life cycle of the product. Especially in the threshold countries and in Third World countries, one of the main tasks of the building industry will be to provide energy-efficient, user-compatible apartments. This has huge market potential.

207
The Skydeck project
Prefabricated modules make different configurations and room divisions possible in residential construction.
(Architect: R. Horden Ass.)

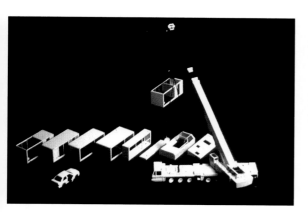

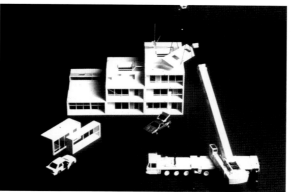

208
Modular design leaves room for open stairwells and two-level rooms.

209
The adaptable house:
A – Living structure
B – Retail structure
C – Office structure (modular,
group and combination
offices)

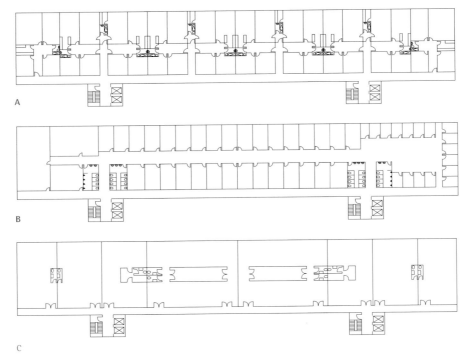

A

B

C

210
Flexible building structure: assigning new uses to floor and interior zones

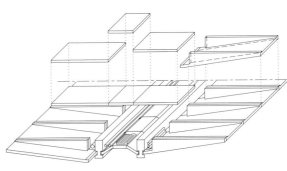

211
Reversible building structure for different uses (office/working/living)

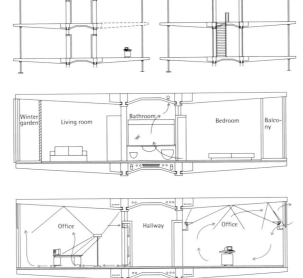

Winter garden | Living room | Bathroom | Bedroom | Balcony

Office | Hallway | Office

212
Support structure with individually changeable components (modular design)

Figures 209 to *212* illustrate the principle of a changeable or adaptable building structure. A building depth of approximately 15 metres provides the best conditions for office, commercial and residential structures. Much thought has been put into creating a flexible structure that allows for changes from floor to floor, on the outside and in the interior, to meet all kinds of requirements. Multi-storey rooms are easily incorporated, as are inner stairwells and moveable wall modules.

Figure 211 is a schematic representation of the installation systems integrated into the rib structure of each floor. Sub-floor systems supply information, heating energy, electricity, cooling energy and fresh air. In this modular design, systems are installed at each level: changes or adaptations on one floor do not affect the floors below. The changeable building structure is composed of individual modules which are in part simply suspended and in part bolted in place. This type of modular framework is feasible in both heavy and light construction. Renovation, expansion and re-use can be achieved by shifting modules, rather than by demolition.

One could comment that none of this is new. And that's quite true. Yet, especially to the lay person, the question begs to be answered: Why hasn't changeable building design advanced further than it has? For the sake of environmental protection, resource conservation and recycling, it is high time that efforts in this direction be renewed.

12.3 Changeable Building Skins

Modular building systems must be complemented by changeable building envelopes, or skins. Anyone who has seen high-rises in Hong Kong is astonished by the variety of façades, a variety that has sprung from necessity and the demand for more living space. Legislation guarantees each inhabitant of Hong Kong a minimal living space of 4 square metres. However, many people are restricted to less space and have found creative ways to expand their living space to the outside. Bamboo structures, steel and aluminium supports and other building materials are often used to expand rooms beyond the façades. *Figure 213* is a schematic illustration of possible façade options to meet user needs. Façades with adjustable or curtained

213
Façade options for different demands (reversible wall units)

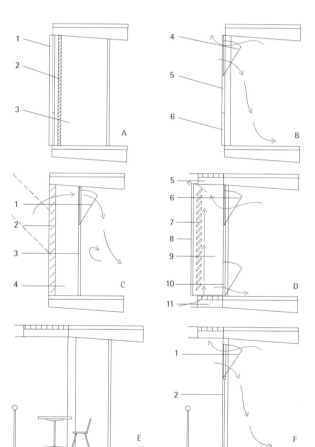

A, B
1 Tempered safety glass with interior sun protection
2 Insulating blind
3 Winter garden
4 Tilt window for night ventilation
5 Insulating glazing
6 Transluzent balustrade component

C, D
1 Tilt window for night ventilation
2 External shading
3 Window component/ insulating glazing
4 Passage
5 Fresh air exit
6 Tilt window for natural ventilation
7 Shading louvres
8 Single glazing as climate façade and sound protection
9 Accessible cavity
10 Double glazed sliding door (insulating glass) with wood frame
11 Fresh air intake

E, F
1 Tilt window for night ventilation
2 Door element

façade elements can be completed in response to user demands and special requirements. *Figure 214* illustrates several basic ideas.

As in the lighting industry, many advances have been made in the area of façades over the past years. Innovative ideas have entered the market, especially

214
The Skydeck project
The exterior skin is easily redesigned or explanded with skylights and balconies.
Arch.: R. Horden Ass.

1 Balkonies glazed or with sun protection
2 Optional glass canopy
3 Gentle roof slope contains tank store
4 Skylight for bathroom
5 - Windows and doors to balcony are double glazed with aluminium frame
   - Exterior walls are masonry or timber framed
   - Partitions are made of hollow concrete blocks
6 Room height can be doubled
7 Building services controlled by central computer with external access

the English-speaking world. Façades have become a widely documented area of expertise for architects, building climatologists, aerophysicists, "façade consultants" and building engineers; teams composed of members from all these fields are searching for the optimal solutions (*see* Chapter 9). There are still some architects who stubbornly persist in the opinion that they alone can develop and plan façades as a whole and for all requirements – but times are changing.

12.4   Changeable Building Services

Building services are not only subject to trends in taste, but also to technical innovation. The topics relevant for architects have already been discussed, as has the need for being able to react to changes. Building services is a complex area that will have to become more responsive to the demand for adaptability, that is, flexible reactivity in the smallest possible units. Basic fit-out and user fit-out formulate the requirements which again are driven by the need to satisfy any demand for adaptation or retrofitting with the least amount of effort, disruption or interruption in operation. The systems catering to future markets and automated buildings will undergo the greatest changes.

12.5 Perspectives

A contemporary project, a high-rise building in Frankfurt (Schneider + Schumacher) that realizes many of the concepts and technologies described here, will serve to round out the topic of mobile buildings

This high-rise is a cylindrical tower approximately 100 metres in height *(Figures 215.1 to 215.2)*. By rotating each floor around the cylindrical core, verandas are created in front of the office areas; the enclosed winter gardens are transformed into multi-storey, spiralling air-filled spaces that achieve interior air flow *(Figures 215.3 to 215.5)*. All areas can be naturally ventilated from the winter gardens *(Figure 215.6)*. At the same time, the winter gardens provide a relationship between interior and exterior. The building can be used for offices, or easily converted to hotel or even apartment use. The most important step for potential conversion to residential use is the use of a flat (girderless) slab floor, tapered towards the core and thus forming a cove large enough to accommodate the entire technical installation. From there, services are distributed either in the floor/ceiling or in the walls to each floor.

Each storey can be divided into independent rental areas of varying proportions. Despite the complexity of the design, the load-bearing structure is simple and cost-efficient. The inner core functions as a bracing tube that runs uninterrupted through all levels. Continuous stanchions are possible by coordinating the stanchion and rotation grids.

The outer "skin" consists of single glazing. Opening elements and defined slits create natural ventilation and prevent overheating. Users can individually open and close the inner façades. The atrium is an additional noise buffer on the lower levels, while serving to counteract high pressures above. The architectural-ly attractive open spaces provide additional internal links. In this manner, several storeys within the whole structure can be defined as a separate building.

215.1
Westhafen tower, photo montage
(Architects: Schneider + Schumacher)

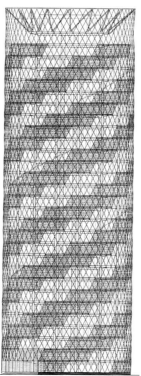

215.2
Elevation

215.3
Section

215.4
Floor plans for different uses

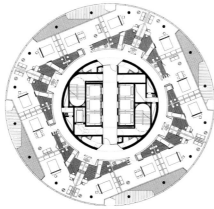

Apartments

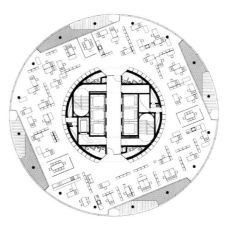

Offices (partitioned)

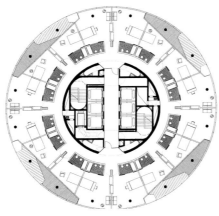

215.5
Façade ventilation

Hotel

Open-plan office

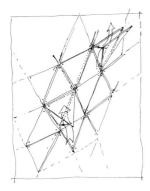

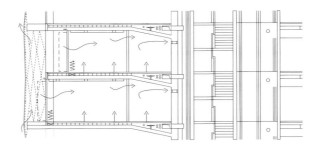

215.6
Climate concept for office areas

Low-Tech – Light-Tech – High-Tech, the title of this book, expresses with confidence that architecture in the information age must be an integrated art. We must search for and discover, investigate and utilize for each individual building, the synergy between these three approaches of vastly different complexity. Sustainable architecture will employ state-of-the-art technologies while taking into account that their use must be justifiable. Such architectural solutions have to satisfy the economic stipulations of the clients, the aesthetic interests of the architects, the new social requirements of the user in the information society and, above all, must respond directly to the urgent ecological challenges we face today.

Low-Tech means designing buildings simply and harnessing the natural resources of the specific environment. Light-Tech is a challenge to use raw materials sparingly and, whenever possible, 100 % recyclable material. When these conditions are met, High-Tech elements and devices can be integrated to create optimal working and living conditions with minimal energy and resource consumption.

It is time to translate these challenges into reality, not only for individual projects but across the board. Urban planning, architecture, construction and technical services are presented with fascinating challenges in the search for a new definition of "form follows function". Architects and engineers in the industrialized countries must develop a global approach, not only to reduce local resource and energy consumption but to provide innovative services worldwide.

Bibliography

Ackermann, Kurt.
Geschoßbauten für Gewerbe und Industrie
Stuttgart:
Deutsche Verlags-Anstalt, 1993.

AIT, Leinfelden-Echterdingen (March 1996).

Allesch, C.; **Keul,** A.; and L. **Oberascher.**
"Aesthetics of Built: A 'Pure Aesthetic' Problem or a Problem of Cultural Psychology?" Paper presented at the 11th International Congress on Empirical Aesthetics of the International Association of Empirical Aesthetics, Budapest, 1990.

Arnheim, R.
Kunst und Sehen.
Berlin: de Gruyter, 1978.

Behling, Sophia and Stefan.
Sol Power: Die Evolution der solaren Architektur.
Munich: Prestel, 1996.

Bott, Helmut, and Volker von **Haas.**
Verdichteter Wohnungsbau.
Stuttgart: Verlag W. Kohlhammer, 1996.

Bund Deutscher Architekten (BDA).
Renaissance der Bahnhöfe.
Exhibition catalogue.
Braunschweig / Wiesbaden:
Vieweg Verlag.

Bundesarchitektenkammer, ed.
Energiegerechtes Bauen und Modernisieren.
Basel: Birkhäuser Verlag, 1996.

Calder, Nigel.
The Manic Sun: Weather Theories Confounded.
Pilkington Press Ltd., 1997.

Daniels, Klaus.
The Technology of Ecological Building. Translated by Elizabeth Schwaiger.
Basel: Birkhäuser Verlag, 1997.
Originally published as
Technologie des ökologischen Bauens (Basel: Birkhäuser Verlag, 1995).

Deutsche Bundesstiftung Umwelt.
Heute für die Zukunft bauen, aber wie? Government publication.
Deutsche Bundesstiftung Umwelt, Osnabrück, 1995.

domus, Sept. 1996.

Fisher, J. D.; **Bell,** P. A.; and A. **Baum.**
Environmental Psychology.
2nd ed. New York: Holt, Rinehart and Winston, 1984.

Fraunhofer Gesellschaft – Institut für Arbeitswirtschaft und Organisation IAO. "Report 1995." Fraunhofer Institut für Arbeitswirtschaft und Organisation IAO, Stuttgart, 1996.

Gates, Bill.
The Road Ahead.
New York: Viking, 1995.

Glässel, Joachim.
Städtische Sonnenräume.
Karlsruhe: C. F. Müller, 1985.

Grub, Hermann.
Unternehmen Grün.
Munich: Callwey Verlag, 1990.

Hegger, Manfred; **Pohl,** Wolfgang; and Stephan **Reiss-Schmidt.**
Vitale Architektur.
Braunschweig: Vieweg & Sohn Verlag, 1988.

Hegger, Manfred, and Rainer **Stuhrmann.**
Im Auftrag der Architektenkammer Baden-Württemberg: Wohnen und Wohnungen bauen. Exhibition catalogue.
Architektenkammer Baden-Württemberg, 1993.

Heller, Eva.
Wie Farben wirken.
Hamburg: Rowohlt, 1989.

Herzog, Thomas, ed. *Die Halle 26.*
Munich: Prestel, 1996

Hoeft, Michael, and Jean-Francois Kaelin.
"Ausstellungspavillion in Brettstapelbauweise"
Schweizer Baublatt 2 (1992).

Horden, Richard.
light tech.
Basel: Birkhäuser, 1995.

Horx, Matthias.
Trendbüro.
Düsseldorf: ECON, 1995.

Ingenhoven Overdiek and Partner.
Evolution Ökologie Architektur.
Aedes, 1996.

Kaplan, S., and R. **Kaplan.**
Cognition and Environment: Functioning in an Uncertain World.
New York: Praeger, 1982.

Kizaoui, Dr.-Ing. J.
Die Akustik in der Lüftungs- und Klimatechnik.
Winnenden: Heizungs-Journal Verlags-GmbH, 1972.

Küller, R., and B. Mikellides.
"Simulated Studies of Color, Arousal, and Comfort."
In: *Environmental Simulation: Research and Policy Issues,* edited by R. W. Marans and D. Stokols.
New York: Plenum Press, 1993.

Meadows, Dennis H.: **Meadows,** Donella L.; **Randers,** Jørgen; and William W. **Behrens.**
The Limits of Growth.
New York: Universe Books, 1972.

Meadows, Dennis H.: **Meadows,** Donella L.; **Randers,** Jørgen; and William W. **Behrens.**
Beyond the Limits. Post Mills, Vermont USA: Chelsea Green Publishers 1992.

Meyer-Bohe, Walter.
Energiesparhäuser.
Stuttgart: DVA Deutsche Verlags-Anstalt, 1996.

Mitchell, William J.
City of Bits.
Basel: Birkhäuser, 1996.

Oberascher, Leonhard.
"Die Sprache der Farbe: Trendfarben, Individualität, Motivation."
DBZ, Special issue 91 (1991).

Oberascher, Leonhard.
"The language of colour."
In: *AIC – COLOR 93*, edited by A. Nemcsis and J. Schanda. Proceeding of the 7th Congress of the International Colour Association, Volume A. Technical University of Budapest, Budapest, 1993.

Oberascher, Leonhard.
"Cyclic Resurgence of Collective Colour Preferences." In: *Color Forecasting: A Survey of International Color Marketing*, edited by H. Linton. New York: Van Nostrand Reinhold, 1994.

Oberascher, Leonhard.
"Farbe als bedeutendes Mittel der Architekturgestaltung."
Bulletin 4 (1994).

Oberascher, Leonhard.
"Farbe in Krankenhaus und Altenheim: Zwei Beispiele der Gestaltung therapeutischer Räume".
DBZ, Special edition, 1(1996).

Oswalt, Philipp, ed.
Wohltemperierte Architektur.
Heidelberg: Verlag C. F. Müller, 1994.

Reich, Robert B.
Die neue Weltwirtschaft.
Frankfurt a. Main: Fischer, 1996.

Rice, Peter, and Hugh **Dutton.**
Transparente Architektur.
Basel: Birkhäuser, 1995.
Originally published as *Le Verre Structurel.*
Paris: Le Moniteur, 1990.

Schlaich, Jörg.
Das Aufwindkraftwerk.
Stuttgart: Deutsche Verlags-Anstalt, 1994.

Schlaich, Jörg, and Rudolf **Bergermann.**
Fußgängerbrücken.
Exhibition catalogue.
Zurich: ETH Zürich, 1994.

Schmidt-Bleek, Friedrich.
Wieviel Umwelt braucht der Mensch?
MIPS – das Maß für ökologisches Wirtschaften.
Basel/Berlin: Birkhäuser Verlag, 1994.

Schneider, Astrid. ed.
Solararchitektur für Europa.
Basel: Birkhäuser Verlag, 1996.

SIA Dokumentation D 0123.
"Hochbaukonstruktionen nach ökologischen Gesichtspunkten."
Zurich: SIA, 1995.

Stoll, Clifford.
Die Wüste Internet.
Frankfurt a. Main: S. Fischer, 1996.

Symposiumsbericht Solararchitektur. Symposium report.
Glashaus, **Herten,**
27. - 28. October 1995.
Tübingen: Verein für grüne Solararchitektur.

von Weizsäcker, E. U.; **Lovins** A. B.; and L. H. **Lovins.**
Faktor vier.
Munich: Droemer Knaur, 1995.

Zoelly, Pierre.
"Les friches industrielles."
Habitation 3 (1989).

Illustration credits

1, 2, 3, 4, 7, 8, 9, 10, 11, 12, 13.1, 14, 15, 16, 17, 18, 19, 21	from UN / World Ressource Institue
5,6	from Spiegel
13.2	from: Ch. Schönwiese
20	from: F. Schmidt-Bleek, Wieviel Umwelt braucht der Mensch? MIPS - das Maß für ökologisches Wirtschaften. Birkhäuser Basel / Berlin 1994
22	from: D. Meadows, The Limits of Growth. Universe Books, New York
23, 24	from: Wuppertal Institut
S. 25	EXPO 2000 Hannover GmbH
S. 31, S. 36	Echtzeit
S. 32	MIT Press / Ian Hunter
27	Archives Ingenhoven Overdiek Kahlen + Partner
28	Holger Knauf, Düsseldorf
31	aus: H.-P. Schmiedel, Wohn-hochhäuser Bd. 1, VEB Verlag für Bauwesen, Berlin (publisher dissolved)
32.2, 32.3, 32.5	Croci & Du Fresne, Bern
33.3, 33.4	Hans Engels, Munich
34, 35	from: P. Oswaldt – Wohltemperierte Architektur
37.1, 37.2, 41, 42.1, 43.1	Sophia und Stefan Behling
37.3, 38.2, 40.2, 44.2	Sophia und Stefan Behling in collaboration with Bruno Schindler: Sol Power: Die Evolution der solaren Architektur, Prestel, Munich/NewYork, 1996
38.1	Bernhard Rudofski, Architektur ohne Architekten, Residenzverlag, Salzburg 1989
39	E. Guidoni, Architettura Primitiva, Electa, Mailand 1979
40.1	P. Oliver, Dwellings, Univ. of Texas Press, London
42.2	from: Mediterranean Architecture
44.1	Living Races of Mankind, Hutchinson, London
46.1, 46.5, 46.6, 46.7, 47.2, 47.5, 48.2, 48.3	A. Vasella
46.3, 46.4, 48.1	from: Klaus Herdeg, Formal structure in indian architecture, Rizzoli International Publications, New York, 1990
47.1, 47.3	from: H. Ronner, S. Jhaveri, A. Vasella; Louis J. Kahn – complete works 1935 – 74, Westview Press Boulder, Colorado 1977
51, 52, 53	Based on drawings by J. Schlaich
57	ETAPLAN, Munich
60	A. Vasella
64, 69, 70, 71, 72, 73	Prof. K.-D. Neumann
65	Wolfgang Reuss, Berlin
66, 67	I. Bimberg
77.1	Markus Meyer, Bremen
77.3, 77.4	Jockers + Partner
77.5	Bisterfeld + Weiss, Kirchheim/Teck
78 - 83	Santi Caleca
84	Verena von Gagern
89	Jörg Hempel, Aachen
S. 102, S.103	Dr. L. Oberascher

105.2, 105.3	W. Huthmacher/Architekton
105.4	Schneider Wessling
106	HouseLab
107	Hans Friedrich Bültmann
108, 111, 112	Ges. für Aerophysik – L. Ilg
115	Jörg Tarrach
117	Seewald / Aerophot Demuss, »Freigegeben Bezirksregierung Braunschweig«
118, 119	nach: Herzog + Partner
120	Eamonn O'Mahoney
122.1	John Norris (oben), Vic Carless (unten)
123.1	Georg Nemec, Freiburg
123.3	Blumer AG
123.5	Rolf Disch, Freiburg
124.4, 124.5	Markus Fischer
125	Museum of London, Picture Library
126	Eamonn O'Mahoney
130.2	based on drawing by Sulzer
132.2	Odilo Schoch
135	J. Weber, Munich
136	Eamonn O'Mahoney
138.1, 138.2	Jörg Tarrach
140	Ken Kirkwood
142.1	von Gerkan, Marg + Partner, Hamburg
142.4, 143.2, 143.3, 144	J. Schlaich
145	J. Natterer
146	K. Wyss, Basel
149, 151 – 153	based on drawing by Frauenhofer Gesellschaft ISE
154.1	Bomin Solar
154.3	D. Leistner / Architekton
zu 154.5	based on drawing by H. Köster
155	H.-G- Friedrich
161, 162, 163.2	Theo Hotz, Zürich
167.1	Ana Maksimiuk (right)
167.1, 167.2	RFR, Paris
168	HPP Hentrich-Petschnigg & Partner KG
171	dpa Deutsche Presseagentur GmbH
172, 175 – 180	P. Steiger, Intep
174	from: SIA Documentation
182	Image Bank, München
193	Holger Knauf, Düsseldorf
197	Michael Gleim, Gießen
198	P. Zoelly, Jürg Gasser
199.1, 199.3	Historisches Archiv Krupp, Essen
199.2, 199.5	H. Kohl
199.4	S. Brügger, Cologne
200, 202	Archives of AS&P
205	Burckhardt + Partner, Zurich
206	from: Forschungsbericht T 2687, Labor für Holztechnik, Fachhochschule Hildesheim/Holzminden
207, 208	Tom Miller
209	Revised by Michael Jung, Küsnacht
214	based on drawing by R. Horden
215.1	OFB, Frankfurt
215.2-6	Schneider + Schumacher, Frankfurt
49.2, 49.3, 50, 55.2, 74, 96, 98, 99, 133, 134, 147,148, 150	from: Technology dof Ecological Building, W. Schwaiger, A. Alber, Ch. Albrecht

Index

ABB Air Handling Equipment
P.O. Box 8131
CH-8050 Zürich-Schweiz
Home Page: www.abb.se/air-handling
Phone: +41 1 319 61 87
Fax: +41 1 319 63 79
E-mail: ulf.bennet
@chibm.mail.abb.com

– Ventilation- and air conditioning products

– Air Handling Units

– Heat-recovery systems

– Fans

– Air Terminals for air intake and air exhaust

– Fan-Coils

– Systems and components for controlled residential ventilation

ABB is a world wide supplier of high quality ventilation and air-conditioning products.

The products are characterized by progressive technology, high quality standards, dependability and economy. Nearly seventy years of experience and numerous pioneered projects have made ABB a leading company in the area of air-conditioning products.

All components are developed and produced by ABB and are thus highly compatible. The product selection ranges from central installation units, various ventilation systems and radial- and axial ventilators to different heat-recovery installations, convector ventilators and cooling convectors.

ABB is a competent partner through first class products, extensive know-how, informative consulting and the certificate of the requirements of the environmental standards according ISO 14001.

DIFA
DEUTSCHE IMMOBILIEN FONDS AG
Valentinskamp 20,
20354 Hamburg
Phone: 040/3 49 19-0, -101
Fax: 040/3 49 19-1 91

DIFA Deutsche Immobilien Fonds AG, Hamburg, or DIFA in short, is a traditional capital investment company that was founded in Hamburg in 1965. As a special credit institution, DIFA is a member of the cooperative banking group of the Volksbanken Raiffeisenbanken and manages four open-ended real estate investment funds. These include two public funds, DIFA-Fonds Nr. 1 and DIFA-GRUND, which are available to a wide spectrum of private investors throughout the Federal Republic of Germany, and two special funds for institutional investors, DIFA-Fonds Nr. 3 for church-financed pension plans and DIFA-Fonds Nr. 4 for the pension schemes of doctors, pharmacists, lawyers and notaries.

Money received from fund investors is invested by DIFA as a trustee in the purchase or project development of stable-value, lucrative commercial real estate, the focus being placed on the services sector. Preference is shown to office buildings in locations with development capacity and to commercial buildings in first-class locations.

The total trust capital in all DIFA funds amounts to some 15 billion marks. The stock in real property covers around 150 objects both at home and abroad. DIFA is the second largest capital investment company for open-ended real estate funds in Germany. The two public funds have attracted more than 300,000 fund investors. Some 200,000 of these have a fixed asset account with DIFA. DIFA funds are regarded by the private investor as asset-value-oriented capital investment for private financial and precautionary planning.

With its activities on international markets, the Dyckerhoff & Widmann AG is one of the most important construction enterprises in the Federal Republic of Germany. It was founded in 1865 and performs work in all fields of construction.

The DYWIDAG Group of Companies comprises a large number of enterprises involved in the widest variety of different work:

- construction of administration and service buildings
- construction of production facilities
- construction of traffic structures
- construction in the field of environmental protection and utilities
- construction of scientific, cultural, sports, welfare and social facilities
- residential buildings
- structural conservation.

DYWIDAG has developed systems which point the way ahead, such as prestressing systems, monocoque systems and free cantilever construction method, as well as slipform and climbing form systems. They provide evidence of our company's technical competence. It is our concern to develop this know-how further and to employ it to meet our client's needs.

Our core activity is the construction business. Our seven main branches provide a comprehensive service in every section of the home market. Foreign business is the responsibility of our main branch "Hauptniederlassung Ausland" and foreign subsidiaries.

As general licensee, the DSI DYWIDAG-Systems International GmbH markets all DYWIDAG systems internationally.

Our precast concrete works division is concerned with the production and sale of precast products and high-quality concrete products.

In addition to construction work, our clients expect services which are becoming increasingly related to meeting clients' needs, ranging from the development of projects to the planning, financing and operating of facilities and to building management. As we are organised to provide integrated services, we can react flexibly to markets that are changing and are continuing to change.

DYWIDAG – we build on Ideas

DYWIDAG

Dyckerhoff & Widmann
Aktiengesellschaft
Postfach 810280
81902 München
Erdinger Landstraße 1
Phone: 089/92 55-1
Fax: 089/92 55-2127

Projecting – Building – Managing

Investors, users and operators do more and more realize that the individual phases in the lifetime of a building must not be contemplated as being isolated units. At present, the trend is to see a building as an integral product, as far as economics are concerned. Such thinking necessiates comprehensive projecting schemes from developing to retro-fitting. For only if architects, civil contractors and mechanical contractors set up and follow an interactive scheme, aesthetic, functional and economical aspects can be combined to achieve optimum results. Comprehensive thinking and multi-disciplinary interaction of all parties involved are prerequisite to continual optimization, in the end leading to minimization of investment costs. KRANTZ-TKT, one of the leading companies in the field of building services, is your competent partner during the significant phases in the lifetime of a building. We have the know-how, pioneer programs and technical equipment that cover the entire range of projecting, building, managing and retro-fitting.

Projecting: Our building simulation program outlines in figures what relationship exists between a building with its physical properties and the projected mechanical systems. Our R&D divisions offer investors, architects, consultants and engineers the opportunity to tests the planned systems and find new solutions together with us.

Our equipment design programs allow to select and design adequate air distribution systems under due consideration of functional requirements, capacity and architectural aspects in the earliest stage of projecting.

Building: Our CAD programs are qualified aids to "live" integrated planning since all building and related data determined during projecting and execution can be transferred to be used for building operation.

Our multi-disciplinary experience as mechanical contractors is the basis for integrated building services planning and execution.

Managing: Our range of integrated facility management covers all activities in connection with operation and maintenance as well as optimization of energy efficiency and systems.

DEUTSCHE BABCOCK

KRANTZ-TKT

GRUPPE **BDAG**

KRANTZ-TKT GMBH
Am Stadion 18-24
51465 Bergisch Gladbach
Germany
Phone: 02202/125-0
Fax: 02202/125-324

RE
ROLAND ERNST

UNTERNEHMENSGRUPPE
ROLAND ERNST

Vangerowstraße 16/1
69115 Heidelberg
Tel.: 0 62 21/903-0
Fax: 0 62 21/90 31 60

STIMULUS

Concentration on core capabilities is the primary aim of present-day companies in their drive to increase competitiveness. Activities which lie outside the focus of the business should be delegated to external service providers who have specialised in these areas.

RESEARCH

Major companies right across Europe are transferring functions to new locations offering economic advantages and meaningful synergies. Our first principal project development task is the correct selection of suitable sites.

FINANCE

Our project development objective is to achieve long-term profits in real terms for all participating partners. Our aim for the duration is to maximize profit opportunities whilst simultaneously minimizing the associated risks. The majority of our projects are therefore conceived as partnerships with participation companies affiliated to the major banks. Shared risk, shared profit: sound practice, in our opinion.

CARE AND MANAGEMENT

Following completion, specialists from the Roland Ernst group of companies ensure that both commercial and technical operations run smoothly. They are the "problem solvers" who deal with every task arising from the operation and management of the building. They also act as competent points of contact for tenants.

PRODUCT SPECTRUM

Our work is oriented towards the requirements of the case. In this respect, we set great store by offering a flexible range of services in all areas of project development. Whether it be residential property, administrative buildings or properties with a social function, hospitals, commercial properties, hotels or leisure facilities: our range of services covers virtually every aspect of private and public residential and commercial construction. We place flexibility in the forefront, because in the real world, the market changes every day.

TRENDS

In years to come, commercial property development will no longer be anonymous administrative affairs; not so much symbols of power or rigid organisation as nodes in a network, information centres and meeting points designed to boost the productivity of a technology-oriented age. Employee performance will go hand in hand with demands on work content and on the working environment in which people spend the greater part of their day. The aesthetics of living will become the aesthetics of working, and vice versa. Our task will entail the project development for such properties, which in the new age will shape the world in which we live and work. We will make these projects a reality in partnership with all those who share our ambition for the future and who value our capacity for achievement.

ROM is a market leader in the field of technical building services and plant construction. All over Germany ist 3,500 employees, including about 1,000 engineers, apply their expertise to the task of creating top-quality engineering achievements – technology for man and the environment. More than 30 branch establishments offer tailor-made solutions.

Business Fields

- Heating Engineering
- Refrigeration
- Ventilation and Air Conditioning
- Fire Protection
- Building Automation
- Instrumentation and Control
- Electrical Engineering
- Clean Room Technology
- Pipeline Systems

- Media Supply Systems
- Sanitary Engineering
- Shipbuilding/Dockbuilding
- Contracting
- Energy Management
- Building Management/Service
- General Contractor: Engineering Environmental Simulation/ Test Stand Technology

Service Areas

Consultancy
Planning
Execution
Building Management/Service
Research & Development

ROM's Central Engineering Department (ZIT) helps to maintain our technical leaderschip. In addition to our work in the field of research and development, our expertise is available to project developers, architects and engineering offices.
You too can make use of our many and various simulation and experimental facilities and our extensive experience gained from innovative construction projects and a large number of research projects.

Range of Services

- Energy simulation for buildings, assessment/optimisation of walling systems, active and passive utilisation of solar energy

- Numerical simulation of currents within rooms and around, through and within buildings

- Facility simulation for optimising room air, heat and cold supply concepts

- Room air current tests, component tests and decedlopment of special components in room-air laboratory

- On-site measurements for assessment of thermal comfort or fault diagnosis, air exchange measurements in naturally ventilated rooms

- Energy consultancy, planning support, concept development

ROM
Technik für
Mensch & Umwelt

ROM-Zentrale
RUD. OTTO MEYER
GmbH & Co. KG
Tilsiter Straße 162
22047 Hamburg
Phone: 040/6949-0
Fax: 040/69492600
e-mail: unteruns@mantis.de
INTERNET: www.rom.de

In the field of technical building systems ZANDER is one of the leading companies in Germany. Headquarters of the firm is Nürnberg. In addition ZANDER has branch offices in Berlin, Hamburg, Isernhagen, Düsseldorf, Dortmund, Koblenz, Frankfurt/Main, Mannheim, Stuttgart, München, Erfurt, Dresden and Leipzig. ZANDER's representations in most parts of Europe are the subsidiaries in Spain, Hungary, Austria and Switzerland. The ZANDER group, which also includes the companies Zander Wärmetechnik Kulmbach GmbH, Zander Umwelt GmbH and Zander Gebäudemanagement GmbH, employs altogether at the moment about 1,400 employees.
ZANDER designs and executes technical plants for buildings and processes. As technical general contractor the experienced staff provide a competent and reliable project handling. The range of performance includes HVAC systems, refrigeration as well as measuring and control plants, energy concepts and the wide range of environmental technology. A main emphasis lies on the realization of complex projects in the cleanroom technology for the pharmaceutical industry.

Besides the planning and implementation of technical plants the operation of buildings is one of ZANDER's main fields of activity. The scope of performance is based on an integral concept. ZANDER takes on all tasks concerning the building and provides the user with a trouble-free comfortable environment.

Overview of the Scope of Performance:
Planning and implementation of technical plants for buildings and processes

- technical general contractor
- ventilation and air-conditioning systems, refrigeration as well as measuring and control plants
- heating technology and energy concepts
- environmental technology
- cleanroom technology

Operation of buildings
- facility management
- service for technical building systems.

ZANDER Klimatechnik AG
Rollnerstrasse 111
D-90408 Nürnberg
Phone: +49/911/3608-0
Fax: +49/911/3608-162
E-mail: info@zktag.de
http://www.zktag.de

ZANDER GEBÄUDEMANAGEMENT
GMBH

ZANDER
Gebäudemanagement GmbH
Rollnerstrasse 111
D-90408 Nürnberg
Phone: +49/911/3608-380
Fax: +49/911/3608-119
E-mail: info_zgm@zktag.de
http://www.zktag.de/zgm

Original edition 1998.
© 2000, first corrected reprint
Birkhäuser - Publishers for Architecture,
P. O. Box 133,
CH-4010 Basel,
Switzerland

Project consulting:
Dr. Andreas Colli
Cover design, Layout:
Ott + Stein, Berlin
*Graphic design, Pictures
and Realization:*
Riemer Design, Munich
Translation:
Elizabeth Schwaiger, Toronto

Printed on acid-free paper
produced from chlorine-free pulp. TCF ∞
Printed in Germany
ISBN 3-7643-6329-0

9 8 7 6 5 4 3 2 1

This book is also available in
a German language edition
(ISBN 3-7643-5809-2).

A CIP catalogue record for this book is
available from the Library of Congress,
Washington D.C., USA

Deutsche Bibliothek Cataloguing-in-Publication Data
Daniels, Klaus:
Low Tech - Light Tech - High Tech : building in the
information age / Klaus Daniels. Engl. transl. by
Elisabeth Schwaiger. - Basel ; Boston ; Berlin :
Birkhäuser, 2000
ISBN 3-7643-6329-0